# NO ONE TO BLAME?

'The gales of war blew a 13-year-old Greek boy to our shores. He was to
become a South African civil rights lawyer of international standing,
a devastating cross-examiner of apartheid's authorised torturers and killers.
Long before the Truth and Reconciliation Commission was visualised,
George Bizos pursued the truth of what was being done to those who suffered
under and had the courage to oppose a racist regime turned brutal tyrant.
When George Bizos won a case, it was not just a professional victory –
it was an imperative of a man whose deep humanity directs his life.
The intimate accounts of major trials in this extraordinary book are
part of our national story we cannot deny: in human responsibility
there never can be nobody to blame.'
– Nadine Gordimer

D1501042

# NO ONE TO BLAME?

In Pursuit of Justice in South Africa

GEORGE BIZOS

*George Bizos*

*For John*

*with my*
*best wishes*

*Johannesburg*
*March 2009*

DAVID PHILIP PUBLISHERS
*Cape Town*

MAYIBUYE BOOKS
*University of the Western Cape, Bellville*

Published 1998 in Southern Africa by David Philip Publishers (Pty) Ltd,
208 Werdmuller Centre, Claremont 7700, South Africa
and Mayibuye Books, University of the Western Cape, Bellville, Cape

Third impression 2000

*Mayibuye Literature and History Series, No. 90*

Copyright © 1998  George Bizos

ISBN 0-86486-319-5

Printed in South Africa by ABC Press, Kinghall Avenue, Epping

# CONTENTS

*To all for whom before and after their deaths*
*justice was not only blind*
*but also deaf and dumb*

# FOREWORD

*by Sydney Kentridge, QC*

THIS book is about a continuing search for truth – the truth about the deaths of the sixty or more people who died in the hands of the Security Police during the years of apartheid in South Africa. It is also about the repeated failure of judicial officers to recognise that truth even when it was staring them in the face.

In South Africa (unlike some other countries) an inquest is held as a matter of course after any death other than from natural causes. The deaths of the political activists who died in Security Police custody were no exception. In each case an inquest was held by a magistrate, often a senior magistrate. As this book shows, in the face of circumstantial and medical evidence pointing plainly to Security Police culpability the magistrates would time after time exonerate the police. In case after case where, to a disinterested observer, the untruthfulness of the police witnesses would have been evident, the magistrates refused to make any finding against them.

Why was this so? Why did the magistrates so readily accept the unconvincing police excuses? There may be many explanations for this apparent credulity. The background and training of the magistrates (in nearly all cases promoted from the ranks of public prosecutors) may have made them reluctant to disbelieve police witnesses, especially when the witnesses were senior officers. In many cases, however, one is driven to conclude that the magistrates had no real desire to reach a true verdict. Consciously or unconsciously they seem to have seen it as their duty to protect the organs of the state at all costs. If this may seem too severe a conclusion, consider the cases of detainees alleged by the police to have committed suicide in detention. The magistrates in those cases do not seem ever to have asked themselves the most obvious question: why should a prisoner commit suicide when (according to the police version) he had the option of remaining silent under interrogation?

The great virtue of this book, however, is that readers may judge for themselves. The evidence, including the cross-examination of the police officers, is set out with meticulous fairness. You may judge for yourselves whether, in truth, 'no one was to blame'.

George Bizos is the only person I know who could have written this book. He was in the thick of most of the forensic battles described. His accounts of the searching-out of evidence in the face of obstructive authority, the cross-examination of the police witnesses and the building-up of each case make absorbing and often exciting reading. My only criticism of the author is that he consistently underplays his own remarkable skill, persistence and courage in the face of an often hostile court and an always hostile establishment. No one did more than this great advocate to keep alive the ideal of justice in South Africa's darkest times.

# PREFACE

Colleagues and friends who heard me relate my disappointment with the exoneration of torturers by inquest magistrates have for years suggested that I should try and get it out of my system through writing. I resisted the temptation partly because our profession has a conservative attitude to publicity for oneself, and because if the truth were to be told, particularly relating to those involved in the judicial process, feathers might be ruffled and eyebrows raised.

Nadine Gordimer, other writers, David and Marie Philip, colleagues – now in high judicial office, or holding leading positions at the Bar both here and in England – encouraged me. They won the day. In our new constitutional dispensation freedom of information is perhaps more important than restrictive professional rules.

Deciding to do it was easier than getting it down on paper. A researcher was needed. Mary Beale, the wife of our son Kimon, indicated, through the good offices of Professor Philip Bonner, that a newly qualified lawyer, Anthony Costa, showed greater interest in contemporary history than in law. Our interview was brief – his legal qualification and his historical research expertise made it unnecessary to interview anyone else.

Julie Khamissa, my secretary, would type what I had dictated, mostly from memory, in the early hours of the morning. Anthony Costa would check whether the records supported my recollections. It didn't come easily; the script went through a number of drafts. Had it not been for the co-operation amongst the three of us, I doubt whether I could have finished it, particularly as I became involved in opposing a number of high-profile amnesty applications.

I am particularly indebted to my colleagues who worked with me in and out of court, whom I mention in the text, particularly Mohamed Navsa in the Goniwe inquest and Patric M. Mtshaulana in the Biko and Goniwe amnesty applications. Without their assistance, it would not have been possible to unravel the often deliberately tangled facts that were advanced by the

Security Police. Clive Plasket and Nicolette Moodie were invaluable during the Goniwe inquest. Miriam Wheeldon, an attorney, joined the Legal Resources Centre (LRC) shortly after the first session of the Biko applications. Her industry and insight into the motivation of the Biko and Goniwe applicants and her advice as to which extracts should be included in the book were of great help. Ramula Patel, counsel for the TRC in the Biko and Cradock Four amnesty applications, was of great help. I thank them all for their encouragement and assistance. I alone must take responsibility for what has finally been written.

Catrin Verloren van Themaat, the LRC librarian, spent much of her spare time digging up material poorly identified by me from the City Library and *The Star* library, both near our offices. Cyrenne Christodoulou helped with the typing.

Allister Sparks, as editor of the *Rand Daily Mail*, courageously reported in full the excesses of the Security Police. He enjoyed the confidence of Dr Jonathan Gluckman and encouraged me to write this book.

David and Marie Philip, probably unwittingly, pressured me by including the title of this book in their list of forthcoming publications almost two years before its birth. They also made helpful suggestions.

Michelle Pickover and Carol Archibald from the Department of Historical Papers at Wits University assisted me and Anthony Costa in locating material.

I would like to thank Russell Martin for imposing the discipline that was needed in the final stages of the preparation of the book. I was reassured by his careful editing and helpful suggestions.

I thank my wife Arethe for her patience, and our sons and daughters-in-law, Damon and Anna, Kimon and Mary, and Alexi and Monique, for urging me on.

George Bizos

# INTRODUCTION

'The struggle of man against power is the struggle of memory against forgetting.'
— Milan Kundera

'We can now deal with our past, establish the truth which has so long been denied us, and lay the basis for genuine reconciliation. Only the truth can put the past to rest.'
— President Nelson Mandela when he signed the Promotion of National Unity and Reconciliation Act on 19 July 1995

A MOTHER produced a blood-stained shirt at the trial of security officers charged with her son's murder. Their lawyer asked her why she had kept it, unwashed, for seven years since his death.

'I was waiting for a day like this,' she said.

Her hope that justice would at last be done was raised by the demise of the regime of the Greek colonels a year earlier.

Many mothers were hoping that the same would happen for them in South Africa. They, their husbands, sons and daughters wanted to know what they had till then been unable to discover: crimes committed against their loved ones had been covered up in the name of justice. Despite numerous inquests over the years, nothing had been revealed, our best efforts thwarted by the conspiracy of silence.

Years before there was talk of a truth and reconciliation commission, I believed that the manner in which justice had been cheated should be exposed. This book was at an advanced stage in 1995 when I began to have doubts whether completing it before the amnesty process was put into operation might present an incomplete picture of what had happened. I also hoped that the conscience of those functionaries who were present with the deceased at the end might lead them to tell the truth. The book was shelved, and I attended one of the first sessions of the Truth and Reconciliation Commission (TRC).

'He slipped while bathing.' So the Security Police told Ben Kgoathe, when he asked what had caused the injury which killed his father, Nicodemus. Middle-aged, dressed in a dark suit, speaking now in English, now in Setswana, Ben Kgoathe told his story to the TRC. Spotlights reflected off the ceiling of Johannesburg's Central Methodist Church, illuminating the room and enabling television cameras to catch his every grimace. But he did not stop. He had waited a long time to tell this story.

Beneath the huge metal cross sat the commissioners, a suitably representative collection of men and women, chosen to hear the harrowing tales of torture, violence and loss. Archbishop Desmond Tutu, the chairperson of the Commission, occupied centre stage, consoling the witnesses, offering them some comfort as they relived their tales of horror. Diminutive, robed in purple, the Archbishop invested the hearings with a mystical element, repeatedly invoking the grace of God, a solvent to wash away the pain of the past.

Journalists scribbled rapidly, trying to catch the words that embodied the memories, let loose once again. Headphones provided access to the simultaneous translations, resulting in a rather strange scene. I don't think Ben Kgoathe noticed any of it.

Nicodemus Kgoathe never came home for the Christmas of 1968. When his children found him in Silverton police station, he was lying on the floor, a dying man. 'He slipped while bathing.' On 5 February 1969 the police arrived in the dusty town of Hebron to tell Mrs Kgoathe that her husband was dead. All the inquiries made by his son brought only threats from the police. 'We'll wring your neck,' they told him.

Ben Kgoathe wanted answers. 'What surprised us', he said, 'was that in 1969 seven people, including my father, died while in custody. Is it possible that people . . . a team of people . . . should die in custody in one year? There could be more, I don't know . . .'

Ben Kgoathe was not alone in wanting to know. Hundreds like him posed similar questions. Only some have been answered during the hearings of the TRC. This book deals with a few cases of people who died at the hands of the state, mainly detainees, and only a small fraction of them. It is a story of pain, torture, violence and death; yet also of hope and whatever claims we can make to truth.

Minister of Justice B.J. Vorster was the driving force behind detention without trial under apartheid. He told his biographer, 'I was not going to send my men into battle with one hand tied behind their backs.' But detention without trial did more than make for a free and fair fight.

The acquittal of the political leaders at the end of the Treason Trial in 1961 probably marked the end of the administration of justice in accordance with generally accepted procedural safeguards, such as habeas corpus. And when the African National Congress (ANC) embarked upon the armed struggle in December 1961, it gave Vorster the excuse he needed, if indeed one was needed, to introduce detention without trial. The Sabotage Act of 1962 was passed to allow house arrest despite heavy criticism, mainly from organisations such as the Congress of Democrats and the Black Sash. They did not carry much weight with the National Party-dominated House of Assembly, which gave birth to the 90-day detention law in 1963. The effect of this legislation was that any police officer above the rank of lieutenant-colonel could, for an initial period of 90 days, detain a person incommunicado and deprive him or her of every possible amenity. Detainees had no right to see a lawyer, a doctor, or members of family. They could not approach the court. The period of 90 days was extended when the courts allowed the police to play a cat and mouse game with detainees – release them, and immediately redetain them. In 1965, 90 days was doubled with the introduction of 180-day detention.

Vorster appointed his old friend Hendrik van den Bergh to head the Security Police, the front line against internal enemies of the republic. Van den Bergh was aware that his new department had a reputation of being 'untouchable'. He was determined to keep control, yet added, 'Many people have attacked me bitterly and accused me of being instrumental in the abrogation of the Rule of Law in South Africa. But we were fighting a revolution in those days. It was not kid glove stuff, it was war . . . as far as I was concerned there was no time for peacetime legal niceties.' In the three years following Van den Bergh's appointment, the Security Police trebled in strength and he himself rose from the rank of lieutenant-colonel to brigadier.

In 1967, section 6 of the Terrorism Act empowered the police to prolong detention without trial for an indefinite period. Generally speaking, a prisoner is at the mercy of his or her captors; that is why in most civilised countries procedural safeguards have been introduced, such as visits by doctors, senior officers, and members of the family, and the companionship of fellow prisoners. Detention without trial in South Africa did away with all that – even judges, who had the right to visit prisoners at any time, were effectively excluded from visiting political detainees.

No wonder that many prisoners died in detention. The only witnesses to the circumstances of their detention were policemen or prison warders; but the shots were called by the Security Police, who were charged with ensuring the safety of the state, and were a law unto themselves. They could hold detainees for as long as they liked, keep them awake by working in shifts, deprive them of reading material, isolate them from humanity.

In South Africa there has to be an inquest whenever there is an unnatural death. The inquests into the deaths of detainees were held by magistrates. Security policemen felt that they could easily fabricate stories, which ordinarily would be an insult to the intelligence of the most gullible, in the confidence that compliant magistrates would swallow them. Slipping on bars of soap, falling down stairs, trying to escape through windows of high-rise buildings, subduing the lonely detainee by means of the equivalent of a scrum of rugby players, are just some of the explanations which were proffered. The detained were not there to speak for themselves. Their isolation made it impossible to produce witnesses, with the notable exception of the Aggett case where evidence of the systematic ill-treatment of detainees was admitted.

Often, however, their bodies revealed much of the truth to forensic experts, of whom the late Dr Jonathan Gluckman was in the forefront. He and a number of his colleagues were able to expose well-rehearsed versions fabricated by the police for the shams they were. Somehow, though, magistrates managed to ignore what was so clear to medical science. Perverse findings were made in many cases, completely against the probabilities and often against any reasonable possibility. What emerged at these inquests often led to public disquiet, even among those who dared not or would not raise their voice against injustice.

Over time the tactics of the Security Police were refined. Torture was concentrated less on the body and more on the mind, where the bruises were invisible even to the pathologist's cold eye. Isolation, sleep deprivation, abuse and comfort in alternating doses, wore down a detainee's mental defences as surely as an iron fist. And, of course, there was always the threat of physical pain to make the treatment that much more effective.

But even these refined methods, the work of professionals who delighted in tormenting their helpless captives, would at times not work too well. The detainee would die, and the spotlight of public inquiry would fall upon the interrogation rooms of the Security Police. Although they almost always got away with it, the political price was too high. For an embattled government, every death was another stripping away of what tattered shreds of legitimacy remained.

Although cleared by the findings of the inquests, the Security Police shied away from the light focused on their activities. A steady stream of deaths in detention through the 1960s peaked in 1969 with seven deaths, including

James Lenkoe and the Imam Haron. No one died in detention the following year. Ahmed Timol and Mtayeni Cuthsela died in 1971. The publicity generated by the Timol inquest led to four quiet years, until the horrors of 1976 and 1977 when thirteen detainees died each year. Then came the death of Steve Biko, whose inquest focused the attention of the world on the brutality of the Security Police, and the number of deaths in detention again fell. One in 1978, none in 1979, one the following year, and then came the 1980s. Escalating pressure externally and internally brought out the iron fist, sanctified by successive states of emergency. The inquest into the death of Dr Neil Aggett in 1982 did little to stem the flow of detainees dying in police custody.

We viewed the Aggett inquest as a victory of sorts, yet in truth it probably hastened the rise of the death squads. In October 1996 the former Police Commissioner, Gen. Johan van der Merwe, became the first top official to confirm what we already knew – that the police had waged a dirty war against the foes of apartheid, believing that 'the enemy had to be destroyed, no matter what'. It was in 1986, according to Brig. Jack Cronjé, one-time Security Police branch commander, that orders came to drop whatever restraint might have been practised by policemen. He told the amnesty committee of the TRC, 'It didn't matter what was done or how we did it, as long as the floodtide of destabilisation, unrest and violence was stopped.' Officers like Cronje passed the orders down the line, releasing a wave of evil whose ripples can still be observed.

Detaining people and forcing confessions out of them either by physical or psychological torture had become counterproductive. The adverse publicity generated by the inquests into the deaths of Timol, Biko, Aggett, Mdluli, Haron and many others probably persuaded the Security Police that they could not afford many more deaths of political detainees. Political assassinations were the answer. If their friends in other totalitarian states disposed of the bodies of their enemies by throwing them into the sea, or burying or burning them beyond recognition, why should they not do the same? To ease their consciences they redefined murder to exclude the killing of enemies of the state.

Assassination could always be blamed on the enemy, the ANC. Disappearance by killing and the absence of the victims' bodies were even more attractive – there was no need for an inquest. The story would be given out that they must have left the country to join the ANC-in-exile. When their families denied this, the state had an answer: the 'exiles' did not want to tell their families and, in any event, the families could not be believed.

Elimination of enemies avoided as well the risk that interrogation methods might be exposed, as in the Aggett inquest, or the threat of a charge of manslaughter or culpable homicide for driving the detainee to suicide. It also did away with the possibility of not securing the conviction of a suspect: any information extracted from a detainee or from friends would not stand up in court even during the apartheid period because of the means by which it had been obtained. It was surely not coincidental that after the Aggett inquest, disappearance of people without trace or shooting of detainees trying to escape became more common.

The first fatal step was the assassination of Rick Turner, whom the Security Police suspected of being an ideologue for the Black Consciousness Movement (BCM). Thereafter the butchering to death of Griffiths Mxenge, the killing of the Cradock Four – Goniwe, Calata, Mkonto and Mhlauli – and the disappearance of the Pebco Three – Sipho Charles Hashe, Qaqawuli Godolozi and Champion Galela, supposed escapees who never showed up again – all became the new way. In the end it did not help; it only accelerated the demise of apartheid.

And so the final weapon in apartheid's secret war – the hit squads, the third force: bands of men who worked outside the law, with implicit sanction, to remove the enemies of the state with as little fuss as possible. Whereas before, suspects had been detained, interrogated and tried, now they were simply eliminated. A bullet in the back of the head, or a parcel bomb, did the job more quickly and, as long as someone else could be blamed, more quietly.

Between 1963 and 1990, 73 detainees are known to have died in detention. The youngest was 16-year-old Dumisani Mbatha, the oldest 63-year-old Ah Yan. They were all male, with the exception of Nobandla Bani. Some were listed as having died of 'natural causes'. The 'natural causes' which led to the deaths of Nicodemus Kgoathe and Solomon Modipane, both detained at Silverton police station in 1969 in connection with the same incident, were precipitated by their falling in the shower and slipping on a piece of soap. Perhaps the strangest case of all is that of the thirteenth victim, an unnamed person who died sometime in 1968, of unnamed causes somewhere in South Africa. The Minister of Police refused to give any further details, robbing that detainee, whoever he or she was, not only of his or her life but also of his or her identity.

Not all of them can be dealt with in one book. A selection has been made to show how the relatives, friends and society as a whole were let down by the administration of justice, either because the conspiracy of silence and outright lying by police officers made it impossible to reach the truth or because the courts too readily believed the fairytales proffered as fact. Apologists of the regime would glibly say, 'But the courts have cleared them!' So they did, but in many instances the courts were clearly wrong on the evidence then available.

This book is about some of those cases, in which the courts refused to answer the question, Who did it? In the face of glaring evidence to the contrary, they resolutely declared that no one was to blame.

CHAPTER 1

# FROM NGUDLE TO TIMOL

⌘

### 'Indians Can't Fly'

AFTER its passage through parliament in 1963, the detention without trial law soon claimed its first victim. On 20 August 1963, two months after the arrest of Walter Sisulu and others at a Rivonia farm, the police detained a 35-year-old Umkhonto weSizwe (MK) commander, Looksmart Solwandle Ngudle, on suspicion of ANC activities. During the night of 4–5 September 1963, he was found hanged in the Pretoria North police cells, hundreds of miles away from his home in Cape Town. His widow, Beauty, heard of his death some ten days later; by then her husband had already been buried.

Wanting answers, Beauty Nomulelo Ngudle went to attorney Joel Carlson. In his investigations, Carlson ran up against a wall of official silence. The department of prisons could not supply information unless they knew when Ngudle was detained and where he had died. When Carlson tried to obtain this information from the Security Police, they denied all knowledge of the matter. And so it went on, as every state department referred Carlson back to the Security Police, and silence.

It was only when the inquest was scheduled that information eventually became available. In the interim, Carlson had interviewed a number of political prisoners who told him how detainees were tortured. Some of the prisoners told Carlson the Security Police had shown them Ngudle's lifeless body as a warning.

In the mid-1990s Govan Mbeki, then Deputy President of the South African Senate, appeared before the Truth and Reconciliation Commission (TRC). A Rivonia trialist, Mbeki had been in Pretoria Central Prison while Ngudle was being held there and the two would occasionally pass each other on the exercise terrain. One day Ngudle dropped a note for Mbeki in which the detainee said that he was being tortured. A fellow Senator of Mbeki's, Christmas Tinto, who had been arrested a week before Ngudle, told the TRC that he saw Ngudle being beaten by policemen. 'They were kicking and beating him as they went up the stairs.' Among those he saw beating Ngudle,

Tinto named Sgt 'Spyker' van Wyk and Sgt Greeff.

Evidence of torture was led at the inquest, but the magistrate was not inter-ested. Counsel for the family was George Lowen, QC, a refugee from Nazi Germany, and a senior advocate at the Johannesburg Bar. The flamboyant, suave Lowen brooked no nonsense and often informed magistrates of this, quite directly. His junior was Ernie Wentzel, a leading liberal who had himself been detained.

It was a difficult inquest, the Security Police doing their utmost to frustrate any possibility of the truth emerging. They brought Ngudle's widow from the Cape and induced her to sign an affidavit that she had never briefed Carlson. Fearing this, Carlson had obtained a power of attorney from the widow and Ngudle's elder brother, who was, according to African indigenous law, her legal guardian.

Not to be discouraged by the failure of this ploy, the government took the unprecedented step of banning a dead person. It was now illegal to quote the late Looksmart Ngudle. Lowen was outraged and decided to withdraw in protest. Ernie later related the story of how Lowen could not himself formally withdraw because he was busy arguing the invalidity of the indictment in the Rivonia Trial on behalf of James Kantor. When Ernie suggested that it was not really necessary for Lowen to come to court and that he would withdraw instead, the older man responded, 'Ernie, you don't know how to withdraw properly.' Ernie spent the morning pacing the corridors of the Pretoria magis-trates' court, making all sorts of excuses to the magistrate for the absence of his senior and pleading with him to wait. George Lowen arrived at 2 o'clock, properly attired with hat and umbrella, with a prepared speech arguing that he could not do justice to the case if he could not quote. The next day pho-tographs appeared in the newspapers of George Lowen leaving the court, bristling with anger.

Perhaps embarrassed by this even cruder ploy, the government relented and permitted the use of statements by Ngudle at the inquest. But Lowen was not to continue. He suffered a heart attack and on his doctor's orders withdrew from the matter. Vernon Berrangé took charge of the case. Although he enjoyed the highest possible reputation as a trial lawyer in criminal cases, Berrangé had never taken silk. The Minister of Justice would probably not have granted him the honour: he had been 'named' as a communist. But Berrangé would also have never given the Minister the pleasure of refusing his application. All the same Berrangé always behaved as a senior member of the Bar, insisting that a junior should be briefed with him.

The state prosecutor, one V. Marinus, favoured by the Security Police for their cases, argued that Ngudle would have been charged with sabotage and his statements had incriminated his former comrades. Since he was facing death by hanging or revenge, suicide was his only way out.

Berrangé took a different tack. He argued, on behalf of the family, that solitary confinement led to mental breakdown. There was nothing in Ngudle's cell apart from a sleeping mat. He had had no reading materials, and was separated from other prisoners. His interrogators, who took him to their head office, were virtually the only people with whom he had had any contact. Detention was a sure way of breaking a person, Berrangé argued. Thus, he concluded, if Ngudle did hang himself, he was driven to it by the police and the detention laws.

The district surgeon, Dr C.J.N. Laubser, said he was satisfied Ngudle had died by hanging; he had found no other injuries on the body. This could not be contested. Because Ngudle had been buried for over a month, the family's pathologist, Dr Hillel Shapiro, was unable to perform an independent autopsy and had to rely on the report of the state pathologist.

Berrangé had a reputation as a fearsome cross-examiner. Maj. Fred van Niekerk of the Security Police was to experience this when questioned on his interrogation methods.

'If a detainee, this man or any other, on being interrogated after he had been detained, says, "I am not under any circumstances prepared to give you any information whatsoever," do you leave him alone or do you take further steps?'

'Well, he's got to be asked again.'

'And again?'

'Yes.'

'And again?'

'Yes.'

'And again?'

'Yes.'

'And again?'

'Yes.'

'I see. The idea being to wear him down, I suppose?'

'I make no comment.'

Berrangé returned to this point of infinite interrogation, when he asked the Major, 'That would be a dreadful thing to happen to a man, wouldn't it, if in fact you were wrong?'

'Yes.'

'It would be, and all that man would be able to see, as far as his future is concerned, would be an endless vista of imprisonment coupled with repeated questioning.'

'Yes.'

Berrangé called Isaac Tlale to testify that he had seen Ngudle at the central police station. Ngudle, he said, had seemed in great pain. Questioned on his own treatment, Tlale told a harrowing tale of torture as the police tried to force him to admit to recruiting for MK. After assaulting him, during which he still denied the allegations, the police told him to undress.

'Did you do so?' asked Berrangé.

'I did so,' responded Tlale.

'And then where were you told to go?'

'I was handcuffed. There were two chairs joined together. I was asked to sit on those two chairs. I was sitting this way . . . ' Tlale indicated how he had sat, with his knees up, his arms wrapped around them. 'My hands were handcuffed,' he continued, 'and in between my knees they inserted a broom handle.'

'Below your knees and above your arms?'

'Above my arms and below my knees.'

'So that you were pinioned then?'

'Yes.'

'What happened to your head?'

'My head was covered with a bag.'

'And what happened to your hands?'

'I could feel that something was tied to my two small fingers.'

'And during this time you were being addressed. Were they talking to you, asking you anything?'

'They were asking me continuously whether I was still denying.'

'Did you continue to deny?'

'I continued denying.'

'What was the next thing you felt?'

'I then felt my body was burning. I felt as if something was shocking me.'

'Have you ever had an electric shock?'

'Yes, I had it when I was repairing a motor car.'

'The same sort of thing?'

'Yes.'

'Can you remember how many times these shocks were put through you?'

'They did it twice.'

'And what happened ultimately?'

'Thereafter I lost my consciousness. The next thing I remember was standing next to a table signing a document.'

'Did anyone hold your hand?'

'One constable was holding my hand.'

'Was this a document that had any writing on it? Or was it blank, or what was it?'

'I could see, on this piece of paper, on top was written my name and address.'

'And the rest, was it blank, or had it writing on it?'

'It was blank.'

'And the sheet of paper on which you signed your name? Was that the same sheet of paper, or can't you remember?'

'It was not the paper which had my name on.'

'And thereafter where did you go?'

'They said I should go and clean myself.'

'Why did you have to go and clean yourself?'

'I had messed myself up.'

'You defecated into your trousers?'

'Yes. I was taken to a latrine. I took a piece of paper and wiped out my trousers.'

'And then you were taken back to your room?'

'Yes.'

But when Berrangé tried to lead further evidence on the matter, the magistrate disputed its relevance. Counsel argued that he was trying to establish 'a system, a technique of torture, used by certain members of the Security Branch, to extract information'. The magistrate was unimpressed – he ruled this irrelevant and Berrangé withdrew in protest. He had tried to show that the only reasonable inference was that if Ngudle had killed himself, it was as a result of the treatment to which he had been subjected. And so the magistrate reached the first in a long series of findings at inquests – no one was to blame.

In many ways the Ngudle inquest was a template on which subsequent Security Police versions at inquests were modelled. The argument of suicide prompted by betrayal was hauled out time and again as the state sought to justify why apparently well-adjusted men would take their own lives. Berrangé's argument about the effects of detention would also resurface, some eighteen years later, in the Aggett inquest. But the most resounding impact of the Ngudle inquest was the finding, which would echo down the years.

It was the same verdict in a case held the following year, one which would have eerie resonances in later years. Suliman Salojee was 32 years old when he fell to his death on 9 September 1964. The young candidate attorney fell sixty feet from the seventh floor of the Johannesburg Security Police headquarters, a building called The Grays, near Main Street, home to Grays Tea.

Grays Building was quite rudimentary, lacking the sophisticated security arrangements that became a feature of the tenth floor at John Vorster Square. It was also the place to which you had to report if you wanted to become a South African citizen. I myself went, but soon thereafter received a letter from F.W. de Klerk's father, then Minister of the Interior, telling me that it was not in the public interest for me to become a South African citizen. A capricious decision that, all else aside, robbed me of a passport or travel document for 32 years.

Detained for two months under the 90-day section of the 1963 law, Salojee had been seen by his wife two weeks before his death. Mrs Rookaya Salojee testified that her husband had been in good spirits and seemed unworried. She was represented at the inquest by George Lowen.

Salojee's interrogator was the notorious Capt. Theuns Swanepoel, better known as 'Rooi Rus'. A stocky and red-faced man (hence his name), he claimed to have questioned Salojee on the day, though he was not in the room, when the detainee fell. When questioned by Lowen on the effects of 90-day detention, Swanepoel exploded: 'I am not prepared to stand here and allow you or anyone else to make propaganda.'

'I am not here to make propaganda,' Lowen replied. 'We are here to find out why a man who was apparently normal should jump from a seventh-floor window. It is not an everyday occurrence.'

Capt. Swanepoel denied assaulting detainees. He refused to answer any questions on interrogation methods. It was an impossible situation. The magistrate did his duty – no one was to blame. Rookaya Salojee was 26 at the time. She was nearing 50 when she told the TRC how she had had a nervous breakdown after Suliman's death, when the Security Police would not leave her alone. 'You will also die, you will also commit suicide,' they told her. 'I'm sorry to say,' she concluded her testimony, 'but I still hate some of the whites. I see a policeman, I hate him.'

In September 1966 Dr Verwoerd, the architect of apartheid, was assassinated in the hallowed halls of the House of Assembly itself by Dimitri Tsafendas. With his tough-talking approach, the securocrat B.J. Vorster mobilised the northern caucus of the National Party to ensure his succession. Now Prime Minister, Vorster kept his old police portfolio. 'I owe it to this House,' he explained to parliament, 'to the people outside and to South Africa our fatherland, in view of the experience I have gained . . . to take personal responsibility for the safety of the state.'

In 1967, the Terrorism Act was passed, empowering police officers to make the period of detention without trial an indefinite one. The Minister of Justice, P.C. Pelser, to whom Vorster had in the meantime relinquished the office, explained that the drastic measures were necessary to ensure the safety of the country. 'We are no longer dealing with Red ideology,' he added, 'but with Red arms.' Even the nominal opposition, the United Party, accepted the legislation in the national interest in order to stave off anarchy. When the lone voice of Helen Suzman protested, Minister Pelser expressed his surprise that she had gone 'so far as to intercede even for terrorists'.

It was never established whether James Lenkoe was a terrorist in any sense of the word. An immigrant from Lesotho, he lived in Soweto and worked for the railways. Everyone agreed that he was never involved in political activity. Everyone, that is, except the omniscient Security Police, who arrived at the Lenkoes' little house in the middle of the night of 5 March 1969. They questioned James Lenkoe, hit him a few times and took him away. A week later his wife received a message to collect his body.

Julia Lenkoe approached Joel Carlson and told him her tragic story. She had watched the police beating her husband when they took him away, for reasons they would not disclose. When she went to visit him in Pretoria prison the following day, she was told she could not see him for 180 days, but should bring clothes and food for him on Sunday. When she arrived with her parcels, she was told that her husband was not there and was sent away. Although her husband had died on 10 March, she was only told on 13 March. She concluded her story by handing over James's belt to Carlson. 'This is my husband's belt,' she told him. 'He had only one and he didn't take it when he was arrested. How can he have hanged himself with this belt?'

When Mrs Lenkoe and her relatives took her late husband's body to be buried in Lesotho, police at the Ficksburg border post refused to permit the men to cross the border. 'My mother and aunt had to carry the coffin to the other side, where they were met by members of my father's family,' Lenkoe's daughter Lorraine later told the TRC.

Jonathan Gluckman was engaged by the family to conduct an autopsy. Counsel was David Soggot. Gluckman brought two peculiar features to light after the post-mortem. One was a small mark on one of Lenkoe's toes which could not be explained. The other was the absence of blood, which would have been produced by a haemorrhage where the neck fractured; this raised the possibility that Lenkoe was hanged *after* he had died.

Although the mark on the toe could have been caused by an electric shock, the evidence was not conclusive. After consulting with the highly respected

American pathologist Prof. Alan Moritz, Gluckman had a spectrographic test conducted in order to check whether the injury was electrothermal. By using samples of skin from Lenkoe's neck and toe, with other samples of skin cauterised during operations, the tests carried out by the South African Bureau of Standards showed a similarity in the cauterised skin and that taken from Lenkoe's toe, all of which revealed a copper content. The injury also made it possible to fix the time of death at no more than twelve hours after the injury had been received. Prof. Moritz agreed with these conclusions, as well as with the suspicion that the hanging was faked.

Counsel for the family were not permitted to have copies of the photograph of Lenkoe's body hanging in his cell. No detailed examination was possible to throw any light on the question whether he had actually hanged himself. What was interesting was that Lenkoe had been dressed in an overall which was not normally worn with a belt and, indeed, did not require one.

When Hieronymus von Praag Koch, the state pathologist with the handlebar moustache, was cross-examined by Soggot, he conceded that his findings were as consistent with hanging while still alive, as after death. He also conceded that a spectrographic test would establish whether the burn (an 'abrasion', he called it) was an electrothermal injury. When Soggot announced that precisely such a test had already been conducted by the South African Bureau of Standards, with a positive finding, Koch was clearly disturbed. The pathologist's discomfort increased when the assessor, Dr J. de Villiers, asked why, in a case of suicidal hanging, Lenkoe's arm was raised. Koch's explanation was that Lenkoe had undergone an instantaneous cadaveric spasm which had caused immediate rigor mortis. This condition was exceedingly rare, and a well-known explanation used in cases of simulated suicide. De Villiers was replaced as the assessor.

As with Salojee, Lenkoe's interrogator was the notorious 'Rooi Rus' Swanepoel, by now a Major in the Security Police. After conducting a search of the cases in which 'Rooi Rus' was involved, Carlson discovered that he had been accused of breaking several limbs, and even threatening to rip open the penis of one man. When testifying, Swanepoel described Lenkoe as a hired assassin, but refused to give any details for security reasons. When Soggot confronted him with the mass of allegations relating to his brutality, Swanepoel was outraged. The prosecutor quickly intervened, claiming that this evidence was inadmissible. In response, Soggot pointed out that he had about twenty affidavits and witnesses who would testify to the truth of their contents. Whenever asked about specific allegations relating to other detainees, the magistrate refused to permit the question.

Hillel Shapiro, a former professor and pathologist, gave evidence that supported Gluckman's findings. A respected figure, Shapiro stood firm, and laid the ground for a surprise witness, Prof. Moritz, who flew in from the United States. Magistrate Tukker was reluctant to reconvene the inquest to allow Moritz to testify before returning to the States. After an application to the Supreme Court, it was agreed that Gluckman would testify first and, if necessary, Moritz would be called. Although the prosecutor, C.G. Jordaan, led Gluckman's evidence, Gluckman was articulate and confident; so much so that Soggot declined to examine his own witness, and Gluckman's testimony stood unchallenged. Moritz's testimony was similar, until Jordaan challenged him on the question of copper traces. The prosecutor put it to Moritz that persons working with metal would have traces of the substance on their skin. When Moritz agreed, Jordaan pushed home his point: 'Then you will agree that if the deceased had constantly come into contact with copper by reason of his work, then his skin would contain more copper?'

Unmoved, the witness replied, 'Yes, but can you tell me what work the deceased did involving the second toe of his right foot?'

This avenue thwarted, the state called the biochemist Prof. Bernard Meyer from Pretoria University, to testify that it would not be possible to determine how much copper would normally be in Lenkoe's body. In order to obtain expert evidence to rebut this somewhat obscure testimony, counsel for the family requested a postponement. But Magistrate Tukker was determined to finish the matter and refused repeated requests for an adjournment.

Because Soggot was busy that morning, the family briefed Willie Oshry, QC to request a postponement on the final day. Oshry also explained that he had not been briefed to question Meyer and had not had time to prepare because of the technical nature of the case. In response, Jordaan petulantly replied that he had been forced to question Dr Moritz at short notice, despite the fact that he (Jordaan) spoke Afrikaans, whereas Moritz was an American with a heavy accent.

When Tukker proved unamenable to this request, Oshry declared that 'bulldozing' was occurring. Tukker was outraged. He warned Oshry, 'Count your words. There is no bulldozing here.'

Soggot's attempts to lead evidence on Maj. Swanepoel's systematic brutality were rejected outright. Jordaan accused Soggot of telling an 'infamous lie' in his application. Soggot kept his cool, and told Jordaan he would not descend to his level. It was all in vain. Tukker declared he had listened to Soggot and all the evidence he was prepared to hear. The matter was closed. Tukker adjourned for a few minutes and returned to give his verdict: James Lenkoe had hanged himself and no one was to blame.

The two-month inquest had been a complete farce. It was not even known what Lenkoe was suspected of having done. The Security Police claimed that they arrested Lenkoe because they believed he was 'a chief figure in the planning of acts of terrorism'. No evidence was ever produced to support this contention. Had the police simply arrested the wrong man, as Carlson suspected? The attorney was disappointed, as he later wrote: 'For me the Lenkoe inquest proceedings demonstrated beyond any doubt that the courts could and would be manipulated by the security police, and laws would be constantly changed to serve their purposes . . . The conduct of the inquest hearings could be considered farcical but for the fact that they were so horrifying.'

Joel Carlson left South Africa in 1970 after years of Security Police harassment. Soon after his departure, his wife and children followed him.

Two months after the death of James Lenkoe, a Cape Town Muslim leader, Imam Abdullah Haron, was detained. He spent 133 days in detention until his death in the cells of the Maitland police station in September 1969. As a respected member of the community, the imam's funeral was attended by over 30 000 people. It was the same day as a minor earthquake in nearby Tulbagh; many saw it as a sign of outrage at Haron's death.

From the post-mortem it emerged that there were 26 separate bruises on the body of the Imam Haron. Ten of these had occurred about ten days before his death; the rest were one to three days old. After much procrastination by the police, the inquest was held in February 1970. It was clear that Haron had been intensely interrogated during the three months he spent in detention. Magistrate J.S.P. Kuhn held that on the available evidence he could not determine how the balance of injuries was caused. The cause of death was found to be natural – a fall down a flight of stairs had produced heart failure in the 46-year-old cleric.

A year later Haron's widow Gamila sued the state for R22 000 in respect of her husband's death. She received an *ex gratia* payment of R5000. 'They took him from me and he stayed in jail for four months – afterwards I saw him as a corpse,' she recalled decades later. 'I can forgive but I can't forget.'

When the Imam Haron died, Ahmed Timol was overseas receiving training as a member of the South African Communist Party (SACP). After his return to South Africa, he served not only as a teacher in a Roodepoort high school, but also as part of the underground. Along with Jeremy Cronin, Timol had been detailed to disseminate propaganda within South Africa. Unlike Cronin, he did not survive.

When Timol left his parents' Roodepoort home one spring evening, he told them he was on the way to the cinema. It was the last time the Timols saw their son alive. That night, Friday 22 October 1971, marked the beginning of a countrywide series of police raids, described as the most extensive since 1964. At about 11 p.m., Ahmed and his companion, Mohamed Salim Essop, were stopped at a police roadblock in Coronationville. On searching the Anglia motor car, police discovered pamphlets belonging to the banned African National Congress and Communist Party. They promptly detained Timol and Essop, and turned them over to the Security Police. At 2.40 p.m. on the next day, Saturday 23 October, Timol was taken to John Vorster Square. What happened next is known only to the members of the police who interrogated Timol over the following days.

Timol's family knew as little as anyone else. They expected their son back that Friday evening. Instead they found the Security Police at their door in the early hours of the next morning. They searched Ahmed's bedroom, saying only, 'We have your son', as they left. The police paid a number of visits to the Timols. When they came again on the Tuesday afternoon prior to his death, Mrs Hawa Timol could bear it no longer. 'I said: "My heart is so sore." I asked where my son was,' she recalled at the inquest.

When she asked why she could not see him, one policeman replied, 'He needs a hiding.'

The shocked Mrs Timol responded, 'I've never hurt my son, so you must not hit him.'

'Because you didn't hit him, we will hit him,' was the policeman's reply.

During the inquest, the policeman concerned, WO Van Rensburg, claimed he had said, 'Look, a child must get a hiding; if you had given him a hiding then you wouldn't be crying now.'

The magistrate found Mrs Timol's version of events unconvincing. It was not unusual for the courts to prefer the evidence of the Security Police.

Mohamed Salim Essop had been arrested along with Ahmed Timol, but the 21-year-old Wits University medical student had seemingly vanished. Essop's parents received an anonymous tip-off that their son was lying ill in the H.F. Verwoerd Hospital in Pretoria, and that a bed had been put across the door to prevent unauthorised people from entering or looking into the ward. According to the informant he was unconscious. The father, Ismail Essop, hurried to Pretoria, climbed onto the bed and looked through the glass panel at the top of the door. He saw his son's upper chest, shoulders and face; it was clear to the father that his son had been injured. Thereupon the Johannesburg attorney Said Cachalia rushed to chambers and asked whether an urgent application could be made by his client for access to his son, and sought protection against further ill-treatment. As was my practice whenever gross violations of human rights were alleged, I approached Isie Maisels, the doyen of the Johannesburg Bar, to ask whether he would take the application.

In the ordinary course of events, the application would have been made to the court in Johannesburg. We did not know who the duty judge would be, but did know that Cecil Margo was presiding in Pretoria. Judge Margo and Isie Maisels knew one another well. Margo had been his junior, and they had both given up their practice to join the armed forces during the Second World War, to fight the Nazis. The press had been informed that the application would be made. Those who were concerned about the safety and well-being of detainees expected young Essop to survive, and to tell his story of what had happened to him – and, by necessary inference, what must have happened to Timol, what had induced him to jump out of a tenth-floor window, if in fact he was not pushed out, as was thought by many.

On our arrival in Pretoria we were met by Frikkie Eloff (later the Hon. Mr Justice Eloff, Judge-President of the Transvaal), who regularly appeared for the Security Police and for farmers who were alleged to have imprisoned and ill-treated labourers on their farms; on behalf of a number of such labourers Maisels and I had brought habeas corpus applications. Eloff handed in a short affidavit by a senior police officer, saying that Essop's son was detained under section 6 of the Terrorism Act, which prohibited access to any person in detention by anyone except the Minister or an officer of the state on official duty. It was stated that no permission would be granted for access to the detainee. There was also a short affidavit by Dr Hieronymus Koch, the pathologist in the employ of the state. He said that there were none of the injuries alleged by the father on the body of the young Essop, whom he had examined. At one stage during the hearing, Maisels remarked caustically, 'Mr Eloff says Mr Essop was not assaulted. I was waiting for him to say Mr Essop slipped on a piece of soap.'

Judge Margo was not impressed by the short affidavits. He indicated during the course of argument that there was public disquiet and felt that it would not be in the interests of justice for him to hold that the courts were powerless to assist a father's access to his comatose son – especially in circumstances where his friend Timol had, according to the Security Police, committed suicide by jumping out of a window. He suggested that there should be discussions, in the hope that some access could be given, and some assurance or undertaking be recorded that his son would not be further ill-treated, if in fact he had been.

During the course of the adjournment, Eloff informed us that none of the

Security Police officers present were able to give such an undertaking or agree to any access and that the only person who could give such permission was the Prime Minister himself, who earlier in his capacity as Minister of Justice had introduced detention without trial and thereby put an end to the writ of habeas corpus. We were requested to be patient, whilst Eloff went off to the Union Buildings to consult with the Prime Minister. He returned empty-handed. He said that the Prime Minister appreciated the judge's concern and thanked him for the opportunity to consider the matter, but that he had a difficulty – if he consented to any relief, he would have to explain to the police who were detaining people without trial, why he had done so. If, on the other hand, the court made an order, he did not have to explain anything to anybody. We were not told whether the Prime Minister was concerned about the anguished parents and the fate of their medical student son.

The court did make an order, restraining the police from further ill-treating Essop, but felt that it could not interfere with the decision depriving Ismail Essop of access to his son. We decided to ask for leave to supplement our papers. This was a result of the judge having said that, despite the affidavit by Dr Koch, the matter obviously required more thorough investigation before a final order was made.

The police, however, rejected both suggestions The Commissioner of Police, Gen. Gideon Joubert, refused to allow any 'outsiders' to see Essop. The detainee, the General added, was free to lay a charge of assault. One lawyer thought this unlikely, commenting, 'In the present climate, would you?' The police went so far as to prevent the deputy sheriff from serving Essop with a copy of the interdict. The interdict was later delivered personally by the registrar of the court. Asked for comment, Gen. P.J. Venter, head of the Security Police, replied, 'I have nothing to say about anything, you will get nothing out of me. My door is closed.'

Ismail Ayob, later attorney to President Nelson Mandela and many other prominent clients, was at the time an articled clerk (the expression 'candidate attorney' having yet to gain currency). Ayob even then showed the determination which has led him to become one of the leading attorneys in South Africa. Our advice to him and his principal, Said Cachalia, was that they had to go to every nurse, doctor, paramedic or any other person who might have seen Essop and ask them to make an affidavit describing his condition.

On the return day of the rule nisi, when a full bench had been constituted, consisting of Judges Bekker and Marais, the matter had to be postponed. Judge Bekker asked a question pregnant with meaning: 'Mnr Eloff, wat makeer Bukofse-hulle in Johannesburg? Hoekom is die applikant se seun Pretoria toe gebring?' [Mr Eloff, what is the matter with Bukofse and his colleagues? Why was the applicant's son brought to Pretoria?] (Bukofse was a district surgeon in Johannesburg.) The full import of his asking why young Essop had been moved from Johannesburg to Pretoria was to become apparent as more evidence emerged.

Ismail Ayob made an affidavit that he had approached no less than 18 persons who had at least by implication agreed that they had seen Essop, but they had been told not to talk to anyone about it and to refuse to make any statement or affidavit on the matter. We asked the court to postpone the matter and to authorise the issue of subpoenas for these persons to come to court. In the meantime, we had heard through Dr Jonathan Gluckman that Essop had been taken to the neurosurgeon Dr C.W. Law. When Law refused to speak about the matter, we asked that he too be subpoenaed. Through the grapevine we understood that he was an honourable man, and that he would not deny that Essop had been injured when he was brought to him. The fact that he was a neurosurgeon was a fairly clear indication of the police's concern that there may have been a head injury. In the earlier hearing, the police had said they had had three neurosurgeons examine Essop, who had been diagnosed with a condition of hysteria. This prompted Maisels to wonder why a neurosurgeon, and not a psychologist, had been called. 'Perhaps he injured his brain by slipping on a piece of soap,' Maisels mused once again.

We had to ignore the caution of not calling a witness with whom one has not had an opportunity of consulting, and called Dr Law as the first witness. Isie Maisels, towering above everyone else in court, was a very direct examiner.

'Dr Law, did you see Mohamed Essop, our client's son?'

'Yes.'

'Did he have any injuries?'

'M'Lords, I can do no better than read the letter that was sent to me by Dr Dennis Vernon Kemp, the district surgeon, who listed sixteen injuries.'

This was the first time we had heard that Essop had been seen by the honest district surgeon Vernon Kemp. We marvelled at Judge Bekker's insight, when earlier on he had wanted to know what was wrong with the district surgeons of Johannesburg and why it was necessary to take Essop to Dr Koch. I tugged at Maisels's gown, and suggested he should ask the judges to authorise a telephonic subpoena on Vernon Kemp, to come to court that very morning. It was so ordered. Our attorney, Said Cachalia, rushed out to phone Dr Kemp. He was there shortly after the mid-morning adjournment, and put into the witness box without consultation. Kemp confirmed the contents of his letter.

But Maisels's forensic *nous* led him to ask a few more questions.

'Where did you see Essop?'

'He was lying comatose in a passage at John Vorster Square, the headquarters of the Security Police in Johannesburg.'

The other question was whether the respondent, Col. P.J. Greyling, and other police officers were in that passage while he was examining and when Dr Kemp ordered Essop to be admitted to hospital. Kemp's reply was positive: 'Yes, they were.'

'Did any of them ask you any questions as to what was wrong with him?'

No, nobody had.

Dr Kemp's evidence was not challenged on any of the material aspects. When Greyling gave evidence, he said that detainees were not ill-treated, that the allegations of torture were an invention of the communists and the liberal press, and he and his fellow police officers regarded people like Essop as their children. The last thing they would do was to ill-treat them. Maisels had the reputation of going directly for the kill. He was asking his questions in English, the Colonel was replying in Afrikaans.

'Tell me, Colonel, after Dr Kemp examined Essop in your presence, did you ask Dr Kemp any questions?'

'Nee, Edelagbare. Wat se vraag moes ek aan hom gestel het?' [No, M'Lord, what question should I have asked him?]

Maisels then suggested the question the policeman could have asked, but he could not resist the temptation of putting it in Afrikaans: 'Sê vir my, dokter, wat makeer my kind?' [Tell me, doctor, what is wrong with my child?]

'Ek het dit nie gedoen nie.' [I didn't do it.]

'Was that because it wasn't necessary for you to ask? You knew that he had been beaten up by your men?'

There seemed no possible answer to Maisels's first blow. Greyling was a hopeless witness. Eloff often complained publicly, and in private, that witnesses such as Greyling did badly because they were at a disadvantage when the questions were not put to them in their mother tongue. An interpreter was offered to Greyling and others. Brian Southwood, then a young advocate at the Pretoria Bar, and now a judge, who had come to court as a spectator, volunteered to act as an interpreter. But the policemen understood the questions in English and they hardly ever waited for the interpreter to translate what Maisels asked.

It was obvious that Dr Koch had lied on oath when he stated that he had not seen any injuries. He excused himself on the basis that he was not asked by the lawyers to say whether there were any injuries on Essop, but merely to deal with the question whether or not young Essop had the specific injuries described by his father in his original affidavit. Koch had merely said that the injuries he saw differed from those described by Essop senior. It was also argued that disclosing the injuries would reveal information about a detainee. This was prohibited by the Terrorism Act unless those holding him consented. The judges hearing the application did not adversely comment on Hieronymus Koch's lack of candour or the correctness or otherwise of his alarming interpretation of the Terrorism Act.

Later, when the *Rand Daily Mail* was making public the serious injuries inflicted on Biko, and his miserable condition before his death, I was stopped in the corridor of the court of appeal by Judge John Trengove, who had been a judge in Pretoria at the time of Essop's case but had not sat as one of the judges who heard it.

'Tell me, Bizos, are you acting for the Biko family?'

'Yes, Judge.'

'Is what the *Daily Mail* is writing true?'

'Yes, and worse, Judge.'

'It serves us right,' Judge Trengove said resignedly. 'If we had dealt with Hieronymus Koch in the Essop case, what happened to Biko might never have occurred.'

Eventually, Essop was released. He made a statement relating what had happened to him: as a result of torture he had collapsed and had become unconscious when the police urinated on him.

The judgment of Judges Marais and Theron (Judge Bekker was no longer available) was read by Judge Theron. It confirmed Judge Margo's order, with costs in favour of the Essop family. The police defence that Essop was merely malingering was rejected. Essop sued for damages. Judge J.H. 'Lammie' Snyman, considered by the profession to be a close friend of Prime Minister Vorster, an enthusiastic supporter of apartheid and later its chief censor, disbelieved Essop. He was sent to prison for his participation in distributing pamphlets. On his release he completed his interrupted medical studies and today is practising medicine.

If Essop had been treated this way, the inference that Timol had suffered a similar fate was inescapable. But even before Essop's fate became known, people were asking questions about Ahmed Timol's death. The news of Timol's fall led to a public outcry and calls for an immediate investigation into the treatment of detainees. As Prof. John Dugard commented, 'The death of yet another detainee in suspicious circumstances again raises the whole question of the methods of interrogation employed by the Security Police.' A Christian clergyman expressed his shock: 'I cannot understand why a young Moslem with a rewarding career before him, whose religion expressly forbids suicide, should have taken such action.' The death of the young school teacher shocked the Indian community: he had been known as a kindly and respectful man, as well as a good cricketer. The funeral drew thousands of people. Timol's brother Mohammed was absent – he too had been detained and was currently sitting in a police cell in Durban.

Not everyone was outraged. The Southern Transvaal moderator of the Dutch Reformed Church was reluctant to comment, calling it 'a matter for the state and the Security Police'. A senior security policeman, Brig. Piet Kruger, denied that detainees were tortured: 'We don't threaten anyone or assault any-one . . . But today we realise that Ahmed Timol is a hero of the communists. We who know the communists know that when they want to go over to vio-lence, they have their people swear an oath to commit suicide rather than name their comrades.'

The government's initial response was silence: the Prime Minister, Minister of Justice Pelser and senior policemen all refused to comment. When John Vorster did speak, he was unrepentant, claiming that the normal legal proce-dure of an inquest by a magistrate was sufficient. 'The Security Police are at present engaged in a comprehensive and serious investigation in connection with terrorism and sabotage,' Vorster commented. 'It is the lawful task of the police to combat terrorism and sabotage, and they will fulfil this task irrespec-tive of any agitation on the part of certain newspapers and individuals to cast suspicion on their activities.'

The *Sunday Times* was unimpressed with this reply, and wrote: 'This kind of sophistry and double talk is not helpful . . . The real charges – and they are serious – he has carefully evaded and these still remain unexplained. How did Mr Ahmed Timol come to fall to his death this week from the tenth floor of John Vorster Square? How did 21-year-old Mr Mohamed Essop come to finish up in hospital after being detained for only a matter of days? . . . Most people must by now be familiar with the long list of shocking, ghastly allegations that deal with the sufferings of detained people. There are enough of these charges to indicate that something is seriously wrong with the system.' Even the Afrikaans pro-National Party press responded with concern, although they were quick to stress that the Security Police should not be prejudged.

Protest and prayer meetings were held throughout South Africa to com-memorate the death of Ahmed Timol. At a prayer meeting held in Vrededorp, one of the organisers said, 'Ahmed Timol has given his life in order that we may reap the fruits of freedom and so that we should one day be able to walk side by side in friendship.' At another meeting, Mrs Helen Suzman spoke out bitterly against the Terrorism Act for having eroded the rule of law ('there is rule by law in South Africa even if there is no rule of law') and given vast powers to the police: 'As long as apartheid exists, so the rule of law will be absent. A government that does not rule by consent will have to rule by force . . . If these basic truths are beginning at long last to dawn on white South Africans, Ahmed Timol will not have died in vain.' On 3 November 1971, the United Nations passed a resolution expressing 'grave indignation and concern' over mistreatment and torture of the opponents of apartheid.

The former head of the Security Police, then in charge of the notorious Bureau for State Security (BOSS), Gen. H.J. van den Bergh, did not share Mrs Suzman's opinions on the Terrorism Act: 'There is nothing wrong with the Terrorism Act. We could not do without it.' Communism, Vorster agreed, needed to be fought and the South African Communist Party was 'one of the oldest communist parties in the world and is very militant'.

Given the level of public concern, it could be expected that the police would at least attempt to investigate Timol's death with a degree of thoroughness. The task was given to the head of the CID, Maj.-Gen. Stoffel Buys. The good General did not disappoint his political masters. Before his investigation was complete, Gen. Buys told *Rapport* that Timol had jumped. The atmosphere in room 1026, the General declared, was the 'most relaxed atmosphere imaginable in such circumstances'. He explained: 'Ahmed Timol was sitting calmly in a chair. There were security men with him. At one stage two of them left the room. Mr Timol suddenly jumped up, aimed at the door. A security man jumped up to intercept him, but the Indian then stormed to the window and jumped through it. He was not scared or injured by anybody at any stage.'

The *Sunday Times* noted this peculiar statement by the General, wryly observing, 'One wonders why General Stoffel Buys, head of the CID, bothers to continue with the official inquiry he is conducting into the death of the political detainee Ahmed Timol, considering that he has already given his finding in advance to a Nationalist Sunday newspaper.' When approached for comment by the *Rand Daily Mail*, Buys was less than friendly. 'Why don't you approach me first instead of going off at a tangent and blackening everybody? You have done your damnedest and already thrown dirt,' he told a reporter.

The magistrate found that the investigation had been impartial, as Gen. Buys was not after all a member of the Security Police. But the vast majority of the people of South Africa, and many throughout the world, found it difficult to believe that Timol had died for the reasons given by the Security Police.

Doubts were even expressed by supporters of the apartheid government.

In accordance with standard procedure, an inquest was held. The Timol family were represented by Isie Maisels and myself; appearing for the police was Fanie Cilliers, who later became an eminent Senior Counsel; the evidence was led by P.A.J. Kotze, the senior public prosecutor. He regularly appeared in political trials in the Eastern Cape and the Transvaal, and was later the chosen magistrate to preside over the Aggett inquest. The magistrate, De Villiers, was an official who had done the ordinary run-of-the-mill criminal cases in the district and regional courts. Together with most of his colleagues, he did not enjoy a reputation of tending to disbelieve police officers.

Fanie Cilliers came to Maisels and me, to say that he considered it his duty to bring to our attention the fact that the police had handed him a document, with instructions to use it, but he had refused to do so. The document appeared on the face of it to have been issued by the Communist Party. Written in disjointed Marxist jargon, the document advised detained members of the Communist Party to complain of ill-treatment and assaults that did not happen, and to commit suicide rather than betray their comrades. The last paragraph was even more self-serving for the police propagandists. It had obviously been drawn up for the purpose of the inquest to explain Essop's supposed malingering and Timol's suicide. It read: 'Rather commit suicide than betray the organisation . . . Vorster and his murderers will not halt our people when we have comrades like Archbishop Hurley, Rowley Arenstein, Vernon Berrangé, Isie Maisels, M.D. Naidoo, George Bizos and others who have been fighting with us since the days of Rivonia.'

Fanie Cilliers did not say that he believed it was a forgery – he could hardly have said so because only his clients really had an interest in forging such a document – but indicated that he considered this last paragraph defamatory, and since his colleagues were involved he felt that he should not make it public. We thanked him for his consideration. The name of a leading Catholic bishop coupled with a group of lawyers known for their participation in the defence of political activists must have been incongruous even to the forgers.

This was not the last time the document surfaced. Five years later the Minister of Justice, Jimmy Kruger, read out portions of it in parliament. The document from which he read was obviously a subsequent edition of the forgery – Archbishop Hurley's name was omitted. The Hon. Minister was attempting to explain 'why these people are continually committing suicide'. His explanation, while no doubt accepted by most of the all-white House, was greeted with incredulity by an outraged Helen Suzman, who dared Kruger to read the document outside parliament. 'You should be ashamed of yourself,' she told the blustering Minister.

The Timol inquest was soon adjourned, as we requested certain documents be made available to us. A call to the magistrate's office to see the affidavits that had been placed before him proved fruitless. He refused to make the information available. Isie Maisels, Said Cachalia, Ismail Ayob and I decided that we had very little to go on without the documents. The magistrate was not even prepared to give us the state pathologist's post-mortem report.

We decided to review the magistrate's refusal. Appearing before the Transvaal Provincial Division in Pretoria, Maisels argued, 'It is this kind of conduct which allows the man in the street to believe that these are proceedings of exoneration and not a matter of making a finding.' The case of *Timol* v *The Magistrate of Johannesburg* became the leading decision on the rights of members of a deceased's family to get information. The judgment is in the names of Judges Cilliers and Marais. Those of us who knew both recognised Judge Kowie Marais's style. The court found that while the magistrate had a discretion in the matter, he had improperly exercised it as he did not even have the documents in his possession when he reached his decision. Inquests were not like criminal trials, said the judges: 'Nevertheless, the inquest must be so thorough that the public and the interested parties are satisfied that there has been a full and fair investigation into the circumstances of the death.' The magistrate was instructed to examine the documents and apply his mind; he did so and duly handed over a set of documents.

When the court at our request moved to conduct an *in loco* inspection in John Vorster Square, the press were barred by the police, despite the magistrate's request that they be present. On leaving room 1026, his father Yussuf Timol said, 'All the sorrows of the past few months welled up in me again when I entered the room from which Ahmed fell.'

Upon the resumption of the inquest the police told their tale. It was Lt.-Col. Van Wyk (who had been a mere lieutenant when he led the raid on the farm in Rivonia) who read the documents seized in the car, and concluded that Timol was in contact with the Central Committee of the Communist Party then exiled in England and was in command of the 'Main Unit' in South Africa. He was thus of 'inestimable value' to the police.

'What this man was guilty of', Van Wyk explained at the inquest, unmoved by the legal principle that a person was innocent until proven guilty, 'was being head of a Main Unit of the Communist Party. He roneoed certain pamphlets and was found in possession of other unlawful documents. He knew how to make pamphlet bombs. In other words, this saboteur had been party to the letting off of bombs which released pamphlets and at the same time activated tapes. He was also in contact with the Communist Party in Britain.' Asked what else, Van Wyk added for good measure, 'I can say that as a self-confessed communist he was involved in a plot to bring about revolution and mass murder in South Africa.' Col. Van Wyk had his man.

Given the importance of their catch, the police decided to keep Timol in the Security Police offices at John Vorster Square. In the past, they explained, communists had escaped from prison or cells, including some whom Van Wyk himself had arrested, such as Harold Wolpe and Arthur Goldreich, the absent main co-conspirators in the Rivonia Trial in which Nelson Mandela and others were sentenced to life imprisonment. Timol was extensively interrogated by a number of police officers, often for over twelve hours each day. Although Col. Van Wyk was in charge of the interrogation, he was assisted by Capts. Richard Bean, J.H. Gloy and J.Z. van Niekerk.

On the night before his death, Timol was guarded by Security Police sergeants Bouwer and Louw, who testified that he slept well; it was warm and he slept in his underwear. At one point they even gave him some of their coffee while the two of them played cards. They both kept watch while their charge slept, or so they claimed. Sleep deprivation was common in the Security Police's interrogation repertoire, and was usually overseen by policemen who were not integral to the questioning process.

I thus put it to Sgt Bouwer, 'If the intention is that a person should sleep, it seems strange to me that two people should have to guard him . . . The office was not a very comfortable place for three persons to spend a night?'

'It is 10 by 18 paces,' he replied.

'It would not even pass municipal regulations. Why was it necessary for two sergeants to spend the night in the room?'

'It is usual for two guards to guard a prisoner. I think this is a regulation.'

'It is a pity it was not kept when Mr Timol jumped from the window.'

Whether or not Timol had slept, his interrogators found him co-operative the following morning, supplying them with names and addresses. The interrogation session that day, 27 October, was the most productive judging by the notes kept by the police.

'If you compare your notes written on the 27th', Maisels put it to Capt. Gloy, 'with those of the two previous days, it is incomparably more than the notes written on the two previous days, put together. On this, the last day of his life, he seems to have answered a large number of questions, which you recorded. He seems to have been more co-operative on the Wednesday than ever before.'

'Judged from the documents it does look that way, but is not really the case. On the two previous days we did not take comprehensive notes. He made hundreds of denials.'

Capt. Gloy's answer confirmed Maisels's question. If Timol was more co-operative, as seemed the case, what had happened that day, or the previous night?

'Even if a man is uncooperative initially, he might talk more once we have got his confidence,' Gloy tried to explain. 'This was our aim with Timol.'

Capt. Van Niekerk claimed he too had tried to win over Timol. At one stage, Van Niekerk explained, Timol had bowed his head and said, 'The prosecutor need only hand in these documents one after the other and I would get at least 20 years.'

But Van Niekerk was there to reassure him.

'My immediate words were, "Get rid of this idea as soon as possible. You might know of a revolution festering and if you give this evidence you could be free tomorrow," ' Van Niekerk added.

'You tried to get his confidence by reassuring him—', I began, when Van Niekerk interjected:

'The police are not persecutors, we are investigators.'

But, the policeman added, Timol was not impressed by his prospects of a light jail term. Again there was no answer to that perennial question, why had he suddenly co-operated?

The police had been trying to establish who the three men referred to in Timol's documents as 'Quentin, Martin and Henry' really were. Capts. Gloy and Van Niekerk were interrogating Timol on just this point that fateful afternoon. Gloy was happy to declare that it had been 'an intensive interrogation' with regard to Quentin, Henry and Martin. But the interrogator could not remember how long it had endured. Between ten minutes and an hour, he proffered. Maisels pointed out that from Gloy's statement it appeared that most of the day was spent on this line of questioning.

'The statement does give that impression,' Gloy responded, 'but it did not happen like that.'

The interrogation was interrupted by Sgt João Rodrigues. A clerk at Security Police headquarters in Pretoria, Rodrigues brought the officers some coffee and their pay cheques. Minutes later there was another visitor to office 1026. Known only as 'Mr X', he declared to Timol that the police knew the identity of Quentin, Martin and Henry. Timol, the police agreed, was shocked when he heard this. It was, Capt. Gloy explained, the 'first and only time' the detainee had expressed this emotion. His eyes were 'wild and staring'. Or, in the equally expressive words of Sgt Rodrigues, 'The Indian appeared shocked when he heard the name . . . He moved his head from side to side and looked bewildered and shocked.'

The interrogators hurried to verify the information they had just received, leaving Sgt Rodrigues to guard the dangerous communist. Rodrigues explained what happened next: 'The Indian asked me if he could go to the toilet. He was sitting on the chair opposite me. We both stood up and I moved to my left around the table. There was a chair in my way. When I looked up I saw the Indian rushing round the table in the direction of the window. I tried to get round the table, but his chair was in the way. Then I tried to get round the other way and another chair was in the way. The Indian already had the window open and was diving through it. When I tried to grab him I fell over the chair. I could not get at him.'

The 30-year-old school teacher lay dead on the southern side of John Vorster Square, ten floors below the room where he had been interrogated for the past four days.

In a matter of seconds Timol had managed to dash across the tiny room, open the window (which was closed because of traffic noise), and hoist himself up and out. It was an incredible story. Sgt Rodrigues was vague on details. 'How it happened I cannot say precisely, it all happened very quickly,' he explained.

Maisels asked him how Timol had opened the window.

'He opened the catch with his hand,' Rodrigues replied.

'Then what did he do?'

'He opened it, and in one movement he dived through, head and arms first.'

Reconsidering, Rodrigues said Timol had fallen more than dived.

'He must have almost wriggled through the window,' Maisels suggested, referring to Timol's height (1.6 m) relative to the window (almost 1 m).

Magistrate De Villiers interrupted, 'I cannot agree. I stood at the window myself.'

'I will argue that point later,' Maisels rejoined.

'I will not allow unfair questions to be put to the witness.'

'I will ask the witness to say what he saw. What did you see?'

'He opened the window and pushed it and then he fell through,' Rodrigues answered.

A strange enough story, made even stranger by the fact that it differed from the one given by Gen. Buys. Buys had claimed that Timol initially made for the door, before jumping through the window. Capt. Gloy had also testified that Rodrigues told him that Timol had made as if he was aiming for the door.

'Did Mr Timol ever aim at the door?' Maisels asked Rodrigues.

'No, not that I saw.'

There must have been a misunderstanding, Rodrigues explained.

Rodrigues, it seemed, had given a number of different versions. Brig. C.W. St John Pattle had conducted his own investigation in the wake of the incident. Rodrigues had given him a different version of events, in which he ran round the table in the opposite direction.

Sgt Rodrigues gave his version to the court, as did Capts. Van Niekerk and Gloy, Brig. Pattle and Gen. Buys. They all cited Rodrigues as their source, despite the anomalies. Which of the various versions, if any, was the truth? Gen. Buys had taken a statement from Sgt Rodrigues two weeks after the incident. 'It seems strange to me', Maisels observed, 'that the most important person, as far as we can see, should be asked two weeks later to make a statement.'

Although Van Niekerk and Gloy claimed to have made notes at the time, they had destroyed these after making their affidavits.

I put it to Capt. Van Niekerk: 'Not even children in Standard Four would write notes out and then throw them into the wastepaper basket. Why, having wasted your time making notes, did you throw them into the wastepaper basket?'

'I did not think them necessary.'

'I am going to put it to you that between these statements there was a substantial change of front as to how Timol met his death.'

The policeman did not have to answer, as Fanie Cilliers interjected, 'I object – this is a fishing expedition.' This was a familiar expression whenever we probed into the happenings in the interrogation rooms of the Security Police.

Gen. Buys downplayed the significance of the different versions, ascribing it all to 'a matter of interpretation'. His cross-examination was cut short when he collapsed in the witness box and had to leave the court. He was never recalled, allegedly on his doctor's instructions. While the Timol family saw this as an act of divine justice, we had our suspicions about the General's collapse. It took him off the hook.

If we accepted that Timol had jumped, in whichever precise sequence of events, the trigger was Mr X's revelation. Why were the mysterious trio of Quentin, Martin and Henry so important? Col. Van Wyk had explained that their full names were Quentin and Henry Jacobsen, twin brothers, and Martin Cohen. He told the court that Quentin Jacobsen and Timol were closely connected and planned acts of sabotage.

Quentin Jacobsen had been arrested on 4 November. In his subsequent trial, he was acquitted. When Maisels explained that Timol's name had not been mentioned in Jacobsen's case, Van Wyk replied he was not involved in that case. He gave the same answer when Maisels pointed out that it had not been alleged that Cohen was an accomplice. All Van Wyk could say was that Jacobsen had been lucky to get off.

Capt. Van Niekerk also claimed that he thought Timol and Jacobsen were conspirators.

'You were wrong,' I told him. 'Mr Jacobsen was acquitted.' It was known that I had defended him and was familiar with the facts and circumstances.

When the magistrate, fearing that I might go off on a tangent, objected to the relevance of this line, I explained, 'Subsequent events have shown that Mr Timol could not possibly have been shocked by the news that Mr Jacobsen was arrested. This is a "terribly" relevant factor. It has been put before you that a man sitting comfortably on a chair was so shocked by this news that he jumped through the window. We are entitled to examine this theory.'

Maj. J.F.C. Fick, who worked with Gen. Buys in the internal investigation, conceded that the police had tried to show a link between Jacobsen and Timol, but had failed. The proffered reason for Timol's plunge had evaporated.

Often the body of a dead detainee on the mortuary slab was more compelling evidence on his behalf than the oral testimony he might have given had he survived the ordeal. His release would inevitably have taken place after his injuries had healed; he would have no witnesses to corroborate his story; and a team of security policemen would claim how well they had treated the detainee, even to the point that they had spent their own money to buy him meat pies and cold drinks.

With the assistance of Dr Jonathan Gluckman, the injuries – carefully noted and subjected to scientific examination – often told a story which could not be controverted, nor easily explained by witnesses whose loyalty to truth and justice was outweighed by their loyalty to the apartheid state, and to their fellow wrongdoers. Such was the case of Ahmed Timol.

After he had fallen ten floors, the fresh injuries on his body could not have been easily attributed to an assault received before he crashed onto the ground. Gluckman had noticed numerous injuries which were not fresh; he explained to us that histologists could date the injuries by the length of the macrophage cells. The healing process comes about as healthy cells make themselves longer in order to devour or replace the injured cells. By measuring the length of the macrophagic cells, you could determine whether the injury was inflicted more than two, four, six, eight, ten or twelve days before.

The scientific evidence showed that the injuries on Timol's body were probably inflicted whilst he was in custody.

Three pathologists testified: the state pathologist Dr Scheepers, Dr Gluckman for the family, and Dr Hieronymus Koch for the police. The main difference of opinion related to the timing of pre-death injuries, which Scheepers and Gluckman dated to the time when Timol was in custody, and Koch dated some days earlier.

In concluding, Maisels said he did not want the court to declare whether Timol had been pushed or thrown: 'All I am asking is for the court to find that it is not known how it came about that he left the window.' Indeed, Maisels continued, the police had left many aspects unexplained. One of these was the discrepancy in statements made by Rodrigues on the day of Timol's death and his evidence in court. 'In my day,' Maisels argued, 'one took a statement from a witness as soon as one could. It is quite inexplicable that no written statement was taken from the man on the spot, Sgt Rodrigues, before 11 November – a fortnight after the occurrence.'

Maisels also pointed out that the police had not explained how Ahmed Timol had sustained his pre-death injuries, which threw doubt on the 'whole cotton-wool case'. Timol had had no injuries prior to his arrest, yet was found to have sustained injuries prior to his death. They could only have occurred during his detention. There was no doubt that Mohamed Essop sustained such injuries; he was hospitalised because of them.

Ultimately, of course, it was the magistrate who was to decide. In a finding that highlighted his basic assumptions, Magistrate De Villiers stated that it was necessary to determine, in the first instance, if the deceased was murdered; if that was not the case, then he fell out of the window by accident; and if that was not the case, then he jumped out himself and committed suicide. To think of murder, he concluded, was absurd, as Timol was a valuable find to the Security Police, who desperately wanted to keep him. The possibility that the deceased fell by accident was also absurd, as it was to accept anything other than that he jumped out the window himself. Assuming that Timol committed suicide, the magistrate continued, he had to determine, if possible on the available evidence, what the deceased's motive had been: was it as a result of his torture or mistreatment by the police, or was it self-reproach, or did he dread a lengthy prison sentence or, lastly, was there a political motive, namely that he did it as a result of the communist ideology?

The magistrate rejected Maisels's suggestions that the internal investigation was a 'whitewashing', saying that it was conducted by members of the South African Police, who were not members of the Security Police. It was difficult for De Villiers to doubt the bona fides of the South African Police.

The magistrate accepted that lesions found on Timol's body may have been caused between one and seven days prior to his death, and the grazes between four and eight days prior to death. If the injuries occurred within four days, then it would have been while in police custody, but all the policemen testified against this, and the court had no reason to doubt their testimony. The medical experts could only speculate that the injuries were inflicted during a 'brawl' when the deceased was pushed around. This, too, was unthinkable. He was a valuable find. He had given valuable information and more was expected.

Although the deceased was interrogated for long hours, he was handled in a 'civilised and humane way'. Therefore, the magistrate concluded, one could not find the reason for suicide in torture or mistreatment. Evidence showed that Timol was a communist and was prominent in the Communist Party as leader of the 'Main Unit' in South Africa. It must therefore be accepted that he was conversant with all orders to members, including the one which said, 'Rather commit suicide than betray the organisation.' Thus the magistrate found that Timol killed himself for a combination of reasons: long jail sentence, giving names and addresses to the police, and the last straw, the revelation of Quentin, Martin and Henry's identity, combined together with the communist ideology.

The magistrate concluded that no one was to blame, although he recommended that the district surgeon visit all detainees, especially to look for evidence of assault, which might prevent long inquests like the present one and unnecessary embarrassment to the police.

The inquest cleared the police, but there were still questions about what had really happened in room 1026. The anomalies in the police story, which we had so carefully exposed, were brushed aside by the confident strokes of a magistrate whose finding was based on two hallowed 'facts': the police were not likely to assault or kill a valuable detainee, and the detainee was likely to kill himself as a result of his 'communist ideology'.

In the absence of justice, rumour and speculation take root. Was Timol accidentally dropped by the police during an interrogation session, as was later claimed by former BOSS agent Gordon Winter? Not known for his reliability, Winter argued that the police were trying to frighten the detainee, when their grip slipped. Much later, a detainee described how he had been held by the ankles by two security policemen and suspended head-down outside a window to look at the ground a number of floors below. The policemen took turns in letting go of one ankle at a time. The victim must have expected that sooner or later they would let both go. He might have struggled. Could Winter have been near the truth?

There was also the story that Timol's body had been mutilated – a gouged eye, the testicles crushed, fingernails torn out. These allegations were publicised in England by a maverick Methodist minister, the Rev. Donald Morton. Twenty-five years later they resurfaced when Mrs Hawa Timol told the Truth and Reconciliation Commission that her son's body had been mutilated. It was also said that the Muslim undertaker who had prepared Timol's body for burial corroborated this story.

When Jonathan Gluckman heard of Morton's allegations, he was outraged. He tried to set the record straight – Timol's body had not been mutilated in the manner described. An affidavit taken by the police from the undertaker at the time confirmed this. Gluckman would not have missed something like this and his integrity was beyond question. Out of a mother's grief came the sorrow that could not be soothed by apartheid justice.

Few were convinced by the outcome of the inquest. As the *Rand Daily Mail* editorial noted after the inquest:

### REAL QUESTIONS STILL REMAIN

'Consider the limitations of the inquest. The magistrate was required to regard Mr. Timol's death as a single incident occurring in a historical vacuum, as it were. He was not permitted to take cognisance of the fact that others have killed themselves while in Security Police hands. He could not seek evidence from other detainees on how they were treated. He could not inquire into why the State has made *ex gratia* payments to several former detainees and one widow of a man who died in detention without there being any public inquiry.

'What the court could – and did – do was hear the evidence of policemen who were with Mr. Timol before he died and at the time of his death. They said he had been considerately treated, and that the police were actually 'trying to win his confidence'. Since, in terms of the Terrorism Act, no one else could visit or talk to him, this sort of evidence could hardly be contradicted.

'Theories that his death was murder or accident were found by the court to be absurd. This is not surprising; few people could have entertained them seriously anyway. As to the motives for suicide, the court permitted itself some speculation. Inevitably, it must again have been based on what police witnesses had to say. No one else was there.'

Perhaps, though, the most powerful comment came from a reader of the *Rand Daily Mail*, Thomas Roderick Scott of Kensington, who wrote shortly after Timol's death:

'My heart goes out to the Timol family in their hour of bereavement . . . But I too am guilty, and so are we all, for it is our silence which lends respectability to the evil of which I accuse the Government and the Security Police. It has taken the death of yet another detainee to wring my Christian conscience sufficiently to give me the courage to raise my voice in protest . . . No longer dare I close my eyes to the naked fascism of a police state in which the mailed fist and jackboot are the order of the day . . . To the Security Police I would say, "Every man's death diminishes me. Seek not, therefore, to know for whom the bell tolls. It tolls for thee." '

The prophecy was partly fulfilled some twenty years later when the Security Police was disbanded. Unhappily most of its members have escaped personal responsibility by clinging on to the conspiracy of silence. We can only hope that the conscience of at least some will lead them to reveal the truth before they are buried like their victims.

For the security policemen and state prosecutors, the Timol inquest was another victory to which they gave expression in their own crass manner. 'The only thing that Lowen and Maisels proved in the Salojee and Timol inquests', ran a 'joke' popular in their quarters, 'was that Indians couldn't fly.' This was repeated in the Bar common room by those members close to the police. Some of the members laughed, although few would admit it today.

Mrs Hawa Timol still carries the burden of her son's death. Aged 78, she appeared before the TRC to recount that horrifying experience. When the police announced her son was dead, she recalled, 'I told them if my body had a zip they could open it to see how I was aching inside.' Speaking in her mother tongue, Gujarati, haltingly, and stifling her tears, Hawa Timol called for the names of her son's killers. 'I still need to know who killed my son,' she said, 'how it was possible that he could commit suicide. I can't be expected to forgive at this stage.' The family were asked how Ahmed's name should be remembered. Their wish: could a school be named in memory of the teacher who gave his life in the struggle against apartheid?

CHAPTER 2

# THE PASSION OF STEVE BIKO

———— ⟨∽⟩⟨∽⟩ ————

'The inquest of Steve Biko was not simply an exceptional event; it
was, in a sense, the revelation of racism, of the way it has
distorted ordinary people, and the way it has destroyed all morality
and decency in a rich and beautiful country.'
– Hilda Bernstein

'The Biko inquest was not a trial in a formal sense, but it became a
trial of the South African system in the court of world opinion.'
– Thomas G. Karis and Gail M. Gerhart

TWENTY-THREE detainees died between Ahmed Timol's fall from the tenth
floor of John Vorster Square in 1971, and Steve Biko's miserable and
lonely death on the cold floor of a cell in Pretoria prison in 1977. Their cases
received various degrees of publicity – but none more than that of Joseph
Mdluli.

Mdluli was a middle-aged hawker suspected of recruiting young men to join
the banned ANC. Policemen paid three visits to Joseph Mdluli's house outside Durban in March 1976. On the first occasion he was arrested and detained; the next day they returned and searched his house; and on the third
day they came to tell his wife that she was a widow.

There was no explanation forthcoming. The autopsy report was kept secret,
the police were silent. Almost three months after Mdluli's death, the Minister
of Justice, Jimmy Kruger, announced that no inquest would be held into the
death. Instead the Natal Attorney-General had decided to charge four policemen with culpable homicide. And so began the trial of Capt. David van Zyl,
Lt. Andrew Taylor, Sgt Mandlakayise Makhanya and Cons. Zabulon Ngobese.

Mdluli had suffered extensive bruising, a fractured thyroid, fractured ribs
and brain haemorrhage. In his testimony, Prof. Issy Gordon, chief government
pathologist for Durban and a Natal University academic, thought that

Mdluli's death could have been caused by a blow to the neck. The police claimed that Mdluli had fallen over a chair.

Despite the extent of the detainee's injuries, the Natal Judge-President, Judge James, acquitted the four policemen. On the police evidence, they had not been present when Mdluli died, having left the room an hour beforehand. But the judge also expressed doubts about the police version and called for further investigation into the matter.

In nearby Pietermaritzburg, the name of Joseph Mdluli featured in a trial under the Terrorism Act, in which it was again alleged that Mdluli was an ANC recruiter. Events took a surprising turn when the state pathologist, Dr B.J. van Straaten, argued that it was impossible that Mdluli's injuries had been caused by falling over a chair, as claimed by the Security Police. When the trial closed in July 1977 and Judge Allan Howard gave his judgment, he referred to Mdluli's death, noting, 'The most probable explanation is that all or most of them [Mdluli's injuries] were inflicted by the Security Police.' When passing sentence, the judge remarked, 'We are satisfied that Mr Mdluli sustained the injuries while in the custody of the Security Police.' It was, however, impossible to say which of the policemen had assaulted Mdluli.

The *Rand Daily Mail* columnist Benjamin Pogrund queried Jimmy Kruger's silence on Mdluli's death. 'Is Mr Mdluli's death to be overlooked as though there was nothing strange about it? Is no one to be held to account for his dying?' In the end, the government threw money at the problem to make it go away. Mrs Lydia Mdluli sued the Minister and the four policemen for just under R30 000. Almost three years to the day since her husband had died, Lydia Mdluli was awarded R15 000 in an out-of-court settlement. Still the silence remained.

It was not only political prisoners who suffered at the hands of the police. This was demonstrated by another case in 1976, when the inquest was held into the death of Soweto businessman Bernard Jabu Vilakazi. He was the son of B.W. Vilakazi, one of the first black academics in South Africa. Suspected of masterminding a number of bank robberies, he was arrested a number of times, but released for lack of evidence. When the perpetrators of one such robbery were arrested, and it was found the money had disappeared, Vilakazi was taken to a police station. A young witness came forward who testified that he had heard Capt. Maree and his investigation team, including a Capt. Kruger, discussing among themselves that it looked as if Vilakazi was going to get off the hook again and that they had better get rid of him.

It was later reported to his widow that her husband had agreed to point out where the gun used in the robbery had been hidden amongst reeds in a swamp in Soweto. Maree and a number of his junior officers took Vilakazi there; he retrieved the gun and pointed it at Maree, who retreated into knee-deep water but nevertheless managed to pump four bullets from his service revolver into Vilakazi's chest. His widow briefed Peet Coetzee and me to represent her at the inquest.

Statements were made available, purporting to have been taken by an investigating officer independent of Maree. When the docket was handed over to us, we discovered that every one of the statements had been written in the same handwriting, which turned out to be that of Capt. Maree. Despite objection we got hold of the investigation diary. It truthfully contradicted the evidence of the investigating officer, who said that he had taken the statements shortly after the event. The record showed that it had taken the investigating officer weeks to get the statements prepared from Capt. Maree, who explained his delay by saying he was very busy.

The firearm that Vilakazi was supposed to have pulled out of the reeds became an exhibit. Capt. Kruger took exception to the cross-examination as to why there was no register of guns at the offices of the notorious Brixton Murder and Robbery Squad. He said that every gun that was obtained was sent for ballistic testing to the forensic laboratories in Pretoria. Believing the young man who gave evidence of the discussion amongst the police officers, we requested the magistrate to subpoena the forensic laboratory to show whether the gun allegedly found by Vilakazi had been sent in for inspection prior to his death. The magistrate replied that we were out of our minds if we thought that the police would have planted a gun on Vilakazi which had already been in their possession. He refused, but said that in order to satisfy us he would ask for an affidavit from the responsible officer at the laboratory stating that this gun had not been with them before.

The magistrate telephoned me in the late afternoon; he asked me if I was sitting down. I said yes, and he read the brief affidavit: Capt. Kruger had sent the gun in ten months previously for examination and upon completion of the tests it had been returned to him at Brixton.

Maree, Kruger and the others who accompanied them upon their murderous trip to the swamp had a simple answer: we don't know what happened to the gun that was returned to Capt. Maree, we don't know how it came to be found in the reeds, and we don't know why it appeared not even to be in working order.

The young prosecutor, Anton Ackermann, unlike some of his most senior colleagues in other cases, asked the magistrate to find that Maree was guilty of murder; the magistrate made such a finding. But the Attorney-General, Mr

J.E. Nöthling, refused to prosecute. Peet Coetzee and our attorney went to interview Nöthling. He regretted that he thought there was insufficient evidence to charge Maree with the murder of Vilakazi. He directed that the investigating officer should be charged with perjury. Although this was an open and shut case, the prosecutor (not Ackermann) managed to lose it. (Ackermann would later successfully prosecute Eugene de Kock and Ferdi Barnard.)

And so the policemen who killed Mdluli and Vilakazi went free. Again, no one was to blame. If the policemen who had killed Mdluli and Vilakazi got off scot-free, why should the policemen who inflicted the injuries on Steve Biko have expected anything less?

The 1960s is known elsewhere in the world as a period of freedom, but in South Africa it was the dark decade in the struggle against apartheid. State repression smashed resistance to the extent that white South Africa entered the 1970s blissfully unaware of the turmoil that was only a few years away. Civil war in Rhodesia, and independence for Mozambique and Angola in 1975, did not bode well for white rule in Africa. At home in South Africa strikes in the Durban area from 1973 heralded a more politically active working class. This new unrest, combined with growing international isolation, did little to shift white voters away from the clutches of the National Party, which was returned to office in 1974. Vorster's new cabinet included Jimmy Kruger, the Minister of Justice, Prisons and Police. Like his boss, Kruger favoured the stick above the carrot.

At the same time as the state was fossilising, new life was emerging in African politics. Alongside the new worker militancy was an equally militant band of black students, led by their most famous member, Bantu Stephen Biko. Born in King William's Town in 1948, Biko still lived there at the time of his detention in the 1970s: he had no choice, having been restricted to the district under security legislation in 1973. His wife Nontsikelelo (Ntsiki to friends) was a nurse and they had two young children.

The state considered Biko dangerous, not because he had ever taken part in violent activities, but because of his formidable intellect. Biko did not invent Black Consciousness. The Mandelas, the Tambos, the Mbekis, the Lembedes and their predecessors, such as Pixley Seme, Sol Plaatje and Josiah Gumede, had through their actions asserted pride in their black identities. But it was Steve Biko who developed and most forcefully articulated the theory of Black Consciousness in South Africa. 'I think basically Black Consciousness', Biko once explained, 'refers itself to the black man and to his situation, and I think the black man is subjected to two forces in this country. He is first of all oppressed by an external world through institutionalised machinery, through laws that restrict him from doing certain things, through heavy work conditions, through poor pay, through very difficult living conditions, through poor education, these are all external to him. And secondly, and this we regard as the most important, the black man in himself has developed a certain state of alienation, he rejects himself, precisely because he attaches the meaning white to all that is good, in other words he associates good and he equates good with white.'

Biko's ideas were expressed in practice. In 1968 he led a walkout from the white-dominated National Union of South African Students (NUSAS) to form a black student body, the South African Students' Organisation (SASO). He was not racist, he often explained, but stressed the need for blacks to liberate themselves. 'Black man, you are on your own' ran SASO's slogan.

After his SASO days, Biko helped found the Black People's Convention, of which he became honorary president. Although his political activities were restricted, he became involved in community programmes in the township where he lived. One of these was the Zanempilo clinic, situated a few miles out of King William's Town, which provided medical services to the community. The clinic was run by Dr Mamphela Ramphele. Although it was not discussed openly, it was common knowledge that Biko and Ramphele were lovers.

The local schemes in which Biko was active were run by a body known as Black Community Programmes (BCP), whose rationale Biko once described:

'Now, the logic here is a simple one, particularly with the community-development projects which form the bulk of the BCP work. It is essentially to answer [the] problem . . . that the Black man is a defeated being who finds it very difficult to lift himself up by his bootstrings. He is alienated – alienated from himself, from his friends and from society in general. He is made to live all the time concerned with matters of existence, concerned with tomorrow, you know, "What shall I eat tomorrow?" Now, we felt that we must attempt to defeat and break this kind of attitude and to instil once more a sense of human dignity within the Black man. So what we did was to design various types of programmes, present these to the Black community with an obvious illustration that these are done by the Black people for the sole purpose of uplifting the Black community. We believe that we teach people by example.'

The 1970s saw the might of the apartheid state pitted against a resurgent popular militancy. Given this climate, it was not long before SASO found itself in the dock. Between August 1975 and December 1976 the state prosecuted nine young blacks for subversion under the Terrorism Act, arguing that the Black Consciousness philosophy propagated by SASO and the BPC would lead to racial confrontation. Biko was the obvious choice to give evidence for the defence.

Over a few days, in one of the great courtroom political statements ever delivered, Biko eloquently outlined the philosophy of Black Consciousness. I heard reports from David Soggot of Biko's testimony for the defence. His evidence impressed Judge Boshoff as well. The judge later confessed to Soggot that when Biko's writings were first published he had not believed that Biko was capable of that sort of intellectual production; he thought that the white activist Rick Turner (later assassinated in his own home) had in fact written these tracts for Biko. Yet, as the trial progressed, Boshoff was so impressed with Biko's intelligence that he changed his mind.

At one stage Judge Boshoff asked Biko, 'But now, why do you refer to people as blacks? Why not brown people? I mean you people are more brown than black.' (The apartheid state and its supporters preferred the word Bantu, anathema to Biko and millions of others.)

Biko replied, 'In the same way as I think white people are more pink and yellow and pale than white.'

'Quite,' said the judge, as if that was the answer he expected.

It was not only black university students who were a threat to the state, but also their younger colleagues in the schools of the country's townships. The increase in the number of high-school students (they resented being referred to as school children or pupils) in the mid-1970s had placed pressure on the educational system, a system which was reviled for the inferior education it provided. When government officials enforced a policy of teaching half of all classes in Afrikaans, the issue was seized upon by angry students. The Soweto Students' Representative Council called a meeting for 16 June. Thousands of school students heeded the call, only to find the police waiting – scared young white men with no qualms about shooting school children. The result was disastrous. In the months that followed, the unrest spread throughout South Africa. Only the full might of state repression could contain the forces unleashed in June 1976, a matter in which those responsible for state security were only too happy to oblige.

One of the instruments forged to bend the spirit of resistance was detention without trial for an indefinite period under section 6 of the Terrorism Act. It was rumoured that the Security Police had perfected a way in which no detainee could escape complete breakdown. This included threats of torture at the time of arrest and suggestions that the captors didn't care a damn if the detainee chose to commit suicide. There would follow a period of complete isolation of two to three weeks. Some detainees confessed that their isolation drove them to a yearning to see their interrogator, even if he had the worst of reputations as a torturer.

The second phase of interrogation consisted of sleep deprivation and physical exhaustion brought on by strenuous exercise to the point of collapse, forced periods of standing on the spot, mixed with foul language and insults, contempt for the detainee's privacy, false information about the loyalty of the detainee's spouse or companion during the period of detention, and often brutality, sparked off by the interrogator's frustration.

Steve Biko was no stranger to these tactics. Prior to his final arrest in August 1977 he had already spent 101 days in detention. He wrote shortly before his death: 'You are either alive and proud or you are dead, and when you are dead, you don't care anyway. And your method of death can be a politicising thing . . . So, if you can overcome the personal fear of death, which is a highly irrational thing, you know, then you're on your way. And in interrogation the same sort of thing applies. I was talking to this policeman, and I told him, "If you want us to make any progress, the best thing is for us to talk. Don't try any form of rough stuff because it just won't work." . . . If they talk to me, well I'm bound to be affected by them as human beings. But the moment they adopt rough stuff, they are imprinting on my mind that they are police. And I only understand one form of dealing with police, and that's to be as unhelpful as possible. So I button up.'

Indeed the Security Police pursued all anti-apartheid activists like bloodhounds. If they could get evidence to convict them of a crime, to put them behind bars for years, this would suit the police's purposes: they would not have to ban them, they would not have to watch them. They believed a political solution lay in prison – then there would be no one to agitate among the masses, who were deemed to be ordinarily law-abiding and compliant.

The Soweto uprising of 1976 only fuelled the flames of police hatred towards Biko: he was considered responsible for the school children's insurrection. The following year they would do their utmost to get him. On the evening of 21 March 1977, he was arrested while buying cigarettes at a café in King William's Town, on charges of defeating the ends of justice, and of persuading or inducing certain state witnesses to give false evidence. He was refused bail. By July 1977, he had appeared four times on charges brought by the Security Police, including one of failing to observe a stop sign while driving. On each occasion he was acquitted of the charge.

Then on 18 August 1977, Biko was again detained with his colleague Peter Jones, at a roadblock on the highway between Cape Town and King William's Town, allegedly for being in breach of his banning order. It is believed that he went to Cape Town to settle differences within the Black Consciousness Movement (BCM). This time he was not acquitted. Before any charges could be laid, he had died in police custody. It was a blow that robbed South Africa of one of its finest sons. He would surely have occupied a senior position in the government of a democratic South Africa. But he was never to see the fulfilment of his aspirations.

Freedom-loving South Africans and the international community were outraged. Even in the atmosphere of repression and suspicion that prevailed in 1977, tributes flowed forth from all quarters for the man many hailed as the true leader of black South Africa. Journalist Donald Woods said of Biko, 'In the three years that I grew to know him, my conviction never wavered that this was the most important political leader in the entire country and quite simply the greatest man I ever had the privilege to know.' United States Senator Dick Clark, chairman of the Senate Foreign Relations Committee's Africa Subcommittee, called Biko's death an 'outrage'. Clark had previously met Biko and described him as a 'remarkable man'. Mangosuthu Buthelezi said, 'I am extremely distressed to hear of Steve's death. I admired him greatly . . . There have been many, many deaths in detention and we as black people are convinced now that for a black man to enter a gaol is almost like entering a grave.'

Percy Qoboza, editor of The World, expressed his shock at the death of 'one of South Africa's most articulate spokesmen of black consciousness, in many ways the spiritual father'. 'I hope that no stone will be left unturned to establish the cause of death,' he commented, probably knowing how unlikely this was. The Black People's Convention issued a fiery statement on the death of their honorary president: 'Mr Biko and other black political martyrs have not died in vain – despite their deaths, they leave the masses with their unconquerable ideas which they successfully preached to those who remain.'

The Biko family were distraught, yet not surprised. Biko's wife, Ntsiki, said, 'I think Steve expected to die in the hands of the Security Police. I think all of us expected it. But Steve was prepared to sacrifice his life for the black cause. He felt his work was so important that even if he died it would be worth it.'

The veteran liberal and author Alan Paton captured the broader implications of Biko's death: 'The Government is making one thing more and more clear. They will treat with no militant black leader whatsoever. They should have a respect for militancy, having had their own Strijdoms and Verwoerds and Vorsters. But they do not. The destination of any militant leader is almost sure to be detention. Any black man who thinks that he has a right equal to any white man to move about South Africa freely, and to share equally in its resources, and to share equally in its government, will end up in detention.

'But there is a possibility more grave than that, the possibility that he may die there. When one examines the statistics, it does indeed seem to be a possibility.'

Amidst this outpouring of grief for the dead man, there came the dissenting voice of the Minister of Justice, Jimmy Kruger. A day after Biko died, Kruger gave an explanation to the press: Biko had been on a hunger strike since 5 September, and had been transferred to Pretoria for treatment, where he died. The following day the Minister addressed the Transvaal congress of the National Party, and he uttered his infamous pronouncement on Biko's death: 'I am not pleased nor am I sorry. It leaves me cold.' This remark came in response to a delegate's congratulation that Kruger was 'so democratic that those who want to starve themselves to death are allowed by him to do so as their democratic right'. Two women from the Black Sash, Esther Levitan and Jill Wentzel (wife of Ernie Wentzel, who was to be one of the three counsel to represent the Biko family), strode into the congress and laid a wreath for Biko at the foot of the platform. Within seconds it had been ripped apart by angry delegates. The crowd hurled abuse as the women left the meeting. *Die Transvaler* expressed its regret at several unfortunate remarks made at the congress. The paranoia of the Nationalists was at its height.

Not content with his pronouncements thus far, Kruger warned a meeting of young Nationalists in Pretoria of the dangers of the Black Consciousness Movement and the Black People's Convention. He said he had a secret BCM document, which advocated that all whites in South Africa must be killed, that 'Uhuru day' was at hand, and that white girls must be raped. Several newspapers called on the Minister to allow others to quote Biko as well, so that people could judge for themselves. 'Strange, isn't it,' mused the *Sunday Times*, 'how all this "damning evidence" in those "secret documents" suddenly popped up when he died.'

Over the following days, Kruger began backtracking as it emerged that some of his senior Nationalist colleagues were unhappy with his unsubtle approach, and the damage it had caused the image of the government. He even stopped commenting on Biko's politics: 'A man has died and it is not for me to start throwing mud at Mr Biko.' But the damage was done. The Minister's explanation was snapped up by the Afrikaans press, who headlined their reports with the 'cause' of Biko's death – a hunger strike. *Die Vaderland* referred to the 'hysterical reaction of certain liberal elements' to Biko's death. Although they did not believe for a moment the police were guilty, they accepted that an inquiry had to be held to prove their innocence. *Beeld* also slammed the English press for their 'venomous' reaction – as did *Die Burger* – and for condemning the police before an inquest was held.

Rumours were rife as to the cause of Biko's death. The *Sunday Express* pointed towards 'severe brain damage'; *The Citizen* inclined towards exonerating the police, reporting a 'kidney illness'. Although the long-awaited autopsy report had yet to be released, we knew what it contained.

As I had appeared in the Timol inquest, the attorney Shun Chetty telephoned me and offered me the brief. The precedent had been set that we were entitled to the documents, but even before this, Shun wanted to know what he should do. I advised him that it was essential that he should contact Jonathan Gluckman to attend the post-mortem. Although Gluckman had a very poor view of Hieronymus Koch (because of Essop and other cases), he respected Prof. J.D. Loubser, the state pathologist who would conduct the autopsy. Shun Chetty was nevertheless sceptical. The call came late to Gluckman – he rushed to the autopsy, arrived while it was in progress, but missed nothing of importance. Gluckman told us that there was evidence of brain damage.

The *Rand Daily Mail* pre-empted the autopsy report by publishing information gained from the doctors who had treated Biko prior to his death. This revealed there were no indications of a hunger strike or dehydration. The evidence instead pointed towards suspected brain damage. Having pipped the long-awaited release of the autopsy report by three days, the *Mail* outraged the Afrikaans press and Nationalist politicians, and was brought before the Press Council on a complaint by Minister Jimmy Kruger.

Sydney Kentridge, SC defended the *Mail* before Judge Oscar Galgut, the chairman of the Press Council. The Minister never even bothered to appear. The *Mail* conceded its headline was ambiguous, but refused to say its report was not correct in contradicting earlier statements by Kruger. Kruger claimed that Biko had refused food and water after 5 September; the *Mail* showed Biko had drunk water in the presence of a doctor on 8 September and was not underweight at the time of his death. Secondly, Kruger claimed the doctors who examined Biko had found nothing specifically wrong with him. Yet the doctors had found symptoms of possible brain damage. 'There is one very good reason why Mr Kruger did not challenge any of these facts,' the *Mail* commented afterwards. 'It is because they are true. We know they are true. And we know Mr Kruger knows they are true.'

In an interview with the *New York Times* on 22 October, Kruger said that the preliminary report on Biko's death gave no indication that assault by the police was a cause of death. 'If there is anything wrong in the Biko case, I will be surprised,' he added. More than six weeks after Biko's death, the autopsy report was forwarded to the Transvaal Attorney-General. According to Associated Press, the autopsy revealed Biko had died from brain injuries. When Jimmy Kruger was first confronted, shortly after his notorious remark, with the details that had leaked out about Biko's condition, he promised a full and fair inquest. He even got into some trouble by telling Fleur de Villiers of the *Sunday Times* that heads might have to roll. Fleur told us that Kruger subsequently approached her and asked whether she had taped his conversation with her. She told him she was not that sort of journalist, but God help him if he denied it. He didn't. The *Rand Daily Mail*'s comment was blunt: 'Kruger's head must be the first to roll.'

On 9 November, Kruger admitted that Biko died of brain damage, but added, 'a man can damage his brain many ways.' Unable to contain his sense of humour, Kruger told a foreign press luncheon, 'I have also felt like banging my head against a brick wall many times, but realising now, with the Biko autopsy, that may be fatal, I haven't done it.'

The inquest opened before the Chief Magistrate of Pretoria, Marthinus Prins, on 27 October, with Profs. Gordon and Olivier as assessors. The police were represented by Retief van Rooyen, SC, assisted by J.M.C. Smit. Evidence was led by the Deputy Attorney-General of the Transvaal, Klaus von Lieres und Wilkau, a favourite of the Security Police. His ability and his enthusiasm for their cause made him a natural to be appointed by the Attorney-General of the Transvaal, no doubt on the suggestion of the Security Police, to lead the evidence on behalf of the state.

As for counsel representing the Biko family, the obvious choice to lead us was Sydney Kentridge. In the years since Timol's case, Sydney had taken silk and had become a leading laywer; he was the number one choice. He was beginning to surpass even Isie Maisels's reputation. Shun Chetty, Ernie Wentzel and I were strongly of the view that he was the man for the job. In the film of the inquest he was played by Albert Finney, but I always thought that Sydney was better as himself. He was busy, as was Ernie, and it fell to me to analyse the affidavits which were handed over by the magistrate.

The affidavits painted a horrific picture. They had been taken after Jimmy Kruger announced the official verdict of a hunger strike. The Security Police from Port Elizabeth had a story to tell, in particular Col. Pieter Goosen, who was in charge of the Security Police in the Eastern Cape, and Maj. Harold Snyman, leader of the interrogation team. There were also affidavits from the doctors who had examined Biko, as well as affidavits by ordinary policemen and prison warders from Port Elizabeth and those at Pretoria prison. It became clear on the first reading of these documents that if anyone had made an attempt to present a near-perfect and consistent story, he had failed miserably.

In their applications for amnesty before the TRC, Snyman and the others later admitted that their affidavits and evidence were false. They had met on the Saturday morning after Biko's death to fabricate a story so as to exculpate themselves and save their country from embarrassment. The fruits of their perjury revealed the rot that had set in in the police force, the National Party government and the administration of justice.

For twenty days following his arrest, Biko was held at the Walmer police station in Port Elizabeth. Naked and manacled, he was not permitted to leave his cell, even to exercise or wash. On the morning of 6 September, Biko was taken to the Security Police offices in the Sanlam Building in Port Elizabeth for interrogation by Maj. Snyman and his team, five in all. Sanlam was situated in the centre of the city, with underground parking, and had already acquired a reputation for the lights of its interrogation rooms being on throughout the night. Biko was interrogated until 6 o'clock that evening, when he was handcuffed and shackled for the night. So the original story went. But in their amnesty applications the security policemen admitted that they had moved the events a day forward in order to avoid criticism for their failure to call the doctor on the 6th. No wonder they failed at the inquest to give an intelligent or coherent account of what happened during the twenty-four hours they had to fill in.

Col. Goosen saw Biko early on the morning of 7 September, after the detainee had been in a 'scuffle' with his captors. The Colonel claimed he feared Biko might have been injured, so he called in the district surgeon, Dr Ivor Lang. After examining Biko, Dr Lang, on Col. Goosen's prompting, made out a medical certificate that there was no evidence of any abnormality or pathology in the patient. By the following day Biko had hardly moved – and his shackles had yet to be taken off. He had not eaten at all.

Dr Lang called in Port Elizabeth's chief district surgeon, Dr Benjamin Tucker, to examine Biko. The trousers Biko had been wearing for the interrogation were soaked with urine, as were his blankets. The doctors decided to transfer him to the prison hospital. That night the prison orderly found Biko fully dressed in the bath – once with water in it, and later in an empty bath.

On the advice of specialist physician Dr Colin Hersch, a lumbar puncture was performed on Biko the following morning, 9 September. A neurosurgeon, Mr Roger Keeley, was consulted by telephone after it emerged that the spinal fluid was filled with blood cells. The neurosurgeon said the signs to date did not indicate brain damage and suggested observation. What might Keeley have found if he had examined him, observed his behaviour and attempted to obtain a history from him?

On 11 September Biko was returned to his cell, where he was discovered lying glassy-eyed, with spittle around his mouth. Col. Goosen decided to transfer him to Pretoria in the back of a Land-Rover. Eleven hours and 1200 kilometres later, Biko was left in the Pretoria prison hospital. Some hours later a young doctor, Andries van Zyl, examined him and ordered that Biko be put on a drip. Later that night he died.

It was clear that Biko suffered his injuries while in the custody of either the Security Police day squad or the night squad. In their affidavits the nearest that emerged to an explanation was the struggle on the morning of 7 September. The night squad stated that nothing had happened the previous night. In fact, as was later revealed at the amnesty hearings, Biko was beaten up on the morning of the 6th.

I took time off and for about three weeks spent all my time preparing for the inquest, working closely with Jonathan Gluckman, Shun Chetty and Ernie Wentzel. (Sydney Kentridge was overseas and only due back a few days before the inquest was scheduled to begin.) Jonathan Gluckman was appalled at the conduct of the doctors. In their affidavits, they admitted some of the facts relating to Biko's injuries, but it also emerged that steps had been taken by Lang and Tucker to hide the fact that Biko had been injured, by submitting the sample from a lumbar puncture under a false name.

There were two aspects of the medical evidence which made the police's and doctors' case patently false. It appeared from the affidavits that early on the morning of 7 September there was a scuffle, although there was no mention of unconsciousness. There were tell-tale signs that this was a cover-up, because it was given out that when Dr Lang was telephoned to come as a matter of urgency, he was informed that Biko had had a stroke. Whether or not the doctors were told that he had been injured the day before was never established, even at the amnesty hearings almost twenty years later.

On the morning of the 7th the pathetic Dr Lang signed a scrap of paper at the instance of Col. Goosen that there was nothing wrong with Biko. It was clear from his affidavit that Biko was injured, that he required medical attention, and that Dr Tucker and Dr Hersch had been called in. But nothing of this was said in the piece of paper filed into the record by Goosen, who was concerned to protect his policemen. It did not matter to him that Dr Lang had perjured himself. And he would get full marks for having outsmarted the naive Dr Lang when, as a Brigadier, he later claimed that the doctors had never informed the police of the severity of Biko's condition. They had told him Biko was feigning illness.

When Sydney returned and I handed him the paginated record, with notes of the suggested cross-examination, in which Dr Lang's false document was highlighted, Sydney, almost in a rage, exclaimed, 'I can't believe it! Show me!' When I showed him the photostat copy of Lang's certificate, he paused, took a copy of the papers, and went to another part of his house to digest them, leaving Ernie, Shun, Jonathan and me in his study. By lunchtime he was on top of the case. He rubbed his hands, a sure sign of his confidence that he would smash the tissue of lies that had been put together.

Jonathan Gluckman had read the police affidavits. Although a pathologist and not a neurologist, his clinical *nous* nevertheless told him that the injury which led to Biko's death would almost invariably have rendered him unconscious. He explained to us what a contracoup injury was: if you knock the head suddenly, and hard enough, and the head turns with sufficient force, the soft brain tissue smashes against the opposite side of the inner skull, and the cells break up and start bleeding. He explained to us that this is what happens when a boxer is knocked out – there is almost invariably unconsciousness. In his opinion, the injury he saw at the post-mortem must inevitably have caused Biko to fall down and remain unconscious for a period of time.

Jonathan recognised this as a weak point in the affidavits and suggested that we should call the leading neuropathologist in the country, Prof. Neville Proctor from Wits University. Prof. Proctor had no doubt that the injury to the brain was so severe that Steve Biko must have been unconscious for a period of up to 20 minutes. This evidence made nonsense of the police version as to how Biko came to be injured. According to them, he had continued with a titanic struggle against a number of his captors for some time before he was subdued. Of course, no one hurt him in any way during this struggle. Gluckman also suggested that we consult the neurosurgeon Rodney Plotkin, an experienced clinician and teacher of neuropathology, who confirmed Prof. Proctor's view.

During the inquest. Prof. Proctor was asked by counsel for the police about an overseas trip one of us was alleged to have made to gather information on the Biko case. The matter was not public knowledge. How could they have known? Sydney Kentridge leapt to his feet, and objected to the question. No explanation was given. We could only conclude our phones were bugged.

We had been informed that police witnesses would have a transmitter on their person, to relay the evidence to their colleagues, sitting in their offices, or in motor cars near the court. When Maj. Harold Snyman went into the witness box, he was carrying a small leather briefcase. He carefully placed it in front of him, on the witness stand. We were tempted to ask what was in it. What a coup it would have been if we had enquired and found a transmitter. But it was too risky to ask. We would have looked paranoid if nothing was found. Sydney decided to ask that it should be taken away from the witness box, without giving any reason. Maj. Harold Snyman's face went beetroot-red.

Although the police always denied using this sort of dirty trick, the practice was exposed by the Appellate Division in the 1977 case of S v Mushimba. The appellants had been convicted of terrorism in Namibia. It turned out that one of the employees of a legal firm representing the accused had passed on witness statements and other confidential documents to the Security Police. Isie Maisels had argued the case and won: the convictions were set aside. When Chief Justice Rumpff noted at the beginning of his judgment, 'This case is happily unique in the history of South African law', this was no doubt more from a lack of evidence than occurrence.

Privilege between client and legal representative did not count for much in Security Police circles.

Two weeks before the Biko inquest was due to start, Jimmy Kruger banned a number of oppositional newspapers and organisations. Whenever organisations are banned and there is no freedom of expression, the courtroom becomes a forum in which political activity is conducted. Biko's inquest was no exception.

The venue for the inquest – the Old Synagogue in Pretoria – was highly charged politically. Here the Treason Trial had been held in the late 1950s, leading to the acquittal of all 156 men and women accused. Here too Winnie Mandela and 21 other activists were acquitted by Judge Bekker and immediately redetained; and in an attempt to re-try them, the plea of autrefois acquit succeeded before Judge Viljoen. Here the first trial under the Terrorism Act was held, against Tuhadeleni and 34 others, in which we argued that South Africa's mandate over South West Africa granted by the League of Nations had lapsed as a result of the passing of a United Nations resolution. At this trial Andimba Toivo ya Toivo annoyed Judge Ludorf intensely by starting off his statement, 'M'Lord, we find ourselves in a foreign country, convicted by a judge who is a stranger to us.' These words found themselves inscribed on a plaque in the lobby of the United Nations and inspired many to help Namibia gain its independence.

From the point of view of the state, the Old Synagogue had the advantage of being somewhat out of the way, and, if there were to be any demonstrations, only a few of Pretoria's loyal citizens would be inconvenienced. From the point of view of those who wanted to display their anger, there was a small advantage: between the portal leading into the Synagogue and the inner edge of the pavement, there was a paved yard which could hold a singing, toyi-toyi-ing, slogan-shouting crowd a few hundred strong. It served a purpose similar to the chorus in an ancient Greek play. At times it sang 'Senzani na?' [What have we done?] to the rhythm and melody of a funeral dirge; at times it sang songs of praise to Steve Biko, to Sydney Kentridge, Ernie and myself, but more often it spat out its contempt and threats to Prime Minister John Vorster, Minister Jimmy Kruger, or one or other of the team of interrogators in the witness box.

When on Monday, 14 November 1977 the Biko inquest began again in earnest after an initial postponement, the Old Synagogue was packed to capacity. Mrs Winnie Kgware, first president of the Black People's Convention, entered the packed courtroom bearing a wreath and a picture of Biko. Biko's mother Alice, his wife Ntsiki and his sister Nobandile, dressed in black, sat staring into space, like icons of grief, generally immobile, listening. The only time the mother reacted was when I showed Prof. Proctor a coloured photograph of the pale red cells of Biko's brain after his skull had been opened for the postmortem. She shook her head and jerked back, reminiscent of the manner in which Biko's head must have turned as a result of the tremendous blow he received.

Reporters took over the front rows and the long benches which had been built for the accused in the Treason Trial. There were more than two hundred people present, among them journalists, diplomats and many followers of Biko. The heat was unbearable, the acoustics intolerable.

The police witnesses – brigadiers, colonels, majors, captains and lieutenants, the centurions appointed to save white civilisation – filed through the witness stand, one by one, absolving themselves of any blame. Lt. Gert Kuhn was the second-in-command at the Walmer police station and the first witness to be called. After Von Lieres had led the witness, Kentridge rose to begin his cross-examination. He did not get very far. His question was in English. Kuhn's first reply was in Afrikaans – he asked to be questioned in Afrikaans. Kentridge suggested an interpreter be found.

The magistrate was puzzled. 'Mr Kentridge, isn't it expected of counsel in our courts to be bilingual?'

'Yes, entirely,' Kentridge responded, 'but I choose to ask my questions in English, one of the official languages of this country.'

When the magistrate asked what authority Kentridge had for this proposition, the advocate was blunt: 'There are no rules about this, other than the provision in the Republic of South Africa Act about the equality of the two official languages.' After some dithering by Prins, Kentridge explained, 'May I say it is not a question of being unable to cross-examine this witness in Afrikaans. Let me say at once that I am quite capable of cross-examining him in Afrikaans. I do not choose to do so.' There was a chorus of approval from the packed court. The insistence by Minister Andries Treurnicht that some school subjects should be taught in Afrikaans had been the immediate cause of the 1976 student uprising. Hearing the leader of the Bar stand up for his right to speak English was viewed as an expression of solidarity with their cause. The court adjourned while an interpreter was found. A song of praise for Kentridge reverberated as the spectators filed out to join those who could not get inside.

When the inquest resumed, the police stuck to their story of the scuffle, an approach which hinged on the explanation of the day squad: Maj. Snyman, Capt. Siebert, WO Marx, WO Beneke and Sgt Nieuwoudt. During the so-called scuffle, so the story ran, Biko had bumped his head, and this was probably when he sustained his injury.

Kentridge was quick to point out that this 'bumping of the head' had not been mentioned in any of the 28 affidavits filed by policemen in the matter. Even the statements taken by the investigating officer, Gen. Kleinhans, who had drawn the police's attention to the question of brain injury, failed to mention that Biko may have bumped his head. Of the five security policemen, none was prepared to say he had seen Biko bump his head. Capt. Siebert claimed that Biko had fallen flat on his face during the scuffle, yet he had not mentioned this in his affidavit to Gen. Kleinhans. WO Marx never saw Biko hit his head against the wall, or fall on his head. And so it went on.

There was an entry in the police occurrences book recording a bump on Biko's head – but the entry was made a day after the incident, by Maj. Snyman. This prompted Kentridge to speculate that the entry had been added only once the police became concerned about Biko's condition. The 'bump' story was finally exploded when, under cross-examination, Snyman was forced to concede that he had not seen Biko's head strike the wall, but was merely drawing 'an inference'. Strangely, the policemen had said nothing of the scuffle to the doctors. Their version to the doctors was that he was shamming. Dr Lang had, after all, given a certificate confirming their self-serving diagnosis. Why, if they believed Biko had been injured in a scuffle and the police were not to blame, had they not informed the doctors?

The account was deficient in other respects as well. Biko had 'gone berserk', Snyman explained, because he had been confronted with certain facts.

Police counsel, Retief van Rooyen, asked Snyman, 'This evidence with which you confronted him, was it based on deductions or facts?'

'It was definitely based on facts. Declarations which were taken from his own friends, people who had worked with him, and were already in our possession.'

Van Rooyen read out a list of allegations regarding the illegal pamphlets which these sworn statements ostensibly proved. The statements were handed in to court. After examining them overnight I noticed something very strange. All the statements had been dated and sworn to after Biko's death. That was all Sydney needed. He addressed the court, asking if Snyman could return 'to explain one simple point'.

'I understand from my learned friend', he explained, 'that . . . the relevance of this is that these were the documents, the sworn statements put to Biko by Maj. Snyman, is that right?'

Van Rooyen replied, 'Yes, our contention is that it is part of the *res gestae* and part of the reason for the sudden eruption.' He obviously had not looked at the date and thought that Kentridge was going to elicit some simple fact to argue against their admissibility.

All that remained was to draw the Major's attention to the date. Kentridge, a master of self-control, could hardly suppress his anger. He deliberately used the Afrikaans word for affidavit to spring the trap that would expose the lie:

'Maj. Snyman, do I understand you right when you say that these *eedsverklarings* are the *eedsverklarings* which you put to Stephen Biko, what I want to know is, was it on the 6th or on the morning of the 7th?'

'It was on the morning of the 7th.'

After Sydney pointed out that the dates ranged from 14 September to 30 September, he declared, 'All of them, in other words, after the death of Mr Biko. These could not have been put to him during his lifetime. What we have got here is a smear prepared after Biko's death, and I think it is a disgrace.'

Maj. Snyman squirmed. He attempted to explain that he did not have the statements in his possession, just the facts. He suggested that he had in mind unsworn statements; but the other policemen had said that on that morning no documents at all were put to Biko. The stench of perjury was unmistakable.

Another crucial element of the police story was Biko's 'confession'. By the evening of the 6th the police claimed that Biko had admitted drawing up the pamphlet of which he had initially denied knowledge. The pamphlet was headed 'August 18th – Commemoration Day' and called for a stayaway to mourn the exiled, jailed and dead. 'Wherever you are, organise yourselves into groups to deal with those who do not heed this appeal. BEAT THEM, burn their books, burn their cars and shops. Show no mercy to informers and other collaborators – they must all be KILLED!" And so it carried on, exhorting bloodshed and mayhem in capital letters. To say that its parentage was questionable was an understatement. But the police maintained that Biko had confessed to authorship of the pamphlet. Kentridge took up the issue with Snyman.

'Well, now, what I am asking is: what methods of persuasion did you use to draw this admission from him?'

'I confronted him with the information we have available.'

'Yes, that may be, but why should he answer you at all, why shouldn't he just whistle at you?'

'Well, when I confronted him with the information, first he denied it but he later said, he later admitted that he really did it.'

'Yes, but that is my point. You confronted him with it and he denied it. Now, how did you persuade him in the course of the day to admit it? Tell us your methods of persuasion, Major.'

'I put the facts to him.'

'Yes, but you said you put the facts to him and he denied it. Then later he admitted it. What do you do, do you make threats?'

'No, I never threatened him.'

'Did you put physical pressure on him?'

'No.'

'Do you, how do you break him down?'

'As I have already said, the legislation gives us an unlimited time period during which we can detain this person. And to put my career on the line and to embarrass the department, even the authorities, wouldn't pay us to assault this man to get information out of him.'

'Right, no, well you have told us then that you don't use physical means. But you see, there wasn't a question of time. Here in the course of a few hours, you got him from a denial to an admission . . . What was to stop Stephen Biko simply saying to you: "Sorry, I am not answering"?'

In his replies the Major was highly evasive.

'I am asking you again: How did you get him to change his mind?'

'I put it to him later that I had statements from his fellow detainees.'

'And did you show them to him?"

'Correct.'

Again the written statements, this time to hide the answer to the question that Snyman was desperate to evade: what can you do to a man who insists on keeping silent?

We inferred from the suspect information given by the security policemen that Biko refused to be intimidated. There was a distinct possibility as well that the Security Police had gone too far in trying to make him talk. Little did we know then that the cause of their wrath was Biko's insistence on sitting on a chair, an impertinence that drove Capt. Siebert to unbridled action against a black man who did not know his place.

Kentridge also questioned Snyman on the fact that Biko was kept naked. Asked why, Snyman replied, 'To prevent detainees committing suicide.'

'To stop them committing suicide in the police cells? For example, with a pair of underpants?' Kentridge shot back.

'No, the person is not wearing underpants, he is completely naked.'

The magistrate tried to explain that Snyman had missed the point. Kentridge tried again, 'Do you suggest that a man could commit suicide with a pair of underpants?'

'It's possible.'

'You know,' Kentridge continued, 'we have seen a lot of statements made by the Special Branch in which it is said that people have committed suicide with their blankets. Do you know about that?'

'Yes, I know that maybe at other places, but we haven't had to deal with that in our section.'

'Yes, but you still let him have blankets?'

'Yes.'

Biko had been kept overnight at Sanlam Building – for security reasons, they said. After 6 o'clock, Lt. Wilken and two other policemen had taken over from Maj. Snyman's team. Snyman claimed this second team was there only to guard Biko. This was an unconvincing story – even the Major agreed that they were 'the night interrogators' at one point.

Kentridge put it to Lt. Wilken: 'Does it not seem strange that a lieutenant and two warrant officers should be detailed to stand watch over a man chained hand and foot?'

Wilken agreed, that under normal circumstances it was.

Wilken claimed that Biko had told him, during the course of the night, that he would make a statement in fifteen minutes' time.

'You must have been pretty pleased that he was prepared to give you a statement?' Kentridge said.

'I was surprised and pleased.'

'That was very good for a non-interrogator,' was Kentridge's comment.

When Lt. Wilken returned to hear the confession from Biko, he found him asleep and did not wake him up. Despite the implausibility of the story, Wilken stuck to his guns – he had not interrogated Biko.

Col. Goosen mentioned this trivial incident of Biko's falling asleep to the Security Police chief, Brig. Zietsman, yet not that he had confessed. Zietsman reported that Goosen had spoken to him telephonically on the Sunday before Biko was sent to Pretoria. 'I also asked Col. Goosen how far the investigation had progressed, whereupon he informed me that at one stage Biko indicated that he wanted fifteen minutes and then he would make a statement, and that after the fifteen minutes he refused to co-operate any further.' Surely if a confession had in fact been made, Wilken would have reported this to Goosen and Goosen in turn to Zietsman.

Under examination Goosen confirmed the content of the conversation, whereupon Kentridge remarked, 'Yes, but you see the significant thing about it is that this was your reply to a question about how far the examination had progressed.'

'That is so.'

'And your reply was a negative reply.'

'I wouldn't say it was negative.'

'Well, it speaks for itself. You see, on the basis of this I suggest that the whole story about Biko having made a confession must be a fabrication.'

'I strongly deny that. I can only comment on what was reported to me by my officers. I never personally conducted an interrogation.'

'Now what I want to suggest is that if Maj. Snyman had reported to you what he reported here in court, what he tried to tell the court about Biko having made a confession, your reply to Brig. Zietsman, when he asked how far the investigation had gone, would have been to say it had reached the stage where he had confessed to sending out the pamphlets.'

'It was a brief, broad discussion with Brig. Zietsman about the background of the detention from the 19th until that Sunday.'

And that was Col. Goosen's explanation.

As it turned out, the portion of the story that Biko was not interrogated during the night of 6–7 September was partly true: not for the reasons given by the security policemen but because he had been seriously injured during the early morning of the 6th. He was confused, inarticulate, incontinent and repeated questions which were put to him rather than trying to answer them, like the echolalia of infants, a sure sign of serious brain damage. That he confessed to serious wrongdoing in this condition is ridiculous. The posthumous attempt to convict him of planning violence failed to convince any reasonable person at the time. The later partial amendments made by the security policemen to their story merely confirmed that outright lies were told, instigated and rehearsed by their superiors.

The Security Police, in their rehearsals for their cross-examination, would have obtained information about the personality of counsel preparing to cross-examine them. The second-in-command of the Security Police, Brig. Johann Coetzee, was the only one connected with the Biko inquest who had any knowledge of Kentridge. Like most leading cross-examiners, Sydney Kentridge used irony as one of his tools of trade. Goosen must have been warned of this; very early on, he avoided a question by saying he was not expected to answer such sarcastic enquiries.

Col. Goosen had already tried to explain why he kept Biko chained up. Kentridge asked him under what power he had had Biko chained for 48 hours. Goosen merely replied, 'I have full powers to ensure a man's safety.'

When Kentridge asked for the statute, Goosen answered, 'We don't work under statutes.'

'Thank you very much. That is always what we suspected,' Kentridge said.

Even the regime's staunch supporter, *The Citizen* newspaper, published the questions and answers that led to this damning admission. As the media throughout the world reported the cross-examination, the brutality, the callousness and the lies of the security policemen were thoroughly exposed.

Worse was to be revealed at the amnesty hearings in Port Elizabeth twenty years later. Biko's arms had been stretched out crucifixion-style against the grille door of the interrogation room. His leg irons were extended by passing the chain across the bars of the door. When the hundreds of spectators at the hearings let out a sound of anguish at this, even Capt. Siebert admitted that it was inhumane.

Towards the end of the inquest, it emerged that a telex had been sent by Col. Goosen to Security Police headquarters in Pretoria. The telex was critical. Not only did it refer to injuries inflicted on Biko at 7 a.m. on the morning of the 7th, but also that he was transported to Pretoria in a 'semi-comatose' condition. The telex, intended only for Security Police eyes, made no mention of shamming.

The telex came to us via a circuitous route. We were trying to determine from whom Jimmy Kruger had obtained his information regarding Biko's death. The magistrate refused to permit us to subpoena Brigs. Zietsman and

Coetzee (to whom Goosen had sent the telex) when suddenly police counsel Van Rooyen piped up, offering us a private consultation with the two Brigadiers.

'Well, this is a very strange and surprising offer, Your Worship,' Sydney responded, 'but if the policemen are prepared to have a private consultation, that is appreciated. Why not have a public consultation, Your Worship? . . . I don't know what the value is of my having a private consultation with them, if they don't undertake to give evidence on the lines of what they tell me in a consultation.'

Sydney undertook to consider the offer, but was anxious to resume the cross-examination of Goosen then in progress.

He asked Goosen why he had not corrected the Minister Kruger's statement about the cause of Biko's death.

'I saw no reason to, as it fell outside my functions.'

'Well, Colonel, in a matter of this importance you must have made some written report to your superiors.'

'I want to understand the question well. Is that in connection with the Biko incident?'

'Yes.'

'At that stage no written report.'

After discussing the affidavits, Sydney got to the point: 'Did you not make any telex report?'

'No.'

Kentridge had already asked Goosen if there was a telex line between Port Elizabeth and Pretoria.

A positive response led him to ask, 'Did you send any telex message concerning Biko at any time?'

'Not at that stage.'

'At any time?'

'I can't remember, I don't believe so. It was dealt with telephonically.'

'What did you say in reply to my question that you did not send a telex at that time? Does that suggest that you sent it some other time?'

'I want to just make it clear that we dealt with it telephonically, between Brig. Coetzee and myself, and at a later stage I delivered consultations or reports telephonically to Brig. Zietsman.'

Goosen knew that he had sent the telex to Security Police headquarters in Pretoria a few days after Biko's death. When he was recalled for further cross-examination he tried to excuse himself, after the existence of the telex had been revealed by Brig. Zietsman, by maintaining that the telex did not concern Biko's death but rather transport arrangements. Thereupon Kentridge read extracts from the telex to Goosen to show how evasive and untruthful he had been when first he gave evidence.

'(1) Transport within a station wagon-type of Land-Rover from which the seat had been removed. Four white members of the Security Branch were present to ensure the maximum safety and comfort of the deceased.

'(2) He was laid on five cell mats, each of which is 1" thick, and they were piled on top of one another.

'(3) He was covered with four blankets and a fifth blanket was made into a pillow for his head.

'(4) The vehicle left the Walmer cells at 6.30 on the 11th for two reasons: firstly, the urgency of the case because Biko's condition had deteriorated since 9.30 on the 11th, when he was admitted to the cell. At the time of his admission he could still walk; later he gave the impression of being in a semi-coma.'

A dying man in a Land-Rover on some mats, travelling over one thousand kilometres with only a bowl of water by his side – this, the Security Police considered comfortable.

After checking the translation with Col. Goosen, Kentridge continued, 'Now I want to suggest that in your original affidavit and your evidence here you would never concede that he was in anything like a semi-coma.'

'I don't believe the term "semi-coma" came out very clearly in the evidence.'

'But this was your word, "semi-coma"?'

'To head office.'

'And you also speak of the urgency of the matter. Now in your evidence here, did you not give the impression that you did not regard the case as really urgent?'

'I viewed it as urgent on medical advice that he must get to an institution with the necessary facilities as quickly as possible.'

The telex also mentioned that the district surgeon had recommended that Biko be moved without delay to a prison so that examination facilities would be available. It also noted that Biko lay down during the journey, did not eat although food was available, was given water twice, and at times was awake and at times appeared to be asleep.

'That is the telex,' Goosen said.

'So that was the report of the journey to Pretoria. Do you think this is in accordance with the statement in your affidavit that at that time on the 11th the general opinion was that there was nothing seriously wrong with him?'

'I think it agrees broadly with my evidence in court. We worried about a condition which could not be diagnosed.'

'Now look at paragraph 3. You said that this telex had nothing to do with his injuries. Paragraph 3 reads "on the 7th of September at 7 a.m. he sustained injuries." Correct?'

'That's the paragraph.'

'These are covered by the occurrences book entry of the 8th of September. The occurrences book entry . . . records that after his injury he refused to speak.'

'That is so.'

'So you are tying up his refusal to speak with his injury?'

'A telex is a highly abbreviated summary. You will notice that the telex is composed by one of my staff officers and by my colleague Maj. Fisher. I broadly agreed completely with the content of the telex.'

Kentridge dealt with the late entry in the occurrences book, before noting that the telex said the injury was 'inflicted' on the detainee on the 7th.

'By the 16th you were talking about an injury which had been inflicted on the detainee?'

'An inference was drawn there.'

'Well, an inference, but an inference that who had inflicted it?'

'Probably in the scuffle in the office.'

'But *toegedien* means that it was inflicted on him?'

'That is a manner of speaking, that is to illustrate clearly to head office.'

The Colonel was unable to explain why the word had been used.

How, after Dr Hersch's examination, could any of the police officers have honestly believed Biko was shamming? And if Col. Goosen believed this, why did he have Biko sent to Pretoria? And he described him in the telex as being in a 'semi-coma'.

The evidence of the doctors was no better than that of the policemen. Kentridge questioned Dr Lang on the certificate he had issued.

'You were told that he [Biko] had refused food and water, that he displayed a weakness of all four limbs and it was feared that he had suffered a stroke. Do you see that?'

'That is correct.'

'Whereas in your certificate all you say is that you were told he would not speak. Well, why didn't you put these other matters in your certificate?'

'I cannot answer, I can't, it is inexplicable.'

The magistrate was incredulous. 'You can't what?' he asked.

'It is inexplicable, I can't explain to you why.'

Dr Lang had to admit that the medical certificate he gave on Biko, which certified no injuries, was 'highly incorrect'.

Lang said that he wanted to send Biko to hospital, but the Security Police refused. He admitted under cross-examination that Col. Goosen's suggestion that Biko was feigning had influenced his perceptions. Hearsay proved more important than his own observations.

Much of Dr Lang's testimony was confused and contradictory. One of the assessors, Prof. Gordon, a highly respected pathologist from the University of Natal, intervened on numerous occasions to remind the doctor what he had already said as he stumbled along. The Professor asked searching questions from time to time. It gave us hope that even though he did not have a vote but was on the bench in an advisory capacity, he would influence the magistrate to make the correct decision.

When Dr Benjamin Tucker, Dr Lang's superior, was called in to see Biko, he too failed to make detailed observations of his patient.

'Did you find out from Biko or from anyone else why he had wet his blankets and mat?' Kentridge enquired.

'No.'

'Did you think he was incontinent?'

'I don't think so.'

'What did you think?'

'I thought that because of his position he had passed water normally in the bed, he was unable to move.'

'What do you mean his position? Because he was chained up?'

'Because he was . . . yes.'

'Did you draw Col. Goosen's attention to this?'

'No.'

Beyond not informing the Colonel, Tucker had not even asked Biko why he had wet his bed. When Kentridge asked him why not, all the doctor could say was, 'Your Worship, I am afraid I cannot answer that question.'

Nor did he ask Biko how his lip was cut.

In his medical report on Biko, Tucker had omitted to mention that the detainee had been handcuffed to a grille, as well as overlooking the abrasions on his ankle, while referring to those on his wrist. When Kentridge questioned him on this, all Tucker could say was that it was an error.

After he was informed that Biko might have suffered a stroke, Tucker conducted a neurological examination and found evidence of a doubtful extensor plantar reflex, a sign of brain damage. Even though Tucker thought Biko might have sustained brain damage he asked neither Biko nor Goosen whether Biko had suffered a head injury.

Kentridge enquired why he had not asked Goosen about this.

'Your Worship,' Tucker replied, 'there was evidence of an injury to his head . . . to his lip, which might have produced . . . or the cause of the injury to his lip may have caused a brain injury or a head injury.'

This was unbelievable. Kentridge was quick to pick up the attack.

'But Dr Tucker, wasn't that all the more reason to investigate it? If you thought the lip injury might have been evidence of a head injury, oughtn't you to have investigated it further?'

'I don't know, from whom?'

'From Col. Goosen?'

'I don't think that I am required to do so.'

'Oh, come!'

'There was this history as given to me of a restraint, and as I said the injury could have come during that period.'

'Why didn't you say to Col. Goosen: "While this man was being restrained, did he by any chance get a blow on the head?" Why didn't you ask a simple question like that?'

'I didn't.'

'Why didn't you?'

'I can only answer by saying that I didn't.'

Tucker had not tried to persuade Goosen to hospitalise Biko in Port Elizabeth after the Colonel announced his intention to send the detainee to Pretoria. When asked why not, Tucker replied, 'I did not consider Biko's condition to be so serious at that time.'

This was despite the fact that there was froth on Biko's mouth, that Biko was apathetic and uncommunicative, and that a physician had found an extensor plantar reflex. Even after receiving the results of the lumbar puncture, Tucker did not attempt to stop the trip.

Kentridge put a hypothetical situation to the doctor: 'Let us assume that you had been seen in Port Elizabeth by a holiday-maker from Pretoria who had a child acting in a bizarre way, the parent might have suspected that the child just didn't want to go back to school, but nonetheless on examination it had been found that the child's left arm was weak, that the child had an extensor plantar reflex, that a lumbar puncture had shown some red cells in the cerebro-spinal fluid, that when doctors were called in for the fourth or fifth time, the child who had been walking the previous day was found lying on the floor, no one could get any sense out of him, he was hyperventilating, there was froth. Take that case, would you possibly have permitted the parent to drive that child 700 miles back to Pretoria?'

'Your Worship, I think that there are certain – there is a certain difference in, shall I say, circumstance.'

'Well, first would you answer my question and then explain the differences. Would you have let the parents drive the child back to Pretoria, or would you insist that the child go into hospital immediately?'

'I would insist that the child go into hospital, yes.'

'May I suggest to you that the only difference between the hypothetical case that I put to you and the case of Stephen Biko was that in the Biko case Col. Goosen insisted that the man not go into a provincial hospital?'

'Your Worship, I wouldn't say insisted. He was averse.'

'Well, why then didn't you stand up for the interests of your patient?'

'Your Worship, I am afraid I am not aware, I don't know whether one in this particular situation, that one can override . . .' Dr Tucker's voice trailed off.

Kentridge filled the silence. 'The Security Police?'

'The decision made by a responsible police officer.'

Even the mode of Biko's transport went unchallenged by the chief district surgeon. Prof. Gordon tried to put his question tactfully. 'Now did it not occur to you there was a – I don't want to embarrass you – but there might well be an ethical responsibility upon you to argue the case to Col. Goosen that if you can't get this man to Pretoria by air, then we should send him to Pretoria by ambulance and we should try and negotiate for an ambulance?'

'That is correct, yes,' Tucker replied.

'Did you attempt to influence the Colonel in any way to try and negotiate for an ambulance?'

'No, I did not.'

Sydney Kentridge questioned Tucker on his ethical standards. 'In terms of the Hippocratic Oath, to which I take it you subscribe, are not the interests of your patient paramount?'

'Yes, Your Worship.'

'But in this case they were subordinated to the interests of security? Is that a fair statement?'

'Yes.'

Dr Tucker had earlier testified that while the Hippocratic Oath was relevant to his ethical conduct, his conduct was actually governed by the rules of the South African Medical and Dental Council (SAMDC). When this was put to Gluckman when he was in the witness box he replied, 'I was somewhat surprised at this. There is nothing in the Hippocratic Oath that conflicts with the rules of the Medical and Dental Council . . . In terms of accepted medical ethics the interest of the patient, and no one else, is paramount.' Gluckman had been elected to the Council repeatedly. He was amongst the leading guardians of the profession's ethical standards.

Drs Lang and Tucker had disgraced themselves. In summing up, Kentridge noted, 'The relationship of the district surgeons to Col. Goosen was one of subservience, bordering on collusion. Their obvious neglect of their patient's interests, and their deference to the requirements of the Security Police, was a breach of their professional duty, which may have contributed to the final result. They should not have tamely accepted Col. Goosen's refusal in any circumstances to send Mr Biko to a proper hospital.'

In addition, both the doctors had attended consultations with counsel for the police. As such, we submitted, very little weight could be given to their testimony.

Our most devastating attack hinged on the likelihood of unconsciousness as a result of Biko's injury. At the hearing Prof. Proctor, holding a cast of a skull Hamlet-like and pointing to the way the blows on the head resulted in the contracoup injury, described how assault upon assault inflicted upon Biko's brain must have led to unconsciousness. 'I would say, as far as medically one can say it, that this patient must have been unconscious.' He was supported by Prof. Ian Simson, head of the Department of Pathology at Pretoria University. The only remaining expert was Prof. Loubser.

Prof. Loubser was Von Lieres's witness. Although Von Lieres asked a number of questions, he did not challenge Prof. Proctor on his opinion about the likelihood of unconsciousness. When Prof. Loubser was called into the witness box he was led by Von Lieres. In an inquest the duty of the representative of the Attorney-General is not to take sides, but to pursue the truth. We expected Von Lieres to ask Prof. Loubser for his response to Prof. Proctor's evidence in relation to the likelihood of unconsciousness. No such question was asked by Von Lieres.

Sydney, Ernie, Shun and I went into a huddle about the cross-examination of Prof. Loubser. Should Sydney ask him if he agreed with Prof. Proctor? If he denied it, it would have opened up an issue which might have weakened the strength of Prof. Proctor's evidence. If he agreed, Prof. Proctor's evidence would have been strengthened and no reasonable person could possibly have believed the police account as to how Biko was injured. We argued the pros and cons amongst ourselves; Sydney was persuaded that he would ask the question, rather than leaving it open. His reason was that Prof. Gordon, the assessor and Professor of Forensic Medicine at Natal University, would no doubt have asked the question if we did not. We had welcomed Prof. Gordon's appointment as an assessor. He was a man of integrity. We didn't know much about the other assessor from Bloemfontein, Prof. J. Olivier but, in the event, had no reason to doubt his competence and impartiality. Unfortunately, assessors sit in an advisory capacity only and have no vote.

After Von Lieres had finished the examination of Prof. Loubser, Kentridge asked whether this meant that Von Lieres had no further questions for the witness. 'Because if he has, with respect, I don't think they should be left to the end,' he said.

The magistrate was confused, noting that Von Lieres had put in all the documents. 'And by his conduct I suggest he has got no further questions at this stage. I can hardly force him to ask questions if he is not inclined to do so.'

Kentridge wanted to get across to Prof. Loubser that we were not hostile to him. He made it clear at the outset. 'What I would like to place on record on behalf of my clients is that we have complete confidence in the thoroughness and integrity of your examination.'

Eventually Sydney put the vital question. 'I want to say that those advising me, Prof. Proctor and also Mr Plotkin, the neurosurgeon, will express the view that on what we have seen of the brain injury in this case, there must have been a period of unconsciousness following it of ten minutes, more likely fifteen to twenty minutes, and possibly up to an hour. Would you agree with that?'

There was a slight smile on Prof. Loubser's face, clearly indicating that he was expecting the question.

'Again, Your Worship, I take notice of the point made. I have no reason to disagree with it.'

The victory was not as absolute as we would have liked. Sydney remarked that the medical authorities he had cited suggested 'that when you have brain damage of this magnitude, it is virtually unthinkable that there is no unconsciousness'.

'My answer was, I have no reason not to agree with that.'

The magistrate supposedly attempted to clarify matters, asking whether it was 'virtually inconceivable that there would not have been an appreciable period of unconsciousness'. This was a much higher test than normally expected.

'That is my personal view,' the enigmatic Professor replied, 'and I agree with that, but the alternative that he was not unconscious is a distinct possibility that I cannot rule out.' We wondered why the magistrate put the question in such absolute terms and whether Prof. Loubser would have conceded the theoretical possibility if the question was differently phrased.

Klaus von Lieres und Wilkau was and is a highly competent advocate. His failure to ask Prof. Loubser the vital question could not have been an oversight. We were certain from the manner in which Prof. Loubser answered the question that the matter had been canvassed by Von Lieres, and Von Lieres knew that Prof. Loubser's answer would be destructive of the story put together by the Security Police.

Von Lieres's conduct was mentioned in our closing argument. Kentridge noted, 'In the task of probing and testing the evidence of the police officers and the witnesses, we had the assistance of the court, but of none of the other counsel in court. All, including the Deputy Attorney-General, appeared to us to ask no question but to repair or extenuate the effect of our cross-examination.'

This observation was not confined to our side. In his report on the inquest, Sir David Napley, former head of the British Law Society, remarked on Von Lieres's conduct: 'It appeared to me, both on a true reading of the Inquest Act and the decision in the case of Timol, that it was his [the Deputy Attorney-General's] duty dispassionately to present, and test, on behalf of the Magistrate, all the relevant available evidence. I may have been wrong but I came away with the clear impression that, on such occasions as he intervened, his questions were directed to preserve the position previously taken up. To this end on occasions he intervened to support the police and doctors although they were already represented by other Counsel.'

After the demise of the apartheid regime, Klaus von Lieres und Wilkau and other Attorneys-General declared that they had never taken instructions from the government of the old regime. Many of us thought that it was not necessary for the government to give instructions in relation to a particular case.

There were differences of opinion amongst the pathologists as to the number of blows which were likely to have been received by Biko – but none concerning the extent of the damage. What more could we ask for? We believed that we had done enough to show that crimes had been committed – culpable homicide or manslaughter, perjury, and attempts to defeat the ends of justice.

Legally, we argued, there was a duty upon the police to explain how Biko had received his injuries. We were confident that we had destroyed the version put forward by the police. The 'scuffle' with the 'bump' tacked on at the end, the 'confession', and the shamming story all had been exposed as the tissue of lies they truly were. Biko's appalling physical condition had clearly emerged. In the light of this, the journey by Land-Rover to Pretoria was nothing less than barbaric.

'It is difficult to comment on these facts in measured terms,' Kentridge said. 'Certainly Col. Goosen's statement, made after the death of Biko was known to him, that everything was done for the comfort and health of Steve

Biko is as cynical a statement as any heard in a court of law.' For all this concern, Biko 'died a miserable and lonely death on a mat on a stone floor in a prison cell'.

The conclusion to our submission evinced our general contempt for the version put forward by the Security Police:

'The police felt confident they could rely upon the doctors to support them. And their confidence was justified. Perhaps strengthened thereby they, with gross impertinence, presented to this court a totally implausible account of Mr Biko's death, starting with a fanciful description of a struggle, violent in the extreme, in which no blow was struck, a bizarre account of an alleged shamming when to any candid observer a man's progress to his death was being seen and described and all the while the refusal to acknowledge the head injury . . . This inquest has exposed grave irregularity and misconduct in the treatment of a single detainee. It has incidentally revealed the dangers to life and liberty involved in the system of holding detainees *incommunicado*. A firm and clear verdict may help to prevent further abuse of the system. In the light of further disquieting evidence before this court, any verdict which can be seen as an exoneration of the Port Elizabeth Security Police will unfortunately be interpreted as a licence to abuse helpless people with impunity. This court cannot allow that to happen.'

Retief van Rooyen, in his closing argument, said there was not a 'tittle' of evidence that Biko had been beaten up. Well, that was his job. He could hardly have responded to the detailed argument we had advanced that his clients could not be believed. B. de V. Pickard had almost nothing to say about the conduct of his clients, the doctors.

In view of the tendency of inquests to exonerate the police, we were not hoping for too much; this was, however, one of our strongest cases. We anxiously awaited the verdict. The family had listened to the evidence without apparent emotion; they were waiting for justice to be done. It was not to be.

On the morning of 2 December, Magistrate Marthinus Prins announced to a packed courtroom:

'This is my finding in terms of the Inquest Act, No. 58 of 1959:

'The identity of the deceased is Stephen Bantu Biko, Black man, approximately 30 years old;

'Date of death: 12 September 1977;

'Cause or likely cause of death: Head injury with associated extensive brain injury, followed by contusion of the blood circulation, disseminated intravascular coagulation as well as renal failure with uraemia. The head injury was probably sustained during the morning of Wednesday, the 7th of September

1977, when the deceased was involved in a scuffle with members of the Security Branch of the South African Police at Port Elizabeth.

'The available evidence does not prove that the death was brought about by any act or omission involving or amounting to an offence on the part of any person. That completes this inquest.'

Three minutes was all it took.

Our worst fears had been confirmed. Whatever hope we may once have held out for judicial checks on the police had been shattered. Sections of the press slated the decision, as did international opinion. The London *Daily Telegraph* found the verdict 'very shocking'. A State Department spokesman in Washington noted, 'It seems inconceivable on the evidence presented that the inquest could render a judgment that no one was responsible.' The *New York Times* commented that the paper had reported that Biko had 'died mysteriously'. 'But now the only mystery remaining after the lengthy magistrate's inquest, now concluded with a whitewash verdict, is which of the security officers who interrogated Mr Biko actually administered the fatal blows.' A number of prominent legal academics, led by those from Afrikaans campuses, called for a full judicial inquiry into Biko's death.

Sir David Napley concluded, 'In short, I was left in no doubt that Mr Biko died as a result of a brain injury inflicted on him by one or more unidentified members of the Security Police.' Sir David presented a full report to Jimmy Kruger. What Kruger did with it we never discovered.

Afrikaans papers urged better treatment of detainees to prevent a recurrence, yet felt the judicial system was unblemished, and accepted the verdict. In an editorial written in English – a most unusual event for the chauvinistic Afrikaner journal – and addressed to the foreign news media, *Die Vaderland* noted with pride, 'The South African judiciary remains a bastion of democracy . . . our judicial system remains unscathed, a remarkable record when one bears in mind that we reside in Africa where there is very little respect for democracy.' In small print at the bottom, the paper added meekly, 'Although we concede that the verdict itself would have been more satisfactory had the presiding magistrate seen fit to analyse evidence and motivate his finding more extensively.'

The furore over his verdict led Magistrate Prins to remark, 'I have only one standard, and that's my conscience.' He was not the first nor the last to wash his hands of an innocent man's blood.

Steve Biko's mother Alice, his wife Ntsiki and his sons, Nkosinathi and Samora, sued the government represented by the Ministers of Health and

Police, alleging wrongful injury on the part of the police and neglect on the part of the doctors. The verdict had been a terrible disappointment, to the family, to the legal and medical profession, and to some judges, not only those opposed to the apartheid policies of the regime. Those disgusted by the magistrate's acceptance of the police fairytale expected the civil trial for damages to show up the magistrate's decision. Their hopes were pinned on a trial that would show Biko's captors and doctors responsible for his death. Mrs Alice Biko, Ntsiki Biko, his brother Khaya and his sister Nobandile were anxious for the trial to take place as soon as possible, so that at least the public record could be set straight.

Sydney, Ernie, Shun and I were also looking forward to the civil trial. Sydney had been devastated by the magistrate's unbelievably brief and patently wrong judgment. He was depressed, and questioned what purpose there was in practising law in South Africa. He later thanked me for my remark that the magistrate's judgment was not what mattered; the world jury had found both the policemen and the doctors guilty of an atrocity. South Africa's justice system, to its shame, let them off.

As far as the civil case went, we feared that we might again not succeed in proving a fatal assault inflicted by the police. The difficulty with showing that medical neglect was the direct cause of Biko's death lay in an opinion expressed by Prof. Loubser during the inquest that the condition of Biko consequent on the injury was irreversible and that even if he had received proper medical attention, he would nevertheless have died. If this was indeed the case, the doctors and Minister of Health would be absolved from liability. In preparation for the civil trial for damages, Sydney asked me whether I could arrange a meeting with the doctors the following Saturday afternoon at two o'clock. I asked Karel Tip, a clerk in Shun Chetty's office, to organise the meeting.

On my arrival at Sydney and Felicia's home, I saw Sydney standing at the top of the stone-paved driveway, waiting for me. A powerful and shining motorbike was parked in the shade. In a hushed voice Sydney told me that Prof. Loubser had arrived for the consultation, pointing to the Professor's motorbike. Who had invited him? I realised that when I asked Karel Tip to arrange for the doctors to be at Sydney's home, he had gone through the list of witnesses and called them all, including Prof. Loubser.

'What are we going to do?' asked Sydney.

I suggested that we hold a short and superficial conference, thank everybody for coming, and break up. Sydney and I went into his study where we found the Professor. I greeted Prof. Loubser politely and we waited for the others, exchanging pleasantries and asking questions about the Professor's interest in motorbikes.

Jonathan Gluckman, Prof. Proctor and Rodney Plotkin all arrived, followed by Shun Chetty and Ernie Wentzel. The doctors appeared not to be concerned about Prof. Loubser's presence. Ernie's expressive face betrayed his amazement. Shun Chetty gave a look of absolute disbelief – Shun considered anyone on the government's side as the enemy. They both remained silent. Sydney, with unaccustomed diffidence, asked, 'Well, who would like to start?'

Almost like a student in his class, Prof. Loubser raised his hand. He said that he was very pleased to be there with his medical colleagues and thanked Sydney for the opportunity to take part in the conference. Something had been worrying him ever since he had testified. He had said that the injury was irreversible and that Biko would not have recovered even if he had been given proper medical attention. He realised, on reconsideration, that he might have been wrong. His opinion, as expressed at the inquest, was based on the condition of the brain at the time of death, as evidenced on postmortem examination. He explained how an injured brain deteriorates if no proper medical attention is given. The process may, in some instances, be reversed with proper care. He might well have been wrong in assuming that the brain was in as bad a condition shortly after the injury was inflicted, and he could not really say whether Biko would have lived or died if he had received proper medical care.

Sydney Kentridge behaved as if that was what he really expected from the Professor. What had meant to be a cautious and brief consultation became a full-blown discussion, not only on medical aspects, but on the legal consequences as well. It became clear that once there was no dispute between Prof. Proctor, Prof. Loubser and Rodney Plotkin, the state was unable to avoid liability, and it would have to pay compensation to the mother, wife and children for the loss of support. Unfortunately, South African law did not then allow a claim for emotional trauma arising from the death of a loved one (although recent attempts are being made to admit such claims under certain circumstances).

For the civil case Van Rooyen was dropped as counsel for the police. He had become involved with the Minister of Foreign Affairs, Pik Botha, in exposing the Information Scandal, in which Minister Connie Mulder and Dr Eschel Rhoodie, Secretary for Information, were involved, and which caused great tensions within the government. He had become *persona non grata* in certain quarters. The government briefed Frank Kirk-Cohen, later to become a judge. Frank telephoned and said that they wanted to settle. He offered

R30 000. We rejected it out of hand. He increased it to R40 000. That too was rejected. Frank then warned that if we did not accept the R40 000, they would pay the amount into court. They would not fight the merits, but confine their defence to the quantum of damages. This was where our case was weakest. The actuary advising us said that we could not justify a claim of over R35 000. He was, I think, more accustomed to assessing loss of earnings in motor collision cases, than dealing with the death of a political leader at the hands of the state.

Steve Biko had been paid very little by the community organisations for which he worked. Frank Kirk-Cohen warned that they would try to show that even this was precarious. He said they would persuade the judge that Steve Biko's future was such that he was unlikely to earn much. The road that he had chosen, according to Kirk-Cohen, would have led him to terms of imprisonment rather than improved earnings as time went on. It would be interesting to ask Judge Frank Kirk-Cohen now what the earnings of Biko might have been in the new South Africa.

We called in the Biko family and explained there was a danger that they could get the worst of both worlds. We advised them that we were convinced the government would not fight the merits of the case and thus a judicial finding against the police and the doctors was not likely to come about. If the court did not award us more than they had chosen to pay into court, the family would have to pay their own and the other side's costs from the date on which the tender was made. With a heavy heart they accepted our advice, and left it to us to raise the amount as high as we possibly could.

The final negotiation was left to Ernie Wentzel, who managed to push them up to R65 000. This was for capital and costs. It sounds like a pittance these days, and hardly to be viewed as proper compensation for the loss of such a man. At the time, however, the Biko family was struggling. His mother was being paid less than R30 a month as a pension for having worked for the better part of her life as a cook in a nurses' home. Ntsiki was not earning very much as a nurse. The children were at school. They needed the money. When Ntsiki heard she would receive R30 000, she announced that she would donate the money to a community project. 'It's all blood money. It doesn't bring Steve back and we miss him terribly,' she explained.

In January 1978 Mamphela Ramphele gave birth to Biko's son and named him Hlumelo – 'the shoot that grows from a dead tree trunk'. Years later I had to apologise to her that we had not communicated with her during the inquest, or in connection with the civil proceedings for compensation. Her and Steve Biko's child would of course have also been entitled to a share. She understood the reasons for our failure to contact her. We were, after all, acting on behalf of the immediate family and did not know what their attitude would have been if we had contacted her.

There was some delay in getting the money to the Bikos. Shun Chetty was closely watched by the Security Police. The victim of many of their dirty tricks, he fled the country before the money was paid to the family. Willy Lane, who was later to be the instructing attorney in the Aggett inquest, was the leader of the attorneys' profession, and saw to it that the money was paid over to the Biko family.

A few months after the finding, I was telephoned by Herbert Fischat, an attorney in Port Elizabeth whom I had never met. He would not discuss the purpose of his visit on the telephone and he flew up one Sunday morning specially to see me. I met him at my office, where he told me that a group of black attorneys in the Eastern Cape were about to make a statement expressing their frustration at the situation in that part of the country. While there had been three well-known advocates in the Biko inquest, and no expense was spared in engaging expert witnesses, Fischat explained, the very people we had exposed as the torturers and killers of Biko were still operating unchecked, without anyone of any seniority in reputation to take them on again. The black attorneys had gone to Ben Kies, counsel practising in Cape Town and the doyen of black practitioners, who suggested to them that they should appoint a representative to come and discuss the matter with me. I was embarrassed and chose not to discuss the matter with him in general terms. I asked him if he had come to offer me work. He looked hard at me, and asked whether I would come; I said yes, that if he had a case and I was available I would do so. He had a case set down for a day the following week, and I agreed to come. A young woman was charged under the Terrorism Act; if convicted she would get five years.

The state's case rested on the evidence of one of her friends, who had also been detained and interrogated in Sanlam Building. During the course of the trial, I asked the slender young woman to describe the room in which she was interrogated. It was the same room in which Biko had been kept, still without a stick of furniture. Carefully, slowly, I extracted from her how she came to make a statement against her friend. She had been threatened, she said, and told that she would meet the same fate as Biko, and after she had repeatedly refused to admit the correctness of what was being alleged against her and her friend, she was grabbed by both her wrists and swung around the room, and allowed to fall flat on her face on the floor. Such witnesses were warned that if they departed from their statement they would be charged and convicted of perjury and jailed for three to five years. The police did not bother to charge her. There had been no other evidence. The prosecutor closed his case and the client was acquitted.

In her case the policeman responsible for injuring her was a junior member of the team, who had not featured in the Biko inquest. Not so in the next case of *S v Khumalo and Others*, in which Capt. Siebert was one of the important *dramatis personae*.

After the Biko inquest and the widespread condemnation of the lack of safeguards for detainees' well-being, indefinite detention under section 6 of the Terrorism Act was used less frequently. There was also provision in the statutes, however, for detention for fourteen days under the Internal Security Act. Eight young men from the Port Elizabeth area were arrested and charged with attempting to leave the country for the purposes of undergoing military training. They were caught near the Botswana border and handed over to Capt. Siebert and other security policemen stationed at Sanlam Building. Confessions were produced from all eight. One, the youngest and arguably the smartest, had an incredible tale to tell.

He was first of all tortured by Capt. Siebert and his team. Then he was taken to a magistrate to make a confession: he told the magistrate from Port Elizabeth that he had nothing to confess and that he had been assaulted by Siebert and his men. He begged the magistrate not to tell the police what he had disclosed. The magistrate acceded to his request, told him that he would not take a statement from the accused, but would make a note of what he had told him, put it in a safe and, if he was brought to court, he would tell his lawyer about it. Although I believed him, I had considerable doubts as to whether the magistrate would have kept his word. Even magistrates, like the Biko doctors, were not anxious to buck the Security Police. I asked Herbert Fischat to approach the magistrate – and there the note was, as the young man had said. But then the state produced a confession from the young man, taken by another magistrate in the nearby town of Uitenhage.

Capt. Siebert and his attendants contended that the eight confessions had been freely and voluntarily made, without any threat or duress or promise made by the police to them. The law had been recently amended to place the onus on an accused to prove that his or her confession was not freely or voluntarily made if it was given to a magistrate. In terms of this provision, the eight confessions were handed in and, despite objection, the state elected and insisted that the accused should give evidence first of their challenge to the confessions. Siebert entered the witness box in rebuttal after the young accused described what had happened between him and the first magistrate.

Siebert therefore had ample opportunity to make up a story about why there was a visit to another magistrate, in a different town, and why the young accused, having refused to confess in the first instance, should have done so on his thirteenth day of detention, the day before he appeared in court. Siebert claimed that the young accused came to him and beseeched him to take him to a magistrate so that he too could make a confession. He felt unhappy that all seven of his co-accused had confessed and he would go to court without having done so.

The upshot of the case was that the confessions were thrown out and the accused were acquitted – but not before Capt. Siebert had a go at me personally. Towards the end of his evidence in chief, the prosecutor asked him whether he was surprised that the accused had made allegations of assault against him and his men. His answer was, 'Yes and no.' He put his hand into the inside pocket of his jacket and drew out a document, and proceeded to explain that the Communist Party had instructed its members and supporters to make false allegations against the police. It was a copy of the document that Minister of Justice Jimmy Kruger had read in parliament and Fanie Cilliers had refused to use in the Timol inquest. I objected to its production on the basis that the accused had already given evidence and it was not suggested that they were members or supporters of the Communist Party or that they knew about the document or had received instructions. As my own name was mentioned in the last paragraph, the reason for its production was not difficult to find.

Nothing ever happened to Capt. Siebert, who subsequently rose to the rank of Brigadier. In 1995, after the adoption of the new democracy, when the country was divided into nine provinces, his name was published in the list of candidates for appointment as provincial Commissioner of Police in Mpumalanga province. There must have been many that wanted to remind those who had to select the commissioner, of Capt. Siebert's service to the apartheid state in Port Elizabeth. In the end he did not get the job. Like many others he took a severance package and retired.

Although the Security Police were untouchable, the doctors were still practising in a profession with its own strict code of ethics. After re-reading the record in the Biko case, the magistrate was moved to refer portions to the South African Medical and Dental Council. The medical profession refused in the first instance to take up the matter of Biko. According to Jonathan Gluckman, the Medical Council's tune changed as a result of what appeared to some to be a deliberate campaign by doctors outside the country. At various medical congresses, foreign doctors would ask their South African colleagues present, with more than a touch of irony, whether they were on the same register as the doctors that were supposed to have treated Biko.

When the Medical and Dental Council finally investigated Drs Lang and Tucker, in October 1979, the doctors applied to the Supreme Court, arguing that the Council's procedures had not been followed. Their application was dismissed by Justice G.A. Coetzee. In April 1980 the Council held its first preliminary investigation, two and a half years after Biko's death. Included with the district surgeons was Dr Colin Hersch. The Council committee found 'no evidence of improper and disgraceful conduct'. Helen Suzman was among those 'utterly astonished' by this finding. In June the full Council met to review the committee's finding. The closed meeting confirmed that no disciplinary action would be taken. This decision, the *Rand Daily Mail* commented, 'makes mumbo-jumbo of the fine phrases of the Hippocratic Oath, phrases which apparently do not preclude doctors in such cases from filling in false medical certificates or ignoring serious signs or from leaving a patient naked, urine-soaked, manacled to a radiator grille, or from being driven 1100 km through the night in the back of a Land-Rover.' Only Dr Hersch welcomed a public inquiry.

With the Council refusing to act, it was left to the Medical Association of South Africa (MASA) to conduct an inquiry into the conduct of Dr Tucker, who was a MASA member. The report found no grounds for expulsion. Concerned members called for the reasoning behind the decision. MASA eventually issued a statement describing Biko's treatment as 'inadequate', but blamed the security laws for curtailing the independence of the physicians. A number of respected doctors resigned from the organisation in protest.

Jonathan Gluckman was a member of the Federal Council of MASA. In a widely publicised statement, he noted, 'I am very aware that mistakes have been made by us in MASA in the handling of the Biko matter.' MASA's Federal Ethical Committee, he explained, would consider holding a full inquiry into the matter. In May 1981 MASA appointed a commission comprising Prof. J.N. de Villiers and Isie Maisels. The government 'strongly advised' Lang and Tucker against testifying. Some three months later the findings were made public. Dr Lang's certificate concerning Biko's condition was described as 'unsatisfactory and incomplete, if not a deliberate *suppressio veri*'. The report also criticised the subordination of doctors to police personnel.

The following year, a group of prominent doctors led by Prof. Frances Ames and Prof. Phillip Tobias again called on the Medical and Dental Council to reopen the investigation. In January 1983 the Council sent questions to the doctors concerned, one of which asked whether they considered themselves responsible to their patients or the Security Police. The Council again refused to reopen the inquiry. Outraged, the group of doctors announced they would approach the Supreme Court, and were supported by Prof. Issy Gordon, one of the assessors in the inquest. The Health Workers' Association planned a similar move.

The application was finally heard in September. The applicants, who were represented by Sydney Kentridge, Dawid de Villiers, QC and also Ismail Mahomed, SC, accused the Council of failing in its duty to take action against the doctors. The high-powered legal team argued that Drs Tucker and Lang had been 'grossly incompetent, insensitive and untruthful' in their treatment of Biko and that in the light of the uncontradicted evidence to that effect, no reasonable and honest council could have decided against a prosecution.

For the Council, Pierre Roux, SC argued that the Council's decision was based on the evidence given at the Biko inquest and was 'legally unassailable'. The court, he submitted, had no jurisdiction over the Council's decisions on professional ethics.

At the end of January 1985, Judge Boshoff delivered his judgment: there was *prima facie* evidence of improper or disgraceful conduct on the part of Drs Lang and Tucker, and the Council was ordered to hold an inquiry. Prof. Ames expressed her delight at the decision because she felt the Council had tried to place itself above the law.

In July the Council opened its inquiry into the conduct of Ivor Lang and Benjamin Tucker. Dr Tucker was found guilty of disgraceful conduct and was suspended from the register for three months (suspended for two years), and Dr Lang was found guilty of improper conduct, cautioned and reprimanded. Tucker was 64 and announced he would retire the following year. Suzman called the sentences 'astonishing and superficial'. In an attempt to salvage its tattered reputation, a full meeting of the Council later that year decided to strike Dr Tucker from the roll. Dr Lang's reprimand was unchanged.

It was not long before Lang's name was again in the news, and again in connection with ill-treatment of detainees. In 1985 Wendy Orr was a young doctor working in the Port Elizabeth district surgeon's office. Her duties included the examination of all new prisoners. Within a few months, Orr noticed a remarkably high number of prisoners who complained of assault by the police and had injuries to confirm their stories. Her immediate superior was Dr Ivor Lang, who was concerned about the number of alleged assaults Dr Orr was recording, and the subsequent police investigations which might follow. The prisons department, more concerned about protecting itself from any claims than the welfare of the detainees, instructed Orr to stop recording prisoners' complaints of assault.

In September 1985 AZAPO marked the eighth anniversary of Biko's death; the response of the Port Elizabeth police was swift and brutal. Many were arrested. All the detainees examined by Dr Orr complained of assaults, and had the wounds to prove it. Driven by desperation at her helplessness, Orr decided to go public. On the strength of Orr's affidavit and those of selected detainees, an application was launched to interdict the police from assaulting detainees. The application was successful. For her trouble, Wendy Orr was suspended from her work with prisoners by Dr Lang. Later that year, she resigned her position, after an anonymous donor paid off her government bursary. Again, Lang had shown whose interests were paramount.

In 1991 Dr Benjamin Tucker petitioned the Medical Council to be reinstated on the roll. In his application, he conceded that he had become 'too closely identified with the interests of the organs of the state, especially the police force'. In his application Dr Tucker wrote that he had been advised that in order to succeed he had to say sorry. 'I hereby do so.' One would have thought that the Biko family were entitled to more than this cliché.

After the inquest, Mrs Ntsiki Biko expressed her disappointment with the judicial process. 'It was declared that nobody was to blame for the fatal lesions on Steve's brain,' she said. 'Nobody was to blame for the vegetable-like condition that he was in when he breathed his last. Nobody was to blame for his death . . . We and the black people of South Africa will not rest until we know how Steve Biko came to meet his death.' She has stayed true to her word.

In the late 1980s I was presented with another opportunity to get at the truth when Col. Snyman again appeared in the witness box to explain what he knew of the brutal murder of Matthew Goniwe and his three companions. I could not resist the temptation to take him back to Biko.

'Where were you during September 1977, Mr Snyman?'

'I can't remember, M'Lord.'

'Oh?'

'But if you can give me more of a clue . . . '

'Where did you work?'

'Security Branch.'

'Security Branch here in Port Elizabeth. You were the officer who was in charge of the interrogation of Steve Biko, not so?'

'I refuse to answer this question, M'Lord.'

'Why? Why do you refuse to answer the question, Mr Snyman?'

'It can incriminate me. Such an inquest was held and I testified there and it can incriminate me, M'Lord.'

'Oh well, do you feel that if you honestly answer any questions I may ask you in relation to the death of Mr Biko, you will incriminate yourself?'

'That is correct, M'Lord . . . '

'Do you remember that you brought a false certificate from Dr Lang to court which said there was nothing wrong with Mr Biko even though he was seriously injured?'

'I refuse to answer the question, M'Lord.'

'Well, can you remember that you brought a telegram to court in which you notified the Commissioner in Pretoria that a blow was inflicted on Biko's head shortly before his death, in order to avoid the accusation?'

'I am not going to answer the question, M'Lord.'

'You can't answer it. Because you feel you may incriminate yourself if you answer that question. Is that what you are saying?'

'That is correct, M'Lord.'

'And you say that you honestly believe that, not so?'

'Correct, M'Lord.'

'Honestly believe that you will incriminate yourself if you testify truthfully about that occurrence?'

'Correct, M'Lord.'

Wide publicity was given to this remarkable resort to the right to remain silent by one who had blatantly refused it to so many detainees. The Biko family, AZAPO and journalists demanded the reopening of the case. Surely, they asked, Snyman's answers amounted to an admission of guilt?

Not so, we had to advise. In the constitutional state about to be established everyone had the right not to incriminate himself or herself. To many, especially the Biko family, the supposed blindness of justice led to her being more easily cheated. Thus when parliament established the TRC in the mid-1990s to bridge the past and the future, by allowing victims and perpetrators to speak, to award amnesty and make reparations, the Biko family expressed their reservations, calling instead for Biko's killers to be tried and punished. Together with AZAPO and others, they applied to the Constitutional Court for the amnesty hearings of the TRC to be declared unconstitutional. They did not succeed, however, the court holding that the interim constitution envisaged the granting of amnesty.

It was the promise of amnesty in fact which lured Biko's killers to approach the TRC. In December 1996 Gideon Nieuwoudt, Harold Snyman, Daniel

Siebert, Ruben Marx and Jacobus Beneke applied for amnesty in respect of the death of Steve Biko. Would the truth finally emerge?

The chief instigator of the applications in the case of Biko seems to have been Nieuwoudt. In 1977 he was a sergeant and a member of the team that dealt with Biko. At the inquest his affidavit was almost a carbon copy of those of the others. We decided at the time not to call him to give oral evidence as we thought he must have been the tail-ender of the team. Even if we got damaging evidence out of him, it would be attributed by our opponents to his junior status. In any event, we were confident that we had enough for the police to be held culpable by Magistrate Prins. Nieuwoudt's subsequent elevation to the rank of colonel, despite the number of detainees' complaints against him, shows that vigour in killing and torture was a recommendation rather than a bar to promotion.

In the 1990s Nieuwoudt was sentenced to twenty years' imprisonment for the murder of three of his black colleagues in the Security Police and an askari (an ANC turncoat) at Motherwell near Port Elizabeth. Now in 1996 he was waiting for his appeal to be heard and was out on R50 000 bail. He decided to apply for amnesty. Although on the evidence at his trial the predominant motive for his actions had been to prevent the disclosure of fraudulent conduct for personal gain – which, if proved before the amnesty committee, would defeat his application – he claimed that he had killed his colleagues to prevent the Security Police from being implicated in the murder of Matthew Goniwe and his three comrades. As the flood of applications poured into the TRC, he could not have been sure that evidence would not be forthcoming to implicate him as well in the abduction and killing of the PEBCO Three. Knowing that he was involved in the death of Biko, mindful that his commander, Col. Harold Snyman, was involved in the PEBCO Three and Goniwe murders, and probably on legal advice, he seems to have approached Snyman, Daniel Siebert, Ruben Marx and Jacobus Beneke to apply for amnesty with him for what had happened to Biko.

Nieuwoudt also applied for amnesty in relation to an assault on Biko's close friend, Peter Jones, arrested with Biko in August 1977. Jones had been kept in solitary confinement for over seventeen months. On his release he recorded how he had been tortured to get him to falsely implicate Biko in the writing and distribution of a pamphlet calling for unbridled violence, which in fact he and Biko had had nothing to do with. Its content and language strongly suggested that it was a forgery by the dirty tricks department within the Security Police.

On release Jones's detailed statement was handed to his attorney, Dullah

Omar, since 1994 the Minister of Justice. It was sent to Sydney Kentridge and me for us to advise whether criminal and civil proceedings should be instituted against Siebert, Nieuwoudt, Beneke, Snyman and Marx. Reluctantly, we advised that no proceedings should be taken, partly because of doubt as to whether the limitation of bringing actions against the police within six months might have barred civil action. Given Magistrate Prins's three-minute judgment, together with other decisions absolving the police, we took a pessimistic view of Peter Jones's prospects of success. His wounds had healed. His torturers would have ganged up to deny his evidence. His solitary confinement deprived him of witnesses to corroborate his version. There would no doubt have been a queue of senior police officers at the police stations where he was kept and many false entries in occurrences books and files. They would have claimed that not only did he have no complaints, but he was treated in a humane manner and with their own money they had bought him fruit and meat pies.

Dullah, Sydney and I decided to let it be, not because we did not believe Peter Jones, but because we believed justice yet again would not be done. Peter Jones's statement was published as an appendix to Donald Woods's book *Biko*. When we heard that Nieuwoudt had applied for amnesty for torturing Peter Jones, I wondered, as I am sure Sydney Kentridge and Dullah Omar did, whether we were right in 1978 in advising Peter Jones not to try to get what was due to him.

The Biko family had had reservations about the Act establishing the TRC. Now there was speculation in the media as to their attitude towards the application for amnesty by Nieuwoudt and colleagues. The family were sceptical whether the truth would be told. Reports that the security policemen would say that the death was accidental convinced them that the 1977 cover-up would continue. So too did a statement by the policemen's attorney, François van der Merwe: 'I must stress that the families of the victims and others should not have high hopes of major disclosures from the applicants regarding the Biko case.' Insult would have been added to injury if the family did not oppose the applications for amnesty.

Bongani Majola, the national director of the Legal Resources Centre (LRC), was approached by a friend on behalf of the Biko family. Bongani and I, in consultation with Wim Trengove, director of the LRC's Constitutional Litigation Unit, agreed that this was a proper case for the Centre to take. Because of my knowledge of the case I was to lead Patric M. Mtshaulana on behalf of the family.

We met at Peter Jones's home in Cape Town with Mrs Ntsiki Biko and her two sons, Nkosinathi and Samora, and Biko's sister, Nobandile. They assured us that they saw no inconsistency in having challenged the validity of the legislation providing for amnesty and now opposing the grant of amnesty. They felt that they could not allow a free ride to those responsible for their loved one's death, knowing that the murderers were going to lie.

Time was running out for the Biko family as well. The twentieth anniversary of Biko's death was less than six months away. If no criminal proceedings were started and the security policemen were guilty only of manslaughter and not murder, no criminal prosecution could be instituted after twenty years. To avoid this, a complaint was lodged with the Attorney-General of the Eastern Cape, L.J. Roberts, SC. If he decided to prosecute, the serving of an indictment would have interrupted the period of prescription. If the policemen were refused amnesty, they could be charged. The Attorney-General of the Eastern Cape, being a practical man, probably thought that no useful purpose would be served in bringing a criminal prosecution on a culpable homicide or manslaughter charge twenty years after the event. He refused to prosecute. The Biko family together with us accepted the decision with some equanimity. We thought that the amnesty applications would at the very least offer unequivocal admissions of guilt The world's judgment would be vindicated that Biko had been tortured, seriously injured and left to die without proper medical attention.

At this time a startling allegation came to the fore that Biko had been poisoned. *Cape Times* reporter Roger Friedman wrote that someone was prepared to say on oath that Biko died as a result of poisoning. The head of the TRC's investigative unit, Dumisa Ntsebeza, confirmed that the TRC was looking into the matter. We told the Biko family that we could not believe the allegation was true. We thought it inconceivable that Dr Jonathan Gluckman, Prof. Proctor and the other doctors would not have seen evidence of it in the thorough post-mortem examination and the tests they had conducted. The TRC's investigative unit had not at that stage come up with anything to suggest there was any truth in the allegation in relation to Biko. But there were reasons to believe that poisoning and disposal of bodies to avoid Biko-type inquests did occur later in the 1980s.

In June 1998 the TRC held hearings into the apartheid regime's chemical warfare and poison programmes. It inquired into the conduct of Dr Wouter Basson, President P.W. Botha's personal physician. He was about to go on trial on charges of murder, conspiracy to murder, fraud and the possession of prohibited drugs. Highly qualified scientists, doctors, army generals and entrepreneurs in the chemical industry had come together to make chemical and biological weapons and poisons. Amongst the intended victims was President Nelson Mandela, in whose food a substance was to be placed that would lead to his being infected by meningitis, and the Secretary General of the South African Council of Churches, Frank Chikane, whose clothing was sprayed with deadly poison; Steve Biko was said to have had poison administered to him that led or contributed to his death.

The name of the police forensic laboratory chief, Lothar Neethling, who had earlier been implicated by Vlakplaas commander Dirk Coetzee, again came to the fore in this regard. By now, few would disagree with Judge Johan Kriegler's finding that Capt. Coetzee was telling the truth when he implicated Gen. Neethling in supplying poisons to the hit squads. The Appellate Division, however, set Kriegler's decision aside. The Judges of Appeal must have felt that an officer and gentleman of such high rank would not stoop so low. The faith of the judges in such old-world values led to the closing down of *Vrye Weekblad* and endangered the continued existence of the *Weekly Mail*.

We will never know whether or not poison was given to Biko. Those who caused his death would not have had any compunction against using it. They may have planned to do so. They may have even started a process of administering small doses to him of a poison difficult to detect at the post-mortem examination. Apartheid's scientists claimed to be capable of producing such poisons.

Be that as it may, the medical evidence and the surrounding circumstances lead to the inevitable conclusion that Biko's death was caused by the use of force that smashed his brain against his skull. The evidence of police officers not in the Security Police and of prison warders, both of whom contradicted the Security Police version at the inquest, gave details of the injured Biko's behaviour. All the reported symptoms were consistent with a violent death rather than poisoning.

We were sent the applications for amnesty made by Snyman, Siebert, Marx, Beneke and Nieuwoudt together with the supporting documents. Each of the applicants was required to fill in a printed form and give full particulars of the act or omission committed with a political objective. Their answers were substantially similar: 'assault on Steve Biko and culpable homicide', 'assault and the death of Steve Biko'. Beneke went a step further – 'murder and assault on activist Steve Biko' – and Nieuwoudt added 'assault on Peter Cyril Jones' and 'defeating the ends of justice/perjury: false statement made on 17 September

1977', covering up what had happened to Biko.

It looked as if they were going to come clean, but this was not to be. Snyman declared that on the Saturday after Biko's death, Col. Goosen asked him to arrange a meeting of all concerned. Goosen told them that the event would have serious consequences, both for the Security Police and the government. Each one was ordered to make a statement suppressing the true facts and depose to an agreed version. Everyone did so. No one asked why they should lie if, as they claimed in their evidence before the amnesty committee, they had done nothing wrong.

There were four main differences between the 1977 and 1997 versions. Biko's injuries were not inflicted on 7 September but on the 6th. He did not continue to struggle after he injured his head against the wall; instead he became confused or semi-conscious. Although everyone had denied that there was any form of assault, it was now admitted that he was struck with a hosepipe by Nieuwoudt. And, above all, the trouble started not because Biko was confronted by affidavits implicating him or because he had confessed to any wrongdoing, but because he insisted on sitting on a chair.

The new version of what happened to Biko was nothing more than a rehash of what the policemen had said in 1977. The main difference was a clumsy attempt to reconcile it with the medical evidence given at the inquest which showed that their version was false. Even they realised that everyone who rejected their story was right and that Magistrate Prins was wrong.

Each one told us about his background. Their parents, their teachers, their church, their political party and its leaders, the officers that trained them, all persuaded them that white Afrikaners must fight for the right to continue living in accordance with their background and upbringing, their inheritance, culture and political way of life. Siebert in particular referred to 26 years' service on the local church council. He had served as a personal bodyguard to Prime Minister Vorster and President Swart, with whom he held political discussions. Whatever the policemen did, they did for the love of their God and their fatherland. They had acted on the express or implied authority of their leaders. In order to come within the terms of the Act, they declared that they had always acted in 'good faith' – without any apparent regard for what this means.

When they were asked at the hearing what political objective they had hoped to achieve by the assault and death of Biko, their answer was best articulated by Siebert, a university graduate: to protect the National Party government and its structures against communist expansionism; to protect South Africa and its Western capitalist system against a violent overthrow by the so-called liberation movements; and to ensure 'the continuation of a normal

Western democracy as I know it'.

In their view Black Consciousness was synonymous with Black Power. Over eighty pages of documents were included in their applications, most of dubious relevance. Two of them, published in the late 1980s, emanated from the State Security Council and its Secretariat. They saw no difference between the security system of the 1980s, which called for the elimination of those perceived to be enemies of the state, and their treatment of Biko in 1977, whilst still protesting that they had not intended to harm him.

The amnesty hearings were set for the week of 6 September 1997. We wondered whether the date was chosen by someone with a sense of history. In contrast to the Old Synagogue in the centre of Pretoria where the inquest had been held, the amnesty applications were to be heard in the Centenary Hall in New Brighton, a black township outside Port Elizabeth. The occasion gave evidence of some of the changes that Steve Biko had lived and died for. The predominantly black audience walked without fear past the many black policemen under the command of both black and white officers. So did the sprinkling of whites, old friends of Biko, but also young people who knew the legend but were thirsty to hear at first hand how he came to die.

Perhaps for other reasons Dr Benjamin Tucker and his wife also came. They were both dressed in their best as if for a religious service, with hats and all. During the adjournment, Dr Tucker sent a message: Would I meet him and shake his hand? I could not bring myself to do it. Contrary to the Hippocratic Oath he had failed to treat Biko. His excuse was that he could not buck the Security Police. His 'apology' to the Medical Council was prompted by advice. Having been reinstated as a doctor and correctly calculating that there was no likelihood of a criminal prosecution, he did not apply for amnesty, nor did assistant district surgeon Lang, who did not bother to come to the hearing. My message to Dr Tucker was that I did not think the time opportune to do what he asked. Tucker somehow managed to corner Peter Jones, one of Biko's closest political colleagues and friends. A picture in colour of Jones and the Tuckers both smiling broadly appeared in the next day's paper. The latter must have felt that the shame he had brought on himself and his profession had been erased. His pose made me feel less guilty for refusing his request.

In Biko's time there had not been a single black judge and only one woman judge in South Africa. But in 1997 the chairman of the amnesty committee was Judge Hassen Mall, one of the first judges appointed to the High Court bench by the Judicial Services Commission under the new constitution. He had been invited by the enlightened Natal Judge-President, the late John

Milne, to take an appointment but refused, not wanting to lend legitimacy to an illegitimate regime. During the hearing Mall was patient and tolerant of counsel, the applicants, witnesses and even of the interjections, murmurs, applause and expressions of displeasure by the crowd, reminiscent of the chorus in an ancient Greek tragedy. On either side of him sat Advocate Denzil Potgieter and Advocate Ntsiki Sandi. They could vote on whether or not to give amnesty and they were expected to give reasons why amnesty would be granted or refused. Quite a difference from Magistrate Prins's inquest court, twenty years earlier, when he alone could decide whether anyone was to blame, and was not obliged to give any reasons.

The five former security policemen took their places on the stage directly opposite us. In their heyday they would not have come to the hall to listen to speeches made by activists. Their black informers would have attended with transmitters hidden on them. One or other of the applicants would have been outside in a car with false numberplates recording the speeches. They stared at us intently, but could not sustain looking into our eyes for as long as they had once done. They had all retired for 'health reasons' and had accepted severance packages granted to them by the newly elected democratic government. The cost to the country was high but it might have been higher if they had remained in service.

Kobus Booyens, a senior advocate appearing for the policemen, was both polite and deferential to the members of the amnesty committee. He objected from time to time, more often than not on the insistence of his instructing attorney, François van der Merwe, who was impatient, fidgety and flippant during the adjournments. Booyens called Col. Harold Snyman to take the oath. He was not the confident man who had given evidence twenty years before. An impression of his face, his tinted glasses and Salvador Dali moustache appears on the cover of Jacques Pauw's book *In the Heart of the Whore*.

Snyman stuck to his basic story that Biko had been injured when he hit his head against a wall during a scuffle, after the enraged detainee had assaulted his captors. Biko, he claimed, was 'unruly, challenging and aggressive' during his interrogation, refusing to answer questions.

'I can't remember how many times it happened,' Snyman testified, 'but Biko tried to sit in a chair, after which Capt. Siebert told him in no uncertain terms to remain standing when we were busy with him. Biko suddenly tried again to sit down on a chair near him. Capt. Siebert grabbed Biko and yanked him out of the chair. He screamed at him to co-operate and that we would not tolerate his attitude. Biko clearly became angry and violently pushed the chair in the direction of Capt. Siebert. While Capt. Siebert tried to block the chair,

Biko threw a punch at him but did not hit him.'

During the ensuing fight, WO Beneke charged in, tackling Biko, who 'fell, stumbled or staggered backwards against the wall.' (If this was intended to explain the contracoup injury caused by blows inflicted above the eye, it did not make sense.) Marx and Nieuwoudt also joined in to subdue the detainee. 'It became a very violent struggle,' Snyman said, telling of punches flying everywhere. In an attempt to handcuff Biko, Snyman explained, the detainee fell, hitting his head against the wall. 'He appeared to be completely confused. He was lying with his head partially against the wall. He looked like someone who had been knocked out in a boxing match.' Biko was speaking in a slow, slurred manner and there was blood on his lip. (Obviously, note had been taken of the evidence of the doctors at the inquest.)

This version of events was so clearly designed to exculpate the policemen, it could not go unchallenged.

'I put it to you that it was not an accidental hitting against the wall. Do you agree with this?' I asked Snyman.

'No, Your Honour,' he replied.

I quoted from Siebert's deposition made to the TRC: 'During the wrestling and fighting I was aware that Det.-Sgt Nieuwoudt hit Biko on the back on a number of occasions with a piece of hosepipe. Thereafter all three of us grabbed Biko and moved with him in the direction of the corner of the office and ran with him into the wall.'

Snyman denied this. Nor had he seen Nieuwoudt strike Biko with the hosepipe.

'In other words', I said, 'the Security Police did nothing wrong. They acted in self-defence – all four of them?'

'That is true,' was Snyman's reply.

Not only was this answer unhelpful to his application for amnesty but, taken together with his answers as to how the confrontation started, it revealed how deep-seated white-supremacist thinking was. Nobody could put it better than Snyman himself in answer to our questions:

'The reason for the scuffle, if it was in fact a scuffle and not a beating up, came about as a result of his refusal to get off the chair. Is that correct?'

'That is correct, Your Honour.'

'That is not a refusal to give information. It is a refusal by a man who thought [as part] of his human dignity as having the right to be seated when there was a chair available.'

'That is correct, Your Honour. His human dignity might well have been violated . . .'

'Yes.'

'The instruction had been from our seniors that we should break him down in order to obtain information from him.'

'But let us just take this step by step. He didn't refuse to answer your questions that led to the scuffle or beating up? Correct?'

'Your Honour, he was resistant and did not want to reply to our questions.'

'He insisted on sitting down. That is the evidence that you have given us, and the scuffle or beating up came about as a result of a stubborn person in your view of not wanting to get up at your request or command?'

'Your Honour, it was clear that he did not want to co-operate with us. It was clear from his behaviour.'

'His behaviour was that he refused to submit to your will that he should not be seated?'

'Your Honour, it had been the instruction that we were not allowed to let him sit down; that we had to break him down in order to obtain the information.'

'Why would his remaining in a seated position – it would just not be possible for you to interrogate him?'

'That is correct, Your Honour. It remains that the instructions were that he was not to be allowed to sit down.'

'Specifically you had an instruction that he should not be allowed to sit down. Is that what you are saying? Or was it your decision that this particular detainee should not sit down?'

'Your Honour, during his interrogation by the interrogation team he was instructed to stand up from the chair.'

'In the background in which you grew up and in which you had a training – we are not talking about now, when you profess to be a democrat, but at that time – was it your general view that a black man had to obey an order of a white man, particularly a white man who was in the Security Police?'

'Your Honour, according to the state system or state order of that time, it had been our thinking that that is the way that things should be done.'

'Yes, your state of mind at that time having regard to the words that you used in your application, was that the late Mr Biko was stubborn, *parmantig* and too big for his boots for a black man?'

'Your Honour, that was the case. That is the impression that he created for us; that he did not really want to listen to us.'

'Yes, but he was a proud man and that your self-respect would have been insulted if he continued sitting on the chair?'

'Your Honour, we had to realise that he was a high-profile person in the

Black Consciousness organisations. He was a president of one of these organisations and by sitting he maintained his own status.'

'I see. So that you were offended, personally offended that you, a white man, had a pretender [to] political power before you and that you were not going to tolerate it and now you told him to get up? Is that correct?'

'That is correct, Your Honour.'

'And had it not been for your personal pride, combined with the personal pride of your fellow security policemen, and he was allowed to sit down, the scuffle or beating up may not have happened at all?'

'Your Honour, our instructions had been very clear from our Commanding Officer with regard to the manner in which we had to break down this person.'

'I want to read your own words in your application at the bottom of page 4 to the top of page 5: "Biko appeared resistant, challenging and aggressive." Was that because he insisted on sitting down?'

'Your Honour, his entire attitude was recalcitrant, challenging and aggressive.'

'Now, did he show all these attitudes but insisting on his right to sit down?'

'Your Honour, when we started with him it already appeared clearly that he was not going to co-operate with us.'

'But he sat down right away.'

'That is correct, Your Honour, and then he was taken from the chair and he was instructed to stand again.'

'Taken from the chair; how was he taken from the chair?'

'Your Honour, it was by one of the members of the investigative team, who grabbed him up from his chair or lifted him up from the chair and told him to remain standing.'

Subdued exclamations of disbelief were heard from the spectators. Devout racists were being shown to be able to lie about many things but not about their hatred and contempt for black people.

'On page 2 of your application, you claim that you have done this in the interests of the National Party government. Could you name anyone in the National Party who advised publicly or even privately that a detainee was not entitled to sit on a chair?' we asked.

'No, Your Honour.'

'You also say that you acted faithfully in accordance with the principles of your church. Can you quote anybody in your church that advocated that a detainee was not entitled to sit on a chair?'

'No, Your Honour.'

'Can you quote anyone in the National Party who suggested to you that a detainee was to be kept naked in his cell and whilst he was being interrogated?'

'Yes, Your Honour. This was an instruction which we received through our Commanding Officer from our head office.'

'Can you please tell me whether anyone in the National Party told you or suggested to you that the detainees were to be kept naked in their cell and naked whilst they were being interrogated by a team of security policemen?'

'No, Your Honour.'

'Did anyone in your church suggest that you might do that?'

'No, Your Honour.'

'You give the impression in your application that you are a God-fearing man who was brought up in a good family which had respect for religion. Am I summarising the position correctly?'

'That is correct, Your Honour.'

'Is committing perjury part and parcel of that upbringing?'

'No, Your Honour.'

'Or committing the crime of defeating the ends of justice?'

'No, Your Honour.'

Snyman admitted that the Security Police had waited almost 24 hours before taking the injured man to a doctor, during which time he was manacled, spread-eagled, to a gate, unable to move or sit down. The interrogators then called their commanding officer, Col. Goosen, who attempted to speak to Biko but could get no response from him. Although the interrogation stopped, he was left in that condition for several hours, probably for the better part of the night.

When I questioned Snyman on this treatment, he replied, 'I would agree that it was inhumane but we were acting under instructions.'

'That's one of the franker answers you have given today,' I replied. 'Was it not a form of torture?'

'That would be correct.'

We adjourned after the cross-examination of Snyman and a portion of Siebert's evidence in chief. The hearings could not continue on 12 September 1997 because it was the twentieth anniversary of the day of Biko's death in Pretoria. A bronze statue of Biko was to be unveiled by President Mandela in East London, and the family invited us to join them. More than ten thousand people were waiting for the President in the Main Square in East London. A small group of young AZAPO members holding up makeshift placards arrived late and vociferously tried to push their way to the front of the crowd. There they continued shouting slogans, toyi-toyi-ing and demanding recognition that Biko was AZAPO's alone. President Mandela, adopting the stance of a school master, admonished them and made it clear during his speech that no particular group could appropriate Biko as their own. He said, 'One of the greatest legacies of the struggle Steve Biko waged was an explosion of pride among the people he represented. People who once looked to Europe and America for inspiration turned their eyes towards Africa.' He said that his death had focused the eyes of the world on the plight of the oppressed people of South Africa. He used the occasion to call for unity amongst the people of South Africa.

Representatives of all the political parties were there. Even some of those who had applied the apartheid policy wanted to be seen at the commemoration service. Mangosuthu Buthelezi, Roelf Meyer and Bantu Holomisa paid homage to Biko by their presence; Peter Gabriel was there to sing his song 'Biko'. Present too were Donald Woods and Sir Richard Attenborough, whose film Cry Freedom helped to make Biko's life, death and vision of South Africa better known to the world. Mamphela Ramphele, now Vice-Chancellor of the University of Cape Town, was also amongst the honoured guests. During lunch there was speculation as to what portfolio would have been assigned to Biko in Mandela's government. With a slightly mischievous smile one guest mused, 'Might it not have been the other way round?'

When the hearings resumed, Daniel Siebert returned to the witness chair. Siebert had obviously prepared himself well and sought to justify himself. He tried hard not to fall into the same trap as Snyman. He had the same difficulty in explaining how the injuries came to be inflicted and how the punches admittedly thrown managed not to land on Biko's head. His answers betrayed his attitude.

'You said, in your application, that you considered that a war was going on. Is that correct?'

'Yes.'

'But now do you, did you ever bother to find out how prisoners are to be treated even in a state of war?'

'That is true, the circumstances of that time and all the things that Mr Bizos has asked motivated one to act in the interests of the state dispensation and in the interest of the community of South Africa and not only the white community, but also in the interests of these people who are sitting here today, that is the black community, because they suffered the most as a result of all the murders, the burning of their vehicles and businesses and houses. It was done in order to protect them. One took a risk of interrogating these people and this was done as a result of the motivation of the organisations that I mentioned, because I believed that the policy of that time, namely apartheid, was an interim measure until it would develop to such an extent or that the politicians of the day come up with better solutions for South Africa.'

'The question, actually, was a simple one. Did you ever bother to find out how, in a war situation, combatants are supposed to treat prisoners from the other side?'

'There is a difference between somebody who is detained during a war situation and one as a result of the interrogation process.'

Judge Mall intervened: 'I think we must just cut this down. Did you ever apply your mind at any stage that South Africa was in a war situation and that the people that you were arresting and detaining were to be treated as prisoners of war?'

'There were diverse principles, we were involved in a total onslaught, the opposition of the day wanted to have themselves qualified as war criminals [sic] and the government of the day did not acknowledge it as such.'

He could not bring himself to call them political prisoners, nor to remember that apartheid, not the liberation struggle, was declared a crime against humanity by the United Nations.

Advocate Mpshe, a black man, must have been surprised to hear that the security policemen were acting on behalf of the black people. He had managed to become an advocate despite Bantu education and all the other obstacles that apartheid had put in his way. He was one of the senior legal practitioners assisting the TRC and the amnesty committee. He asked Siebert: 'Now, what was this dispensation which you were protecting at the time?'

'The structures of the state. As Mr Bizos referred to earlier, the dissatisfaction regarding education, the own management of affairs, management of own affairs, as it was called, there were lots of things which caused dissatisfaction at the time and which gave rise to unrest, to strikes, to boycotts and stayaway actions and the like, and the continuing violence and strikes had a negative influence on foreign investments.'

Mpshe referred Siebert to his application in which it appeared, 'By the above-mentioned objectives to ensure the existence of a normal Western democracy as I knew it, to maintain the above and to ensure its survival.'

He then asked: 'Was there any democracy in the country at that stage?'

'With all due respect, Chairperson, it could be a difference of opinion and maybe I should make so bold as to ask what the position is today from the perspective of a white person. So, I do not really want to comment on that. According to my opinion there was a democracy at the time in the country. Admittedly, black people were, to some extent, excluded.'

Before Mpshe could formulate his next question, Judge Mall intervened: 'I do not think there will be, this Committee needs much persuasion as to whether the previous regime was a democracy or not.'

Mpshe wanted to know from Judge Mall what he really meant. Judge Mall made it abundantly clear: 'I am just telling you, you do not have to persuade this Committee on whether South Africa was a democracy or not at that time.'

Mpshe thanked the Judge and said he had no further questions.

Even whilst in detention in 1977 Peter Jones identified Siebert as the one likely to have inflicted the fatal blow on Biko. Jones himself had suffered at Siebert's hands. He told Julian Rademeyer of the *Eastern Province Herald* when asked what he thought of Siebert: 'He is an ideologue, a holy man who believes passionately in his cause. He is a much more substantial person in terms of his knowledge, his depth, his viciousness and his capacity for violence.'.

The next applicant to testify was Ruben Marx. The grandfatherly figure of Marx moved uncomfortably on his seat when asked what had happened in the interrogation room. He was quick to say: 'I did not see anything. When they handcuffed him to the iron grid, I left. I said that I had had enough of this whole business.'

'You actually [dissociated] yourself from what Mr Siebert did?'

'Yes, I did, I did not want to associate myself with that.'

'Because you say that your experience with Mr Biko was that he was a quiet and civilised person.'

'I met him in '74 at an Anglican farm . . . Lt. Marais and WO Ferreira and I went to fetch four persons: Steve Biko, [Bokwe] Mafuna, and I cannot remember the other two. In any case, when we arrived there, I asked, "Who is in charge here?" and this big man came out and said, "I am in charge." "Please do ask them just to keep quiet that I can do my" – I identified myself – "please do ask them to keep quiet, I have got a job to be done here." He put his hands up and just as if you turned off an electrical switch, they were all quiet and I saw that this was a disciplined man.'

'What did you see Mr Siebert doing wrong in that office, Mr Marx?'

'I was there very seldom, I do not, I know, in the first place, he was sitting on the side and I was, if I was on the other side I would have asked him if he wanted some tea or to smoke or something, I would have created a good atmosphere so that one could have a starting point. It is of no use to tell the man to, just to stand up. Mr Siebert is hearing what I am saying, but this is my own personal opinion. One, I will not say that one would have won his trust, but one would have at least had mutual respect for one another.'

'It seems to me, Mr Marx, that this is not the first time we meet, of course. You may remember we met before, but you are the old type of policeman.'

'I do still remember that day, yes.'

'And you do not go about doing your police work like these ambitious young men did it?'

'Well, we are still of the older generation. You had to look after your work otherwise they would just have fired you. You could not just hit a person left and right. I worked in the black areas and I am still here today. There is not an explosive situation which one cannot diffuse in a very diplomatic way. I worked in New Brighton, all over.'

'No, we understand fully, Mr Marx.'

Judge Mall intervened: 'You have said nice things about him, give him a chance to say nice things about you.'

'We will have a chat afterwards, Mr Chairman.'

'Ja.'

We had met in the case in which Siebert had managed to extract confessions from eight detainees. These were subsequently held to be inadmissible. One of the reasons for this was that Marx accepted the testimony of the accused, men from Port Elizabeth who insisted they had been in the vicinity of the South Africa–Botswana border for an innocent purpose. During the trial Siebert could not explain in cross-examination why they had changed their minds soon after he started interrogating them and confessed to going out of the country for military training.

Ruben Marx stagnated in the police force, while Siebert became a Brigadier. Age and education may explain the difference but surely Siebert's enthusiasm must have counted for some of his rapid promotion to the top.

Marx felt that he had done nothing wrong. He applied for amnesty because the others asked him to do so. We had our doubts whether he was as benign as he claimed: Peter Jones was to testify at the hearings that Marx took part in his torture.

Beneke was the last to testify. He had taken early retirement from the police, apparently to become a successful businessman, and was separately represented. He did not follow the example of Marx, but stuck to the new version of the other three. Attempts to get details of what had happened failed. The three would not tie themselves down to any detail. To them it was a scuffle.

None of them could bring himself to admit that Biko was punched in a manner which would have led to brain damage.

At the inquest no one had spoken of the presence of one or two pieces of hosepipe in the interrogation room. In his application to the amnesty committee Beneke said that Nieuwoudt hit Biko with a cut-off piece of hosepipe over his back for the purpose of restraining him. He would not say how many times Nieuwoudt struck him.

We asked: 'Can you please explain to us how you made an attempt to restrain someone by hitting him with a hosepipe on the back so hard that it actually left tramlines on his skin?'

'I did not hit him with the hosepipe. Sgt Nieuwoudt did. He also hit me in the process and I had similar marks. I cannot take responsibility for his actions.'

'Well, on how many occasions were you hit with the hosepipe?'

'Twice.'

'Well, far from the correctness of the suggestion that Mr Biko had gone berserk, it would appear that the person that had really gone berserk in that room was Mr Nieuwoudt.'

'I do not know.'

'Where were your injuries sustained, on what part of your body as a result of your being hit by Mr Nieuwoudt?'

'It was on my back.'

'How hard were the blows?'

'It is difficult to describe, they were reasonably hard.'

'Did they leave tramline-like injuries on your skin?'

'Yes, it did.'

'Did you ask Mr Nieuwoudt what had gone wrong with him that he managed to strike at least two blows on you and possibly a number of blows on Mr Biko, what had gone wrong with him, did you ask him?'

'I did not speak to him about that.'

'Why not?'

'I accepted this as part of the incident that took place.'

Judge Mall intervened: 'In other words, you assumed that the blows were not meant for you, they were meant for Mr Biko? You got hurt accidentally?'

'That is correct.'

He admitted that he had seen the hosepipe there before but said that it was used to siphon petrol for the very Land-Rover which transported Biko to Pretoria. No credible explanation could be given as to why it was in the interrogation room.

Peter Jones had a different story to tell. There were two pieces of hosepipe in the interrogation room, one green, the other black. There was an 'in' joke amongst those who tortured him: the one pipe was known as 'green power' and the other as 'black power'. Judging by the pain he suffered, one of the pipes contained a metallic substance, probably a chain.

Jones gave a detailed account of how not only Nieuwoudt but the others as well took part in a series of assaults on him for the purpose of getting him to write a statement implicating Biko and himself in a conspiracy to produce a pamphlet calling for unbridled violence. Patric Mtshaulana led his evidence. Jones described how Siebert became enraged when he read the statement that Jones had prepared overnight. He ordered two coloured policemen to put him 'on the bricks'. The five that dealt with Biko came into the room.

Judge Mall asked: 'Yes?'

'They asked the two coloured Security Police to leave the room and I was instructed to stand on two half-bricks that were then put next to each other. I was pulled by some of them, we had a bit of a struggle, eventually I stood on the two half-bricks and I was made to lift two steel chairs, one was put in reverse on top of the other, two of them lifted it and I was made to hold it above my head.'

'These half-bricks on which you had to stand, I imagine a brick broken into half, it has a smooth side and a serrated edge. On which edge would you have …'

'On the smooth side, narrow side.'

'You would have stood on the smooth side?'

'Yes.'

Patric Mtshaulana took over: 'Yes, continue.'

'I was warned that if these chairs should come down or if I should let it fall, I would get it, which I interpreted as a threat, and the questioning then resumed between Siebert and Snyman . . .'

'Were they questioning you about your statement or about something else?'

'They were questioning me specifically about the pamphlet that they knew they had sufficient acknowledgement and evidence from independent sources, but I was required to independently confirm these things; and when I continued denying that we were involved in any pamphlet, we were in Cape Town, we had nothing to do with any pamphlet, they got very angry. Siebert got up and kicked me on my leg. By that stage, the chairs had long ago come down to the level of my shoulders, because I couldn't keep it up . . .'

'You say that at that time Mr Siebert started kicking you?'

'Yes.'

'It fell down, one [chair] fell right to the other side and it struck Snyman and one also struck Siebert, he then started shouting, that did I want to fight, and I will get a fight. He started hitting me, I grabbed his hands and pulled it down and I told him that there was no need for this. I was co-operating. I was answering their specific questions. He then called the others, and they grabbed me. This is now Nieuwoudt and Beneke, he shouted to them to again handcuff me. I was handcuffed. Siebert then removed his watch, rolled up his sleeves, he approached me and started hitting me with heavy blows with open hands, left and right for a very long period, for a prolonged period. That very rapidly led to a most vicious assault by all five people in the room. We had Siebert standing in front of me, and hitting my face. We had Nieuwoudt on the left of me attacking my head and my back. There was Beneke with a black hosepipe hitting me on the back and the bottom, and to the left and right of Siebert respectively . . . '

'Start again. You said Mr Siebert was hitting you with open hands on the face.'

'To the face.'

'Yes.'

'Siebert was to the left – sorry, Nieuwoudt was to the left and rear of me, attacking my head and my back.'

'With what?'

'With a green hosepipe. Beneke was to the right rear, attacking my back and bottom with a black hosepipe. And to the left and right of Siebert, respectively, was Snyman and Marx, who were basically delivering blows and kicking to keep me aligned, in position. During this massive assault, we were moving all over the room and falling all over the room and eventually I just ended up with my back turned to them, facing the wall and everybody panting and me moaning and groaning on the one side as a result.'

'And, at the end of this assault, did you then give them the information they wanted?'

'They asked if I was then ready to give them a statement, a satisfactory statement. I indicated yes, they gave me paper and a pen and for the rest of that day, which was then several hours that I had, I then prepared a second statement.'

During the course of the assaults Siebert in particular used abusive language. Biko was referred to as a 'kaffir' and he, Jones, a 'hotnot'.

The cross-examination by police counsel Booyens was in the main conducted in an apologetic tone. He nevertheless suggested that Jones may have exaggerated in order to justify his making a statement. It was put to him that Nieuwoudt alone assaulted him and was not present at any assault that may have been committed by any of the others. Jones was angered by the suggestion.

He had to keep his tears back when, glaring at Booyens and Nieuwoudt sitting next to him, he said:

'Sir, if I can respond, my attendance at these hearings, I believe, are completely incidental and of a minor nature. This entire hearing is about the fact that a very important person in the life of this country died and lost his life. My show is a side-show, I would never have even bothered to come here and talk about this, if it was not for the fact that there were blatant lies and inaccuracies by these people.'

Each of Biko's murderers said something which he must have believed was a sort of apology.

Snyman declared: 'I am convinced in my heart that our behaviour was wrong and I'm sorry for what happened.'

The words of the others were not much different. None of them made an unequivocal apology or a sincere expression of regret or contrition. The best that they could say for themselves was that they were unduly influenced by the political climate then existing. None of it was convincing. Nor was their insistence that they had done nothing wrong and that it was a mere accident or misfortune.

Under the apartheid regime security policemen who gave evidence before the courts looked up to the magistrates and judges, at the country's coat of arms with the motto 'Ex unitate vires – Unity in strength'. The only unity they believed in was, in their own words, 'white Afrikaner unity'. They regarded other whites as lesser citizens, some of us to be tolerated, but not welcome, and the blacks as their servants. Before the amnesty committee they had to look at a banner, 'Truth: The Road to Reconciliation.'

Not many of us were convinced, however, that the truth was told. The chalk circle, standing on bricks, holding up chairs and other ways of sapping the physical and moral strength of lonely detainees were well known to the Security Police. We know what the same team did to Peter Jones during the same period. What would have restrained them from applying the same methods to Steve Biko? We can only hope that one or more of them will once again come forward and say what really happened to Biko. Why should he have been treated differently from Jones? Was Biko asked to lift the chair above his head? Did he drop it? Was he handcuffed and then beaten up? Was Siebert the captain of the team? We may never know.

CHAPTER 3

# NEIL HUDSON AGGETT

☙❧

*'I Am Also an Idealist'*

*'The Aggett inquest was a mirror held up to reflect the unimagined
depths of depravity, brutality and destruction employed by the
Security Police.'*

– Helen Joseph

*'The vast propaganda machine of the state creates a situation in
which people do not know their own history. For instance, we have
lived through the period in which Neil Aggett died. What steps have
we taken to ensure that the lessons of today will be taught to our
children?'*

– Dullah Omar

I N THE government's campaign against its internal enemies, real or imagined, those with links to African trade unions came in for close scrutiny.
The state was convinced they were acting on orders from the liberation movements to disrupt the economy and foment unrest. In the early seventies the
National Union of South African Students (NUSAS) had started a programme called the Wages Commission, which served as training ground for a
professional approach to trade union organisation. It attracted a number of
socially conscious young people including the Johannesburg doctor Neil
Hudson Aggett, who was the secretary of the Transvaal branch of the African
Food and Canning Workers' Union. The Security Police tried to prove that
the NUSAS leadership was guilty of furthering the objects of the ANC and
the Communist Party by unlawfully attempting to bring about economic
changes, encouraging the formation of trade unions for Africans for whom the
government had created special toothless structures. Charles Nupen and Karel
Tip, two NUSAS presidents, Glenn Moss, the president of the Wits Students'
Representative Council, Cedric de Beer, a student leader, and Eddie Webster,
a sociology lecturer at the same university, were acquitted of that and other

charges, including calling for the release of political prisoners. Their ten-month trial, in which Arthur Chaskalson, Denis Kuny, Raymond Tucker, Geoff Budlender and I were involved, confirmed the view that doing the same kind of work as that of an unlawful organisation did not make one guilty unless the prosecution proved one did it on behalf of the banned organisation.

Aggett had been under surveillance for a few years before his eventual detention on 27 November 1981. Legal sophistry was not going to prevent the Security Police from tracking down young whites making common cause with African revolutionaries. For six months prior to this, he had been watched constantly, followed by up to five cars at a time. The catalyst in his arrest was the decision to charge the ANC activist Barbara Hogan. Facing charges of treason, terrorism and furthering the aims of the ANC, she admitted to being an ANC member. It appeared from her trial that she had compiled a list of names, headed 'Close Comrades', of people sympathetic to the struggle. The police discovered the list and detained most of those mentioned. One of the names was Neil Aggett.

The new decade, the 1980s, was the last stage of the apartheid state and, in many ways, the one which saw the fiercest battles between the regime and its opponents. Prime Minister John Vorster's marathon term of office ended in 1978 when, tarnished by the revelations of the Information Scandal, he was packed off to become State President, a mere figurehead. Vorster's successor as Prime Minister was the Minister of Defence, P.W. Botha, later to become known as 'die groot krokodil'. Botha rode out the storm surrounding the scandal and pulled together his deeply divided National Party with the promise of reform. The Afrikaner, he announced with trademark stoniness, had to 'adapt or die'. But along with reform came repression – the carrot and the stick became the hallmark of Botha's regime. In the new jargon of the day, the government was facing a 'total onslaught' which could only be fought with a 'total strategy'. Detention without trial remained an integral part of the strategy.

In an attempt to placate critics of the detention system, the state appointed a commission under Chief Justice Rabie 'to enquire into and to report and make recommendations on the necessity, adequacy, fairness and efficacy of the legislation pertaining to the internal security of the Republic of South Africa'. The hearings were held in camera and canvassed primarily the views of those in favour of the system – no former detainees testified before the Rabie Commission. Much weight was given to the claim by the police that 'the information they obtained by means of interrogation in detention is the most powerful, and to a large extent their only, weapon for anticipating and combating activities endangering the State which are planned and organised outside the borders of the Republic, and that without it they would not be able to carry out the task which they have to perform in the interests of the security of the country.'

The Rabie Commission was impressed that the Terrorism Act made provision for regular visits of detainees by a magistrate, circumstances permitting. There were also inspectors of detainees who called on those in detention to ascertain whether they were being properly cared for. Police officers were also responsible for the supervision of detainees in their custody. The Commission heard evidence from magistrates, inspectors and police officers, who testified to the measures they took to safeguard detainees' lives. The report of the Rabie Commission was published on 3 February 1982, the same day that Minister of Police Louis le Grange was questioned in parliament on the treatment of detainees. 'I should like to say to the Hon. Members,' the Hon. Minister remarked, 'that the detainees in police cells or in prisons are being detained under the most favourable conditions possible . . . All reasonable precautions are being taken to prevent any of them from injuring themselves or from being injured in some other way or from committing suicide. Surely Hon. Members are aware of the serious circumstances in the past. We were all faced with this, but during the past two and a half years there has not been a single case of this nature.' Two days later Dr Neil Hudson Aggett was found hanging from the bars of the steel grille in his cell in John Vorster Square. He had spent 70 days in detention. He was the first white person to die in detention.

Neil's father, Aubrey Aggett, had some means of his own. He engaged his own attorneys, the prestigious firm of Bell, Dewar and Hall, one of Johannesburg's oldest. The senior partner was William Lane, who took a personal interest in the case. He had a good rapport with Mr Aggett and kept him informed of developments. Lane asked me to handle the inquest. Along with Lane, we had the services of David Dison, a junior partner who moved in activist circles and did a lot of work with detainees, and James Sutherland, a typical young white South African, hardly exposed to any political activity, but who became an ardent human rights lawyer as a result of these experiences. Denis Kuny was briefed with me, and Mohamed Navsa was his pupil. This team worked very hard to produce the almost twenty statements from former detainees which we hoped would provide similar factual evidence. Mohamed Navsa researched the law as to whether driving one to suicide was culpable homicide or murder, while his principal, Denis Kuny, shared the cross-examination with me. Denis and Mohamed spoke much better Afrikaans than I did. I relied heavily on their assistance when we discussed the cross-examination and the evidence to be led by us.

The Timol experience suggested to us that if we accepted the police version that there had been a suicide, we could open up a wider inquiry into the general treatment of the detainee than if we limited ourselves to an allegation that he was killed by the police. Magistrates were anxious to confine cross-examination to what was directly relevant to the issue. They would try to stop cross-examination about the length of periods of interrogation, deprivation of food or reading matter, on the basis that it was not relevant to the cause of death. We decided that the inquiry could be broadened if the circumstances of the detention could be said to have led to or induced the suicide, in much the way Vernon Berrangé had argued in the Ngudle inquest. Questions in relation to the general treatment of the detainee could not be blocked if the issue was whether, even though he or she might have committed suicide, those responsible for his detention could be held criminally liable for the death if they induced the person to commit suicide.

This approach was not free of legal difficulty, but an even greater difficulty had been encountered in a number of cases in the decade between Timol's death in 1971 and Aggett's in 1982, in persuading the relatives of the deceased detainee to let us conduct the case on the assumption that their loved one might have committed suicide. We came to the conclusion, after lengthy discussions with Dr Gluckman, that the probabilities tended to show that Aggett might well have committed suicide. There was another reason that led me to this view. On the floor of Neil Aggett's cell was Nikos Kazantzakis's *Zorba the Greek*, open at page 246, dealing with the suicide of the young man whose passionate love for the widow had been rejected:

'Every minute death was dying and being reborn, just like life. For thousands of years the young girls and boys have danced beneath the tender foliage of the trees in spring – beneath the poplars, firs, oaks, planes and slender palms – and they will go on dancing for thousands more years, their faces consumed with desire. Faces change, crumble, return to earth; but others rise to take their place. There is only one dancer, but he has a thousand masks. He is always twenty. He is immortal.'

Were these thoughts on the unending cycle of life and death, a message left by Neil Aggett for those he knew and loved? Or was it intended for a wider audience: affirming that a single life may be lost but others will rise to take his or her place?

When we put the problem to Mr Aubrey Aggett, Neil's father, his initial reaction was no different from those in the past. At first he could not believe it. Although he was reluctant to accept the possibility that his son had committed suicide, he listened carefully to what we had to say about making it easier to expose the ill-treatment that was meted out to detainees, more particularly to his son.

We explained that if we adopted the view that it was suicide, the police might be held legally responsible, the evidence of other detainees, detained at or about the same time, and interrogated by the same team, might become admissible, and the inquest would take more the form of an indictment against detention without trial. His wife Joy, Neil's mother, was in tears, hardly in a state to take part in the decision. He looked at me sternly. I was not sure what was going through his mind. He looked at his daughter Jill, who nodded. With a deliberate and almost a commanding voice, he said, 'Do it.'

Neil's companion, Dr Liz Floyd, also believed that he was driven to suicide. For one thing, the Security Police encouraged speculation about suicide by openly speaking about it. The lift in John Vorster Square could go no further than the ninth floor: one had to walk up a flight of stairs to the tenth floor where the interrogations took place. After Liz Floyd was herself detained the security policeman taking her upstairs drew her attention specially to a wire-mesh grille above the handrail. 'We put it up to prevent people (like Timol) jumping to their death.' Liz had never thought of suicide before. Every time she walked up or down those stairs, fear would strike her again.

Aggett's death sparked a wave of protests, but the government, in typically stubborn fashion, rejected a move by the Progressive Federal Party (PFP) to hold a snap debate in parliament on the matter. The Food and Canning Workers' Union called a work stoppage for half an hour on Thursday 11 February 1982 at 11.30 a.m. This was observed by about 85 000 workers across the country.

Thousands packed St Mary's Cathedral in Johannesburg for Aggett's funeral on 13 February, with thousands more lining the route to Westpark Cemetery. The general secretary of the Food and Canning Workers' Union, Jan Theron, went to the heart of the matter in his tribute, saying, 'Forty-five people have died in detention before Neil Aggett. Has any inquest prevented his death, has any inquest placed the guilt for the death where it lies? Let's put the blame where it lies – with the Government.' Although Aggett's parents were uncomfortable with the 'political' nature of the funeral, Bishop Tutu saw it as a sign of hope for South Africa, 'an incredible demonstration of affection and regard for a young white man by thousands of blacks'.

In the opinion of the *Sunday Times*, 'Once again South Africa has failed the basic test of any democracy: the way it treats the helpless in its society. For none is more helpless than the prisoner detained without trial at the whim of the authorities, with access neither to the courts nor to those who have his welfare at heart . . . This week for the 46th time in South Africa's dismal history of detention that peculiarly cruel and inhuman punishment claimed a victim: a man in the prime of his life whose only proven "offence" appears to have been his involvement with a black trade union.'

As so often happened, Aggett's death hit his family hardest. His sister, Jill Burger, said, 'To me and my family, Neil's period of detention was a nightmare . . . Knowing that a loved one is being held under such circumstances and at the mercy of policemen who are accountable to no one is an agonising experience. There wasn't an hour when I didn't think of him sitting alone in his grim cell while I enjoyed the freedom of going where and when I wanted in the glorious sunshine.' Their mother Joy visited Aggett on New Year's Eve at John Vorster Square, with her daughter Jill. It was the last time she saw her son alive. 'We sat very close to him. Dear Jilly, she made us squash up next to him, and we held his hands.' All she could say after his death was, 'They could not understand my sensitive son.'

Liz Floyd, Aggett's companion, was detained with him in the early hours of the morning. She was still in detention when she heard of Neil's death, and was not permitted to attend his funeral. 'After I heard of Aggett's death I am scared to go back to John Vorster Square because of Neil's death. I am scared to be left on my own'

The picture that emerged of Neil Aggett was echoed around the country: his dedication to his medical and trade union work, his relentless schedule and uncompromising principles. In the words of Liz Floyd, 'He was a very gentle person, a very intelligent person. He was very warm to people, although he wouldn't be the kind of person who would go around being very friendly to everybody. If he got close to somebody, he would be very warm to them, and considerate. He thought about things a lot. He was very concerned about what was going on around him . . . '

Unfortunately for Dr Aggett, the police were less thoughtful about the welfare of their detainees, especially in view of their over-riding desire to extract information. It was precisely this desire resulting in an interminable interrogation which, we argued, was responsible for Aggett's suicide. Having accepted that Aggett might have hanged himself, we contended that the Security Police were responsible for causing his death at the end of seventy days of detention.

In terms of the law, the police are responsible for the mental and physical health of a detainee. The two policemen charged by us with betraying this trust were Maj. Arthur Benoni Cronwright, who was in overall charge of the investigation and interrogation of Aggett, and Lt. Stephan Peter Whitehead, the officer directly in charge of Aggett's interrogation, especially during the last ten days of Aggett's life. The risks of detainees committing suicide were well known and the police should have taken precautions. Despite this, they placed Aggett under intense physical and emotional pressures, never assessing whether he could withstand them. Suicide is not a crime in South African law and one cannot punish the deed. But inciting or aiding someone to commit suicide may be murder, attempted murder or culpable homicide, depending on the facts.

With detained trade unionists the Security Police had very little to go on, so they would try to extract incriminating evidence through intensive interrogation. Liz Floyd pointed out that Aggett might have survived if, indeed, he was doing something unlawful, which he would have been able to confess to to satisfy the lust of his captors. 'When in solitary confinement,' Floyd explained, 'the outside world ceases to exist. Survival while in detention means contact with people. The authorities tend to deny you such contact. They try to break you down during interrogation. Before, I could not understand why detainees committed suicide. When you are inside yourself, you realise the difference between life and death is very small indeed.'

What had happened to Neil Aggett during his time on the tenth floor of John Vorster Square? We could only attempt to reconstruct the events of his detention from the often contradictory testimony that emerged during the inquest, his complaints to officials and other detainees to whom he furtively spoke, and the experiences of some other detainees interrogated by members of the same team.

The first phase of interrogation took place from 15 December 1981 under the control of Capt. Martin Naudé from the East London Security Police. Aggett had no complaints during this period, and when visited by a friend, Yvette Breytenbach, on 24 December, he confirmed he was planning to holiday with her and her boyfriend in February. A week later, Aggett was visited by his mother and sister. Everyone agreed that he seemed to be in good spirits, considering the circumstances; even Capt. Naudé seemed pleased with Aggett's statements. Hardly a suicide risk according to the picture given by those who knew him.

The New Year came and, with it, a new period of interrogation from 4 January until 8 January. On the first day of this phase, Aggett reported that he had been assaulted. He later described the events of that day in a statement taken from him:

'On the 82.01.04 a black member of the force called Chauke came to fetch me at the cells and took me to the tenth floor, room 1012. Present in the room were Lt. Whitehead, the black policeman Chauke, and a railway police sergeant called Schalk.

'I was interrogated by Lt. Whitehead and every time that he asked me a question and I denied it, he accused me of calling him a liar. Then this Schalk would assault me, he hit me with his open hand in my face. And I fell against the table with my back and I could feel a scab on my back. He also assaulted me with his fists by hitting me on the side of my temple and my chest. He also kicked me with his knee on the side of my thigh. This Schalk wore a watch which cut my right forearm and it was bleeding. Later this Schalk went to wash off the blood that was on him. While I was assaulted by him he grabbed me by the scrotum and squeezed my testicles.'

Aggett told fellow-detainee Auret van Heerden of his experience, but he was unable to tell his story to the inspector of detainees, Abraham Mouton, who was denied access to Aggett on the very day he was assaulted. WO MacPherson told Mouton that Aggett was 'not available for an interview'. At that very moment the detainee was on the tenth floor of John Vorster, undergoing interrogation. Why were the police so anxious to keep the inspector away on the very day that Aggett had complained of an assault? There could only be one answer.

It was not the first time that the inspector and the magistrate were to be fobbed off by the Security Police when they tried to visit Aggett. Two days later Magistrate Wessels was also turned away by MacPherson when he tried to see Aggett. In his testimony MacPherson claimed he would have fetched Aggett if the magistrate and the inspector had told him to do so. Neither of them had indicated they would wait for him to return with the detainee.

We asked the head of the Johannesburg Security Police, Brig. Hendrik Muller, about the magistrates who visited detainees.

'Have you ever seen a magistrate on the tenth floor of John Vorster Square?'

'I can't recall having seen one, sir.'

'But now, but that is where most of the interrogation takes place – let's take some basic things: people are detained for the purposes of being interrogated?'

'Yes, sir.'

'Most if not all of the interrogation takes place on the ninth and tenth floors of John Vorster Square?'

'Tenth floor, Your Worship.'

'Tenth floor, and you've never seen the inspector of detainees there and you've never seen a magistrate there?'

'I haven't seen them there, no.'

'Well, in how many years?'

'Nearly six years, sir.'

How seriously did magistrates and inspectors of detainees take their duties to protect them?

The visiting magistrate finally saw Aggett a fortnight later, on 18 January, and recorded his complaint regarding the assault on the 4th. Aggett had an injury on his forearm to corroborate his allegations, an injury which was consistent with one found at the post-mortem examination. The letter from the magistrate containing Aggett's allegations took a week to reach John Vorster Square, hardly more than a kilometre away from the Magistrates' Court. It was now 25 January and Maj. Cronwright, who was in charge of the investigation, informed the interrogator, Lt. Stephan Whitehead, of the complaint.

This was the same day that the detainee Maurice Smithers reported seeing Aggett assaulted on the tenth floor. In a note which he smuggled out and which reached Helen Suzman, Smithers reported, 'I saw him being interrogated . . . He was standing all the time. Later he was still standing except he was naked. He was made to do push-ups, a substantial number. He was hit either with a belt or a rolled-up newspaper while doing them.' Suzman made the note public in parliament. The government indignantly denied the allegations, demanding the name of the detainee who had written the note. Adriaan Vlok, later the uncouth Minister of Police, remarked casually that he could not understand why detainees in solitary confinement were lonely when they were being interrogated for hours on end. Smithers was released from detention on 26 March, and served with a banning order on 13 April, the first day of the inquest.

Security Police Cons. Mohanwe Maketla was in the room with Smithers when the assault occurred. Maketla denied witnessing the assault, but under cross-examination admitted that if he had seen such an assault, he would have done nothing about it since he had instructions to guard Smithers.

'You could have stood at the door and shouted for help,' the Constable was told in cross-examination.

'I couldn't have,' Maketla replied. 'We don't make a noise when we are working.'

'What is more important, good manners or preventing someone from being assaulted?'

'Good manners,' came the reply.

Lt. Caswell Magoro of the Security Police initially denied having seen Aggett on 25 January. After he was confronted with a register which he had signed on removing Aggett from his cell, Magoro eventually admitted that he had taken Aggett to the tenth floor. The well-rehearsed police version was showing strains, visible to all, except, as it happened, the presiding magistrate. He rejected Smithers's evidence and excused the shortcomings of that given by the policemen.

By this time Aggett had written and indexed a statement 75 pages long. The police were not satisfied; Aggett added 28 more pages. These too, it turned out, were insufficient for Aggett's ambitious young interrogator. Lt. Whitehead had been with the Security Police for about six years and was only promoted to lieutenant in December 1981. He was a determined man when he assumed command of Aggett's interrogation on Monday 25 January, the day he heard of Aggett's complaint to the magistrate and the same day that Smithers saw Aggett assaulted on the tenth floor. The suspect whom Whitehead had been watching for three years was finally within his grasp; here, at last, was a chance to prove that Aggett was involved in the illegal activity he had long suspected. Auret van Heerden testified that Whitehead and Aggett did not have a 'happy' relationship; indeed, Aggett feared Whitehead. Aggett believed that Whitehead was responsible for the withdrawal of certain privileges, such as withholding his surgery textbooks. Despite this, Lt. Whitehead claimed to have got on well with Aggett. Dr Liz Floyd was contemptuous of Whitehead. She considered him a limited man, in some ways unsure of himself, who compensated by trying to bully people.

Whitehead oversaw the final stretch of interrogation, the 'long weekend' which finally broke Neil Aggett. From 28 until 31 January, Aggett did not leave the tenth floor, did not change his clothing, nor did he wash or have any exercise. For 62 hours he had no contact with anyone save his interrogators. During this 'long weekend' Aggett was interrogated by different teams, from 8.25 p.m. until 2.40 p.m. and again from 4 p.m. until midnight, on the Thursday; from 6 a.m. until midnight the following day; and on Saturday from 6 a.m. until about 11.30 p.m. This, at least, was the police's version. In his affidavit of 4 February, Neil Aggett described the hell of the 'long weekend':

'I was kept awake since the morning of the 28th January, 1982 to the 30th January, 1982. During the night of the 29th January, 1982 Lieut. Whitehead and another Security Sergeant, whose name I don't know, and another black male, also a policeman, were present when Lieut. Whitehead blindfolded me with a towel. They made me sit down and handcuffed me behind my back. I was shocked through the handcuffs. I don't know what they used to shock me with. I was shocked a few times. I have a scratch on my left pulse (radial nerve) where I was injured while being handcuffed. The scab on my back and the scar on my pulse as well as the scar on my forearm were the only injuries that I received as a result of this assault. I complained in the cells to Warrant Officer MacPherson who is working at the cells, about my back. I was not seen by a doctor.'

The Minister of Police attempted to have Aggett's final statement declared inadmissible, after the magistrate had ruled otherwise. In an application to the Supreme Court, the counsel for the police, Piet Schabort, SC, argued that the statement should not be made public in 'the interests of national security', as publication would disclose the working methods and techniques of the Security Police. He said the good name of the police was at stake, and it was not possible to cross-examine the man who made the statement. The application itself caused a sensation, leading to suspicion that the state was attempting to hide something. As the *Rand Daily Mail* commented, 'The Minister and the Security Police want to operate without scrutiny, especially when embarrassment or worse is possible. Even when a man has died in their custody. No matter what happens at the inquest now, that central, chilling fact has been well established.'

Judges Frikkie Eloff and Richard Goldstone, sitting in Pretoria, held that they would not lightly interfere with another court's activities, and there were no such grounds in this case. We were thus permitted to cross-examine the district surgeon Vernon Kemp on the contents of the statement; and the police were forced to offer a different version of the long weekend. When asked about being kept in an interrogation room for 62 hours, the doctor replied, 'My own personal view is that I should hate it to happen to me.' The police never asked Dr Kemp for his opinion on the effects of intensive interrogation.

They could not deny that Aggett had spent all this time in the interrogation room because of the entries in the occurrences book kept by the ordinary policemen in charge of the police cells. These kept a good and honest record. There was no love lost between the arrogant Security Police and those in uniform, whose rank was not respected and who were jealous of the privileges enjoyed by the security policemen. Highly improbable explanations had to be thought out.

In his initial affidavit, Whitehead claimed that 'intensive interrogation' was needed for the 'continuity' of the investigation, not realising that his colleagues would disavow the technique of 'intensive interrogation' when they gave evidence. During his own evidence, Whitehead claimed that Aggett had requested a prolonged session so that he could 'open his heart' and conclude the investigation. Whitehead and Cronwright both testified that they had wanted to gain Aggett's co-operation; we pointed out that prior to this, Aggett had been writing statements regularly, even indexing them – hardly an unco-operative detainee.

Lt. Whitehead's treatment of Aggett during this 'intensive interrogation' did not bother him.

'Did anybody warn you', we asked, 'that detainees require to be away from their interrogators so that the anxiety that is created in the interrogation situation may be wiped out by peaceful sleep away from the interrogator? Did anybody tell you that?'

'Your Worship, no one told me that, but I just want to correct that a detainee does not feel anxious while in detention.'

'Oh, I see, you as an interrogator thought that no anxiety whatsoever comes about in the persons that you interrogate on the tenth floor, is that your answer?'

'Your Worship, I merely said no anxiety is created.'

We asked Whitehead if he was aware of the dangers of lengthy interrogation, of how far he could go. He had completed an interrogation course, he replied.

'Did anybody warn you of the danger of interrogating persons about their innermost personal secrets and their personal emotions with other human beings?'

'Your Worship, I have already indicated to the court that I completed an interrogation course.'

'Did anyone warn you of the danger of getting people in interrogation to disclose to you their private lives?'

'Your Worship, during the course we were instructed on all dangers of interrogation.'

Was it really necessary, we asked the policeman, to interrogate a person on their personal relationships?

Yes, Whitehead replied; in order to test their truthfulness.

Neil Aggett's chief interrogator, the one who may well have driven him to take his own life, was unaware how many people had died in detention, most of them allegedly by committing suicide. When asked if he was aware of the risk that by being pushed too hard during interrogation a detainee might choose to take his own life rather than face the continuous barrage of questions, Lt. Whitehead replied, 'No, Your Worship, because people are not pushed too far.'

The plump, bespectacled 25-year-old Lieutenant never looked me in the eye, directing all his answers to the magistrate. Whitehead was an elusive witness, often taking refuge in linguistic confusion, as the questions were put in English and he answered in Afrikaans. The atmosphere in the courtroom was tense, and the magistrate had occasion to warn me about my manner of cross-examination, particularly after I told Whitehead, 'You have been in the witness box for three and a half hours. Dr Aggett was questioned for 62 hours. You have a long way to go.'

During the course of questioning, we drew attention to the discrepancies between Whitehead's exhaustive affidavit and his testimony. In the former, he made no mention of Aggett's desire to 'open his heart' or his request for continued interrogation; yet, in his evidence, these were the reasons he gave for the lengthy interrogation. His affidavit also made no mention of the 'betrayal of comrades' hypothesis which Whitehead used to explain Aggett's suicide. These lacunae were to prove unimportant in the magistrate's finding.

That Whitehead was a thoroughly unsavoury character emerged from his conduct after Aggett's death: he admitted entering illegally the Somerset West home of Aggett's parents in March 1982. Whitehead, we submitted, was a person who was prepared to misuse his position as a police officer, and had no qualms about flouting the law. The Aggetts' domestic worker complained that she was threatened, and that force was used to allow the intruders to remove documents. Aubrey Aggett was incensed by this sort of behaviour and laid a criminal charge of illegal entry. William Lane asked the Attorney-General, 'Why do you refuse to prosecute?' The Attorney-General replied that there was a tape of a conversation between the domestic worker and the police which contradicted her statement. William Lane asked for the transcript. They sent a copy, which made the case against the police even worse. The police had vilified the Aggetts to their domestic worker and gave her money to keep their visit a secret.

Whilst being cross-examined in relation to this incident, Whitehead excused himself for the reason that the police had been asked to do this by the lawyers as a way to get documents which would help their psychiatrist, Prof. Jan Plomp, build up a personality profile of Aggett. Piet Schabort had no hesitation in standing up in open court and discrediting his client. Schabort approached me to say that he hoped I accepted his assurance that he and Schalk Burger, his junior, had nothing to do with it. I, of course, accepted without any reservation. He also told me he had been asked by the Minister of Justice and Police, Louis le Grange, to apologise to Mr Aggett for the invasion of his privacy and to say that the Minister was prepared to grant Mr Aggett an audience to apologise to him personally. By this time Aubrey Aggett had heard a lot of the evidence about his son's ill-treatment, and he asked me to tell Schabort to inform the Minister that he was not interested in any apology from the Minister in charge of the people who had caused his son's death. When I told him, Schabort said he understood how the old man felt. Although of a conservative background, Piet Schabort showed a tremendous respect for justice when he was appointed to the bench. Together with Ismail Mahomed, he chaired the plenary meetings of CODESA, at which the interim South African constitution was adopted in 1993.

At one stage during the inquest I was carrying very heavy bags from the parking area, some distance away from the Magistrates' Court, when Schabort came up and sympathised with me, saying that the police had arranged for him to park within the courtyard, and that he would get a place there for me. Consistent with my attitude to the Security Police, I said no thank you. Schabort wanted to know why. My reply was a question in response: 'How do you think Mr and Mrs Aggett, Jill Burger and Liz Floyd would feel if they saw me accepting a favour from your clients?'

In July 1983 Det.-Sgt Paul Erasmus was fined R200 for entering and searching the Aggett home in Somerset West without a warrant. A similar charge against Whitehead was withdrawn, an outcome which added insult to injury for the Aggetts.

Convinced of Aggett's guilt, Whitehead set out to extract a confession from the detainee. But he was not alone. He was assisted by Warrant Officers De Bruyn and Carr, both of whom had never been involved in the investigation. What, we asked, were they doing? Carr had been accused by other detainees of ill-treatment, which gave weight to the suspicion that Carr and De Bruyn's role was primarily one of intimidation and to prevent Aggett from sleeping. Most of the police officers interrogating Aggett knew little or nothing about him or his trade union activities. One of the interrogators, WO Lukas, justified his presence on the grounds that he had special knowledge of a proposed 'Trade Union Centre'. When cross-examined on his 'special knowledge' he declined to answer, saying it was secret information. The centre, however, was common knowledge and was mentioned by Aggett in his affidavits. This patently false explanation of Lukas's presence lent weight to our suspicion that he was required for some other purpose.

The interrogators worked in shifts, breaking down what little resistance Aggett had left. Although the Security Police denied using a shift system, the evidence suggested otherwise. Some of the policemen had been approached the day before Aggett's death and were asked to be available at certain times.

We asked the head of the Security Police in Johannesburg, Brig. Muller, about one of his officers, Capt. Andries Struwig, who had been found by the

Appellate Division to have forced a witness and an accused to make false confessions on charges of murder that might have led to their execution. Brig. Muller said that despite this, Capt. Struwig 'is acceptable to me as a member of my staff'. He would feel safe leaving a detainee in the hands of Capt. Struwig. Another of Aggett's interrogators admitted that he had been convicted of assaulting a magistrate, to whom he later paid damages in a civil suit. These were the kind of men who were entrusted with the lives of those they had been taught to hate.

Maj. Arthur Cronwright testified to authorising the 'long weekend' because he had been told by Whitehead that Aggett had asked for an extended session of interrogation. The police, Cronwright claimed, were not anxious to finish the interrogation speedily.

'Your Worship,' Cronwright declared, 'it would make no difference to me if it took another year.'

'You can't be serious about that.'

'I am completely, completely serious about that.'

In September 1997 I examined the former Police Commissioner, Gen. Johann Coetzee, before the TRC about his knowledge of the deaths of hundreds of activists. He chose to come up to me afterwards and tell me that he did not have any ill-feeling towards me for doing my job, for which I thanked him. He said he always respected me despite the fact that his juniors had tried to persuade him that I was the head of the Communist Party. I told him I knew this because Maj. Cronwright had said so in the Aggett inquest. 'Oh, he was a madman,' Coetzee replied. I regret now that I did not take the opportunity to ask him, if he knew Cronwright was mad, why he, Gen. Coetzee, as head of the Security Police, had allowed him to be the commander of the interrogation unit that tortured so many detainees including Neil Aggett.

The police claimed the 62-hour interrogation session with Aggett was a success: Aggett had confessed and implicated a number of his comrades. These disclosures, they argued, had led to Aggett's suicide, as, once more, they employed their old favourite, the 'betrayal of comrades' syndrome. There was, however, no evidence, apart from that of Lt. Whitehead and WO Deetlefs, that Aggett made such disclosures. The documents which might have supported this were never made available, as the police claimed privilege. The four pages of notes taken by Deetlefs were never released. There were other questions. Why was the information given to Deetlefs, who had hardly participated in the interrogation? Why did the Commissioner of Police not act on the information he received and arrest the people 'betrayed' by Aggett? Why, if Aggett was being co-operative, did he not write the names himself? These questions went unanswered.

Cronwright at one stage claimed he had withheld statements of Aggett's which would link 'a very respected person in this court today' to the South African Communist Party. (The expression 'a respected person from the northern suburbs' had been used by Judge Ludorf to the *Sunday Times* reporter Maggie Smith shortly after his early retirement to refer to Bram Fischer. He told her that he knew who the leader of the Communist Party was and, although he was not prepared to mention the name, 'it was a respected person' living in the northern suburbs of Johannesburg.) I asked Cronwright why he had not detained him. Cronwright threatened that he would get 'the respected person' yet. I wished him the best of British luck. The way Cronwright looked at me and my response did not go unnoticed by Joe Lelyveld, the *New York Times* correspondent. He told me, 'That was meant for you!' I agreed, and added that, as I did not know Aggett at all, I knew that they were lying about the names he was said to have given.

When the police eventually released the statements made by Aggett (excluding the supposedly crucial four pages), they were hardly the evidence of a man revealing all. The Security Police produced two copies of a 'confession' allegedly written by Aggett, one handwritten and one an unsigned typed copy. There were important differences between the two, which we found very suspicious. In the handwritten version, for example, Aggett had written, 'I support the Marxist ideology and therefore am a communist. I am also an idealist.' The sentence was removed from the typed version: the 'editor' must have realised that idealism and Marxism are incompatible bedfellows, and Aggett was either confused or was recording a contradiction in order to prove that he was forced to write the first. The Police Directorate of Public Relations urged several newspapers to print the typed 'confession', especially the part where Aggett admitted to being a communist. This passage, the police said, was 'the crux of the whole thing'. Few newspapers fell for this crude ploy. The police's action was criticised by the PFP MP David Dalling, who was also critical of the SABC's coverage of the statement, which had been extensive, in contrast to its limited coverage of other evidence. What was important for the administration of justice, Dalling concluded, 'is not that Dr Aggett was a communist but rather what happened to him while he was in police custody.'

The language used in the Aggett 'confession' was particularly revealing, even suggesting that it had been partly composed by Aggett's interrogators. Drawing on a statement by the Wits politics lecturer Tom Lodge, we argued that a communist would not describe Marxism as 'an ideology'. And the addition of the words 'I am also an idealist' was intended to make nonsense of the statement which preceded it. We also argued that the word 'communistic' which appeared elsewhere in his statement was pejorative and most likely a direct translation from the Afrikaans 'kommunistiese'. Whitehead denied everything, even the obvious.

If the police story was accepted, it did not explain why Aggett had 'confessed' when he did. It was the same question Sydney Kentridge had put to Maj. Harold Snyman during the Biko inquest: 'Why should he answer you at all, why shouldn't he just whistle at you?' The same answer would be given: they would confront him with information, which we were asked in the Aggett case to believe was kept back until the day before he committed suicide.

In their effort to prove Aggett's guilt, Cronwright claimed he had evidence that Aggett belonged to an ANC cell in the Witwatersrand. Yet Aggett's initial statement to Capt. Naudé had made no mention of the fact.

'Your Worship,' the Major explained, 'all I can surmise is that he didn't want to say anything about that.'

But, we responded, would the interrogator not have asked the detainee about this document and noted that Aggett had denied it or refused to discuss it?

'It is not necessary to put it in the statement, because it's a negative answer, Your Worship.'

'Oh?'

Cronwright explained that section 6 detainees had to answer all questions to the satisfaction of the Commissioner of Police. A negative answer did not meet this requirement. It was clear that the police would keep asking the same questions until they got the answers they wanted.

After the 'long weekend' of interrogation Aggett was no longer the same man. His fellow detainees gave evidence of his changed mood in the days prior to his death. He did not greet them, seldom ate his food and, at times, would stare blankly at the wall. A magistrate was prevented from seeing him on 1 February. When Auret van Heerden saw Aggett that same day, the latter looked frightened; in a hushed conversation, Aggett made a motion like breaking a twig and said, 'I have broken.' He added, 'They must not ask me any more questions', before bursting into tears. The next day, Van Heerden thought Aggett looked like a zombie. 'Physically, he looked depressed, his shoulders were slumped, he walked with very little purpose, his feet dragged, he shuffled along and his response to things going on around him, to me in particular, was very removed. I found difficulty getting through to him.' Van

Heerden was afraid that if he complained to the police about what had happened to Aggett, he (Van Heerden) would suffer.

On the morning before he died, Aggett was visited by Sgt. Aletta Blom, who took down his final statement, albeit in broken English. 'She must have cut a very poor picture to Dr Aggett, whatever his condition,' we argued. 'He could not have believed he would get much protection.'

That evening, Aggett left his dinner untouched. We know that he read from *Zorba*, and that he appeared deeply depressed. The following morning he was dead.

One of the distinguishing features of Aggett's case was the admission of 'similar fact evidence', that is, evidence given by other detainees on their treatment by Maj. Cronwright's investigation team at John Vorster Square. To this end, the court allowed the evidence of Prema Naidoo, Shirish Nanabhai, Sisa Njikelana, Thabo Lerumo and Gabriel Ngwenya, all of whom complained of ill-treatment at the hands of the Security Police. Some of them underwent similar interrogation procedures, and suffered similar injuries to Aggett, which were suggestive of electric shocks. The injuries described by Nanabhai and Njikelana were apparent, in Nanabhai's case, to the district surgeon Dr Jacobson. Yet the police denied ever having administered such treatment. We argued that the police were lying. 'If they are lying in regard to this aspect, then in all probability they are lying in regard to other aspects of the ill-treatment of Nanabhai and Njikelana and it follows from this that there is a strong probability that the police are engaged in a conspiracy of silence in regard to the treatment of Dr Aggett.' It was highly unlikely that this evidence was fabricated, as the affidavits were made mainly while still in prison; and Dr Jacobson had verified Nanabhai's wound. Although we had affidavits from a number of others, the magistrate ruled them inadmissible.

It is difficult to accept the reasons given by the magistrate for disallowing the further evidence to prove the systematic torture of detainees. Counsel for the Security Police objected that the proceedings were being conducted by us as if we were before a commission of inquiry into detention without trial rather than an inquest to determine whether anyone was responsible for the death of Dr Neil Aggett. The complaint was not without substance. We offered no apology as we were entitled to lead similar fact evidence. We agreed that it was the best we could do seeing that the police refused access to detainees by relatives, doctors and lawyers, and even turned magistrates and inspectors away.

The magistrate in the Aggett case had had enough. The graphic accounts of torture were an embarrassment to the system. The magistrate's impatience

*Above*: Isie Maisels, George Bizos and Jonathan Gluckman at the Timol inquest
*Below*: Ahmed Timol and Imam Abdullah Haron (photos: Mayibuye Centre)

Bantu Stephen Biko (photo: Mayibuye Centre)

Biko's mother, wife and son in mourning (photo: Mayibuye Centre)

*Left:* Sydney Kentridge at the time of the Biko inquest
*Below and opposite:* Neil Aggett's funeral
(photos: Mayibuye Centre)

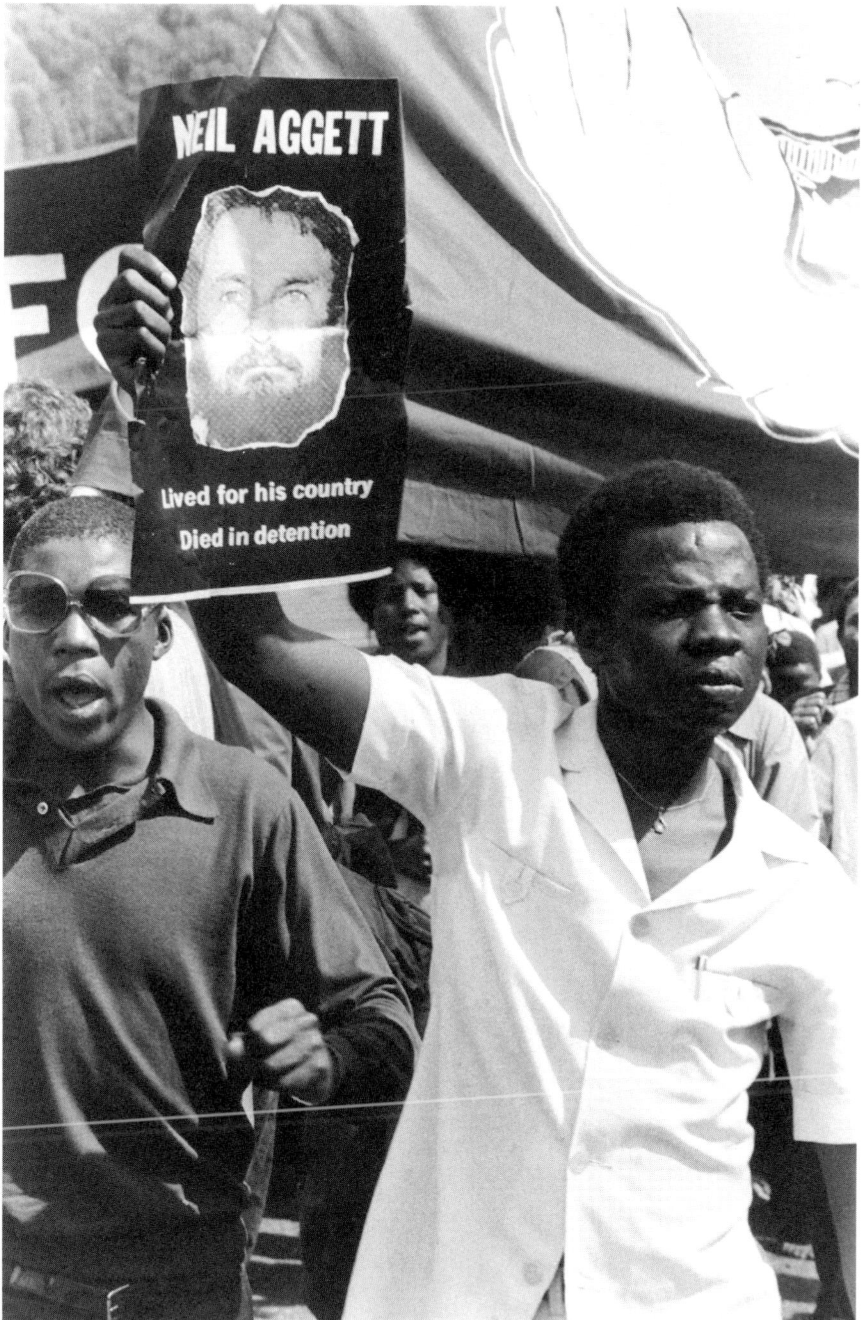
NEIL AGGETT
Lived for his country
Died in detention

*Above*: Matthew Goniwe
*Below*: The funeral of the Cradock Four (photos: Mayibuye Centre)

*Above*: Mrs Nyameka Goniwe with George Bizos at the TRC amnesty hearings
*Below*: Mrs Calata, Mrs Mkonto and Mrs Mhlauli

Craig Williamson passing the blame for various killings on to Louis le Grange and Col. Piet Goosen at the TRC amnesty hearings (Cartoon by Zapiro)

became obvious when we asked for leave to introduce a piece of evidence discovered by Dr Jonathan Gluckman whilst waiting in a physiotherapist's consulting rooms. He removed the small rubber covering off a machine used for electrotherapy. The metal thus exposed revealed a pattern identical to that described by Dr Jacobson as 'multiple punctate little scales each the size of a pen's head', which he found on Shirish Nanabhai's arms: Nanabhai said that he had been given electric shocks. Here was corroboration at last, or so we thought. But not the magistrate, who in his judgment, disbelieving him, said: 'We cannot rule out the possibility that Mr Nanabhai expected the police and was well prepared when they arrived and perhaps equipped [himself] with the two marks on his arms.'

Auret van Heerden was one of those who gave evidence of Aggett's condition; we were not permitted, however, to lead evidence of his own treatment in detention. In his inadmissible affidavit, he described his treatment by Maj. Abrie, Capt. Olivier from East London, Capt. Visser from John Vorster Square, and WO Prince from Springs:

'They then placed a canvas bank bag over my head; it was a fawn or light-brown coloured bank bag, with the name of an Afrikaans banking concern which I cannot remember. The bag was a little bit too small and so Capt. Visser actually tore it at the corners to ensure that it would fit completely over my head.

'They then wet the bag . . . Once the bag was wet it was very difficult to breathe through it. They then began applying shocks, initially to the soles of my feet, my wrists and my forearms but as the shocking continued they began placing the electrodes on the nape of my neck and at the base of my spine.

'As the shock was applied I began screaming compulsively and could not stop myself. I made a conscious attempt to stop screaming but I simply could not. As I screamed I found that I could not breathe. I also could not see anything because the bag was over my head. The feeling of claustrophobia was extreme and I found myself panicking because the shocks were pulsating through my body . . .

'As more and more water was applied to the bag I found myself lying on the floor in a pool of water with the current travelling up and down my body, being conducted by the water and at the same time screaming and being unable to breathe. I'm not sure how they gauged how long I could actually withstand the shocks or how long it would be before I in fact suffocated, but at a certain stage they stopped administering the shocks and took the bag off. They would then immediately begin firing questions at me . . .

'If I did not give them an answer which they wanted they would then start to put the bag back over my head.'

The litany of torture continues for a further ten pages.

Having adduced evidence of systematic torture by the squad of security policemen operating out of John Vorster Square, we hoped to establish that Neil Aggett had suffered a similar fate. And, implicitly, that other detainees would also share this fate unless the activities of the Security Police were denounced. We concluded our argument with a plea for the rule of law to be observed, arguing that 'this court's finding will clearly show that we are all subject to the law of the land and its processes which protect the dignity of human life'. The police, we hoped, were not above the law; we were to be sadly disappointed.

The inquest lasted 42 days, extended over six months. The magistrate, Piet Kotzé, began his judgment on 20 December, in front of a packed courtroom. Most of those present were journalists, local and foreign. Helen Suzman and other politicians were also there, as were Aggett's parents; and so too Maj. Cronwright, resplendent in his green suit. The magistrate must have been aware of the criticisms made by Magistrate Marthinus Prins's three-minute judgment in the Biko inquest. He was going to make sure that he would not be criticised on the grounds of brevity. The reading of his judgment of 187 pages went into a second day.

The magistrate accepted the evidence relating to Aggett's arrest and detention, and the finding of his body. 'The most important question for decision', he continued, 'is what happened to Aggett at John Vorster Square Police Station since his arrival on the 11th December 1981 until the night of his death, the 4th February 1982. On this issue we have two conflicting versions.' It soon emerged which version was more to Kotzé's liking.

In weighing up the evidence, the magistrate dealt with the credibility of different witnesses. Almost every witness called at our instance was disbelieved by Magistrate Kotzé, who was particularly scathing of the detainees who testified. Prema Naidoo was criticised for failing to complain to the district surgeon, and because he was 'a person with strong feelings against the Security Police . . . the possibility of bias can therefore not be excluded'. Scars found on the body of Shirish Nanabhai, and confirmed by Dr Jacobson, were discounted because it was not possible to say how they were caused, and Jacobson had found only two marks, not four, as Nanabhai had claimed.

So it went on, as one witness after another was dismissed on the grounds of minor inconsistencies in testimony, shiftiness on the stand, failure to complain to the inspector and mere bias against the Security Police. Sisa

Njikelana, Gabriel Ngwenya and Thabo Lerumo were each, in turn, written off as unreliable witnesses. Piet Schabort and Schalk Burger had scored against them in cross-examination. We could have no complaint: their clients were entitled to the best defence available, and they got it.

P.G. Haasbroek, SC and André de Vries, who were appointed by the Attorney-General to lead the evidence, did not do much more than call the witnesses and read their statements into the record. Sydney Kentridge's remark in the Biko case was equally applicable: it was left to us alone to prove the evidence of the policemen. Yet the other witnesses were treated differently. Denis Kuny objected to André de Vries's questioning of one of the witnesses called by us because it was cross-examination.

In the magistrate's judgment Maurice Smithers, a fellow detainee, was taken to task for discrepancies between his initial note, his affidavit and his testimony. In his note, he had stated that he had seen Aggett hit with a newspaper, but in evidence he said that it appeared to be a newspaper but that he was not sure. 'If Mr Smithers was not sure what it was,' Kotzé intoned, 'why did he make a positive statement in his note that it was rolled-up newspaper?' The magistrate would not make an allowance for the necessity for brevity in a note, hurriedly written on a scrap of paper and smuggled out of a high security fortress.

When it came to the police witnesses, Kotzé was impressed by the degree of corroboration which their evidence offered one another. Whatever discrepancies existed were wiped away by the magic wand of corroboration. Whitehead, one of the last of the policemen to give evidence, had indeed done better than we had expected. Although he could not explain away the inherent improbabilities in his version, he was consistent with himself and the other members of the squad in relating how they had kept Dr Aggett on the tenth floor for 62 hours. His success was partly explained in the 1990s when a special investigation team under Transvaal Attorney-General Jan D'Oliveira was established to look into security force hit squads, and it was revealed that my chambers had been bugged during the Aggett inquest. The police would play the transcript of our discussions in preparation of cross-examination and rehearse the possible answers with plenty of time to choose the most plausible. We were deprived of the element of surprise, the cross-examiner's strongest weapon. Of course the magistrate could not have known then, and I am absolutely certain that neither Piet Schabort nor Schalk Burger even suspected it, otherwise they would have thrown their brief back to the State Attorney. I had reason to believe that my office was bugged from time to time on the off-chance that the Security Police might pick up something of interest. But I never imagined that they would go as far as they reportedly did to defeat the ends of justice.

Although he planned to treat the evidence of Cronwright and Whitehead 'with caution', the magistrate felt they had been through a 'thorough and merciless' cross-examination by myself and was impressed, in particular, with the way Whitehead dealt with the situation, and the corroboration offered by other police witnesses.

Magistrate Kotzé moved on to examine Aggett's account of his ill-treatment to Magistrate Wessels, which was contrasted with what he allegedly told Auret van Heerden. Although Kotzé concluded, 'The discrepancies between these two versions are so conspicuous that they do not call for comment', the main differences seemed to lie in the amount of detail and the name of the policeman who assaulted Aggett. In his statement Aggett said, 'The assault was by a sergeant of the Railway Police. His first name is Schalk', whereas Van Heerden reported that Aggett had said he was assaulted by 'a Railway policeman . . . by the name of Van Schalkwyk, I am not sure of his rank'. That this should be a discrepancy was quite odd because by Van Schalkwyk's own admission, Aggett used to call him 'Schalk'.

The magistrate did not accept the evidence regarding a *modus operandi* among the Security Police for conducting assaults. Some detainees were in his view unreliable witnesses, while others had not been ill-treated. 'We must try to find the truth on facts, not on innuendo or slander,' Kotzé remarked. He was unable to find that Aggett was assaulted in the manner described by Smithers, and declared the scar on Aggett's arm could be placed, according to expert evidence, at any time between three weeks and three months.

Kotzé recognised that it was problematic that the complaint made on 18 January had been dealt with so slowly, but held that this delay alone had no effect on the events which followed. Regarding the pathetic police investigation into Aggett's death, Kotzé merely said, 'It is a fact of life that we find degrees of experience and zeal in every profession.' In the same breath he applied this little aphorism to Aggett's interrogation: 'It was suggested that some of the policemen who interrogated Dr Aggett was [sic] not competent to do it. It is a fact of life that we find degrees of competence in every profession . . . This suggestion was coupled with the allegation that these policemen were present only to intimidate and keep Dr Aggett awake. We have no reliable facts to substantiate this allegation.'

The lies of WO MacPherson which had kept the inspector away from Aggett were dismissed as carelessness; 'an inference that it was done in pursuance of a conspiracy by the interrogators is possible but such conspiracy is denied by the witnesses whose evidence I cannot reject.' Once again the word of the Security Police was accepted as the truth, however improbable.

The magistrate was unable to find that the 'long weekend' occurred without Aggett's consent. All the police witnesses, including those not involved with the Security Police, saw no change in Aggett after this interrogation. In addition he had made a rational statement to Sgt Blom the day before he died. The policemen were clearly not aware of Aggett's condition; and, the magistrate held, there was no reasonable possibility that they ought to have foreseen Aggett's suicide.

Not only did the magistrate exonerate Cronwright and Whitehead, but he went on to suggest that Auret van Heerden was not blameless in Aggett's suicide. Kotzé remarked that Van Heerden's name appeared on Barbara Hogan's list as a 'person under discipline' and that 'Ex facie the document, Mr Van Heerden's position seems to be superior to that of Dr Aggett'. Did the magistrate mean that Van Heerden was Aggett's superior in the ANC and feared any revelations the latter might make? Kotzé remarked, 'I do not refer to this document to convey that I believe in the truth of the information but merely to emphasise the existence thereof.' Van Heerden had admitted that he was suspected of disloyalty, which led the magistrate to muse, 'In these circumstances one can expect him to do something to save face.'

In Magistrate Kotzé's scenario, Van Heerden was both worried by Aggett's revelation that he had 'broken' and concerned about the need to 'save face'. Here was a perfect opportunity to solve both problems. Once he realised Aggett was a suicide risk, Kotzé continued, Van Heerden should have informed the police immediately. 'Is it really possible that a man with honest and honourable motives would behave like this if he really cared? In the case of Mr Van Heerden one might be inclined to say that there was a duty on him to raise alarm on the night of 4th February, 1982 but of course a moral duty will not suffice in legal proceedings,' Kotzé concluded with palpable disappointment.

On the evidence of the police psychiatrist Prof. Plomp, Kotzé took refuge in the 'betrayed comrades' hypothesis: 'He [Aggett] was a man who was devoted to a cause, who worked with a number of close associates to achieve his goals. During the period of detention he had to disclose particulars of his activities and, more important, the names of his associates. These disclosures must have brought about a feeling of uncertainty about his future and the realisation that steps could be taken against his associates. The possibility of a sense of guilt towards his associates, a sense of betrayal of his friends and associates, is large. He had to face some of his associates and to admit the disclosures, an anticipation or feeling of rejection by them cannot be excluded. Unfortunately it was during this crucial period that he had to be informed *inter alia* that a friend could not afford to provide him with a portable radio in the cell.'

With 'associates' replacing 'comrades', it was a classic judgment based on 'revelations' which were never revealed. In a final moment of *schadenfreude*, Magistrate Kotzé had managed to rope another of Aggett's 'associates' into the circle of blame; the police, at any rate, were innocent. It was an unbelievable judgment.

The verdict was slammed by the official opposition; Helen Suzman called the finding 'totally outrageous', adding, 'It was beyond the expectations of even the police, whose counsel only asked for an open verdict.' Bishop Tutu found the verdict 'quite shattering'. The Southern African Catholic Bishops' Conference and the South African Council of Churches blamed the system of detention for Aggett's death.

What was perhaps most outrageous was the magistrate's suggestion that Van Heerden was morally culpable, not the police. Even a conservative newspaper called this apportionment of blame *'belaglik'* – laughable. A Wits law lecturer saw this as a fundamental flaw in Piet Kotzé's own moral code, his insularity and lack of empathy.

Judicial officers rarely write a judgment which they believe is wrong. Piet Kotzé, like most of us, was a product of his background. He was a competent and zealous prosecutor in the Eastern Cape in the 1960s when hundreds were sent to Robben Island for supporting the banned ANC. In fairness, Kotzé was not less zealous in ordinary criminal cases. In the 1970s he came to Johannesburg. He was allotted the prestigious north-eastern corner office on the ground floor of the Magistrates' Courts directly opposite to where the offices of Mandela and Tambo had been situated until 1961. He presided in most of the important political cases in the Regional Court and was obviously overseeing his less experienced colleagues. The regional magistrates who usually conducted political trials were not chosen at random but by the Security Police. The latter asked the control prosecutor to set the matter down in a given court, which they knew was usually presided over by one whom they trusted. All these magistrates had started their careers as prosecutors. Most had prosecuted political cases and knew at least some of the senior security policemen. They were all civil servants. Their legal qualifications were in the main obtained at the Justice College run by the department. We were told that one of the lessons taught there was that defence counsel were not to be trusted, especially those from the Johannesburg Bar. Piet Kotzé, while a prosecutor, behaved towards us as if he had taken the lesson seriously. None of these practices were likely to produce independent and legitimate judicial officers.

They were all white, almost all of them Afrikaners, in a multiracial and multilingual society in which the criminal law was used to maintain an unjust system. From an early age they were taught that South Africa belonged to them. The likes of Aggett, Floyd and Smithers were their guests, the Naidoos and Nanabhais less welcome, and the Ngwenyas, Lerumos and Njikelanas their servants known only by their first names. Of course not all Afrikaners remained within the laager. There were some, like Bram Fischer and Beyers Naudé, Afrikaners to the core, who rejected apartheid as unjust and foresaw its demise. There was young Auret van Heerden who joined the ANC, according to Barbara Hogan's note. They were the exceptions and beyond the pale. They were all a danger to Afrikaner racial and cultural purity, which had to be preserved at all costs.

It must have been difficult for Magistrate Piet Kotzé to rise above his background. Had he done so, his reasoning and findings would have been different. His decision that Aggett was not hanged by his captors is clearly correct. On the evidence before him no reasonable court could have come to a different conclusion. But his decision that Neil Aggett was not tortured by the Security Police and brought thereby to commit suicide is as clearly wrong. Detainees were not more likely to be untruthful because of their commitment to a cause than security policemen, whose loyalty to each other and the evil system they were called upon to preserve may have been greater than their loyalty to the truth. No matter how many policemen said that Aggett consented to a 62-hour session in the interrogation room, they could not and should not have been believed. There was not only Aggett's own statement contradicting this but evidence of a widely used system of breaking down the detainees' resistance so that they would subscribe to what their interrogators wanted from them.

In the Aggett case, the vital questions on the probabilities were not posed in the judgment nor were the answers convincing. If Aggett was well treated and co-operative, why did he complain of being assaulted? Why was the inspector of detainees kept away from him so shortly after he said he had been assaulted? Why was an inept young policewoman, junior to those against whom the complaint was made, assigned to investigate it? Why did she make the contents of the statement known to the suspects? Why were teams arranged for another session during the following weekend other than to repeat the 62-hour performance? Might this have been the trigger for the suicide rather than the 'betrayal of his comrades' story of the security policemen for whom there was some evidence that it was an afterthought?

The judgment emphasised that those who gave evidence of electric shocks, assaults and insults to their persons were not consistent with themselves. They either did not complain at all, or complained to some and not to others, or got some of the detail wrong. The magistrate thought it unnecessary to look at the evidence before him, at the writings and opinions of doctors, psychiatrists and clinical psychologists that detainees lived in fear, not knowing whom to trust from day to day, nor how their conditions might change for the worse.

How else could the statement of Lerumo to the inspector of detainees Abraham Mouton be explained: 'A chain was put around my neck by security policeman Malherbe. I was threatened that if I do not speak the truth I will be killed. I do not want Malherbe to be charged. I forgave him.' And another former detainee, Ismail Momoniat, again to Mouton: 'The Security Police have not been good to me when I was detained the first week but I do not want to talk about it.' He was not asked why not. And again Ngwenya to Mouton: 'I want an English Bible, that is all. I was beaten up on 27 November 1981, but I do not want to lay a charge or say anything about it.' Again, he was not asked why not.

Dr Liz Floyd reported two days after Dr Neil Aggett's death: 'Last Thursday at John Vorster Square three security policemen threatened me. One said he will make me stand day and night if necessary for three days to make me talk. Two said I would get a five-year sentence because I was withholding information. One was Lt. Whitehead and one Capt. Olivier.' She was told while being interrogated that she would continue standing for a long time because she was 'cheeky'. She stood for one hour but was allowed to sit when she informed them that she had arthritis. She added: 'The Security Police did not assault me physically, only mentally.'

Magistrate Kotzé did not weigh up the evidence of these witnesses as well as that of Smithers and Van Heerden by posing the question: Is this evidence not consistent with the purpose of detention without trial or with the police admissions that they do not record 'negative' answers or with uncertainty in the detainees' minds whether complaining would help them or exacerbate their suffering? Above all, the magistrate's lengthy analysis and then rejection of their evidence because of contradictions of detail make his judgment no more credible than the three-minute effort of Magistrate Prins in the Biko inquest.

It was left to Liz Floyd to ask the question the police had been unable to answer: 'If the Security Police treated [Neil] the way the magistrate accepted they did, why did he die and why have over 50 other people died in detention?' Her anger was matched only by her sorrow. 'It will take a very long time to get over Neil.'

Sitting silently in the courtroom, Neil Aggett's parents could hardly believe their ears. Retired, conservative farmers, they had spent a large portion of their savings in legal costs, as they sought to learn the truth about their son's death. They reaped a bitter harvest. They had left Kenya to avoid living under a black government, and had voted for the National Party in 1981. They disapproved of their son's politics and lifestyle; but the hell they were plunged into by his death changed their lives forever. Neil's father, Aubrey Aggett, said, 'The magistrate's findings are beyond my understanding . . . I am only a farmer, but I cannot accept the verdict.'

The Minister of Justice, Kobie Coetsee, was unmoved. 'Justice took its course,' he said. The *Rand Daily Mail* thought otherwise:

'So, after South Africa's longest inquest, we know at last where blame for the death in detention of Dr Neil Aggett might lie.

'On a fellow detainee. A man who realised a day before the trade unionist died that his friend had suicidal tendencies and did not inform his captors. A man who himself was cowed and living in fear and helplessness. A man who was kept under guard day and night in one of the world's strictest security systems. Yes, this is the man who, the Aggett inquest magistrate found yesterday, might have had some moral responsibility for the suicide.

'Not the Security Police whose job it was to protect, keep alive and produce in court a man whose alleged confession would surely have helped convict others. Not the men in whose hands 51 detainees had already died and who are among the most experienced in the world when it comes to dealing with most forms of suicide and death in detention, including men slipping on soap, falling down stairs, throwing themselves out of buildings, and hanging themselves in their cells.'

Auret van Heerden had also been detained and tortured, but he was still alive and he instituted a civil claim for damages. His claim foundered on the rock of corroboration erected by the Security Police, and was finally destroyed by a photograph produced by the police. The photo showed Van Heerden having coffee in a Pretoria coffee bar with a security policeman. They explained that he was an informer who was well treated, even taken out for coffee. Would they have ill-treated such a valuable person?

When I was defending Dr Fabian Ribeiro on a charge under the Terrorism Act in Pretoria, the investigating officer regularly asked me to go and have coffee with him. It may have been at the same place where Auret van Heerden was photographed, near the Security Police headquarters. I repeatedly refused. I instinctively felt that it was wrong to have social contact with anyone involved with detention without trial, even though there may not have been specific evidence brought to my notice that the investigating officer had tortured any detainee. When that evidence came out in Auret van Heerden's case, I was glad that I never took up the invitation.

I was told, from time to time, that detainees were asked who was going to defend them. When any of them mentioned my name, they would be warned against employing me. They were told the judges did not like me, I would not give them a proper defence, and their jail sentences would inevitably be longer. I know of no one who took their advice.

When it became clear that I would defend Barbara Hogan, the author of the list on which Neil Aggett's name had appeared, the Security Police subpoenaed me to give evidence before a magistrate of what I had said, according to them, at a meeting at Wits University in support of the 'Free Mandela Campaign'. As I stepped out of court an attempt was made to serve the subpoena on me by the very Deetlefs to whom it was claimed the vital information had been disclosed by Aggett. I told him to go away. It was improper to serve a process on counsel whilst in his robes at the door of the court. I had read this in some book. Deetlefs was taken aback. As he turned away I told him that he no doubt knew where my office was. He was there at the end of the court day. I let him wait in the reception area until I had disrobed in my office. I took the subpoena and he left. Members of the Security Police expected to be treated with respect, if not awe.

I was outraged and immediately dictated an affidavit in which I explained that I knew nothing about the ANC, other than what I had learnt in my professional capacity, and I had addressed the meeting on the subject of the legal treatment of political prisoners. I further explained that I believed ulterior motives lay behind the subpoena: no attempt had been made to question me on any 'information' I might have, and the suggestion that I was furthering the aims of an unlawful organisation was 'patently ludicrous'. 'To require me at this stage, having been briefed for the defence, to be interviewed by persons whom I may be obliged to cross-examine in that very defence', I concluded, 'is calculated to embarrass me in the exercise of my duties as an advocate.'

The senior prosecutor, André de Vries, who had signed the subpoena, had no answer when Johan Kriegler, then chairman of the Bar Council, enquired why I was never asked to make a statement and why a subpoena was issued. The Security Police really called the tune, even in relation to prosecutors, few of whom could stand up to them. De Vries told Kriegler I could ignore the subpoena.

Whenever in a high-profile case our family was subjected to comparatively minor dirty tricks, we suspected the Security Police. My wife Arethe and I would be told on the phone that the speaker was a friend of one of our sons, Kimon, Damon or Alexi, and that he was detained at John Vorster Square. A couple of questions about how the caller knew would be followed by such hesitant answers that we ignored the call. Once it was easy to do so because our three sons were at home. In the late 1970s a friend of theirs, whose voice was known to us, phoned to say that Damon and Alexi had been arrested at the Johannesburg railway station for distributing pamphlets earlier in the day. As I was about to set off to the police station they drove in. Damon's first words, with a broad smile, were, 'Father, they may hate you, but I want to tell you that they respect you.'

Damon and Alexi took turns in filling me in. Alexi, a first-year engineering student and looking even younger than his 18 years, was arrested by a sergeant in uniform, who took away his batch of pamphlets. Alexi waved to his older brother, who immediately went to him. Damon was then also taken. They were not asked their names, nor told why they were arrested, nor to where they would be taken. They were locked in the back of the police van and driven to John Vorster Square to the office of a Capt. Van Rensburg of the Security Police. They were asked to give their names.

'Are you related to Advocate George Bizos?' Van Rensburg asked.

'Yes, he is our father.'

'O God, nee [O God, no],' was his immediate response.

He composed himself and continued in the most polite manner: 'Now don't go and tell your father you were arrested. I want to make it clear that you are free to go and don't have to answer any questions. The sergeant brought you here because we want to know who issued these pamphlets. If you want to you can tell us.'

'That's easy,' said Damon, 'look at the bottom: it says "Issued by the Students' Representative Council, University of the Witwatersrand."'

'Yes, thank you,' said the Captain. 'Are you prepared to tell us who actually did it?

'The full council decided. I am the vice-president.'

'Thank you,' said Capt. Van Rensburg again.

He instructed the sergeant to take them back to where they were when he invited them to come with him and asked them to give me his best regards. Alexi, not to be outdone, asked that the pamphlets should be returned to him or he should be issued with a receipt. He got the pamphlets back.

Months later I went to the John Vorster Square charge office to see an awaiting-trial prisoner in preparation for an application for bail. The jovial middle-aged sergeant behind the counter greeted me by name and asked me how my two boys were. I asked him if he was the one who had taken them to Capt. Van Rensburg. Yes, he had. He thanked me for not making trouble for him. He was proud of his clean record, of not having complaints in his personal file. He said he had only done what he had been asked to do by the Security Police. I assured him that the police would not have much trouble from the likes of me if they treated everyone's children with the consideration with which they had treated ours.

Other students in similar circumstances would have been at least interrogated, threatened with detention, questioned about their families and friends, about political activity on the campus and the influence of their lecturers. If a weakness emerged they would be invited to do their patriotic duty by reporting on them all. They were assured that they would be rewarded. If the bait was not taken the parting words would be: 'If you know what's good for you, keep quiet. We don't want to read about this in tomorrow's *Rand Daily Mail*.' If you were black you would have been slapped around, and much worse if you had a copy of the Freedom Charter.

The Aggett inquest had cleared the Security Police, but it implicitly exposed Judge Rabie and his Commission. The very inspectors and magistrates in whom the Chief Justice had so much faith were of no help to Neil Aggett. When they eventually saw Aggett, his complaint was handled so poorly that the safeguards were exposed for the sham they were. The claim by the police that they were concerned with the welfare of detainees was also exposed as callous. 'Who would watch the watchers?' asked a report published by Lawyers for Human Rights.

The recommendations of the Rabie report were incorporated in the Internal Security Act of 1982, which repealed, among others, the Terrorism Act. But the Internal Security Act did not mean the end of detention without trial. This was a period of 'total onslaught', the credo used to justify almost any measure in defence of 'white civilisation'. Section 29 of the Internal Security Act provided for indefinite detention.

So ineffective were the precautions contained in the new legislation that the Medical Association of South Africa in mid-1982 established a committee to report on the medical dangers of detention. Chaired by Professor S.A.S. Strauss, the seven-man committee included Prof. J.D. Loubser and Dr Jonathan Gluckman. The Johannesburg Bar Council was asked to make representations to the committee. Johan Kriegler asked me to accompany him to relate what evidence those of us who usually did political trials had heard from detainees. The medical profession did not want to be involved in another Biko fiasco.

The report of the MASA committee found that despite the Internal Security Act and the directives issued by the Minister of Law and Order, 'there are insufficient safeguards in the existing legislation to ensure that maltreatment of detainees does not occur without those responsible having to account for their actions before a court of law. Persuasive evidence has been put before the committee that where harsh methods are employed in the detention and interrogation of detainees, including isolation and sensory deprivation for relatively lengthy periods of time, this may have extremely serious, and possibly permanent, effects on the mental and physical health of a detainee.'

Isolation combined with the cessation of normal routine, and the strain of intensive interrogation, could lead to serious mental breakdown or even suicide. It was the duty of medical practitioners, the report noted, to practise preventive medicine. This was equally true for those primarily responsible for the medical care of detainees – the district surgeons. While acknowledging the difficulties faced by these practitioners, the committee categorically rejected the suggestion that a 'conspiracy' existed between district surgeons and the police. But in implying that no district surgeon ever covered up for the Security Police, especially outside the metropolitan areas, the committee had presumed too much faith in some doctors. The committee recommended a number of additional measures to protect the health of detainees. These included the recommendations that regular weekly physical and psychiatric assessments be held of detainees in isolation, that interrogation be taped by closed-circuit television, that detainees could, if requested, be examined by private doctors of their choice in the presence of the district surgeon, and adequate facilities be provided for the proper medical and psychiatric treatment of detainees. Few of these recommendations were ever implemented.

A year after Aggett's death, a memorial service was held at Wits University, which was attended by over a thousand people. Neil Aggett's name was added to the list of dead detainees, as he took his place among the heroes of the struggle. But for an old white farmer from Somerset West, this was little consolation. 'I'm bitter as hell about it,' Aggett's father said afterwards. 'The government are the biggest liars that ever lived. Sooner or later, there is going to be a helluva blow-up here. Violence breeds violence and the government is getting more and more violent and people will react with violence . . . From the day he died, I have woken up every morning with the memory of the terrible torture I believe my son was subjected to.'

Liz Floyd later said that the security police felt no remorse, only anger. Because of the embarrassment to the system, they began shifting their tactics, turning to murder and 'disappearances'. They were determined not to have another Neil Aggett. Indeed, the adverse publicity which they had earned led to their adoption of the Chilean and Argentinian ways of dealing with the 'enemies of the state': kill them, bury them secretly, say they escaped or deny they were in custody, blame their deaths or disappearance on the enemy, the ANC. There would be no inquests, no cross-examinations, no adverse publicity. The State Security Council, the Generals, propagandists, and gullible magistrates and judges would protect those that tortured and killed for their country's sake. But things did not always work out this way.

Liz Floyd believes the TRC should have been called the Truth and Recognition Commission. Although reconciliation may have occurred in small doses, recognition that the police tortured, maimed, lied and defeated the ends of justice is recorded in their own words on film and on paper. Justice was cheated but hopefully history will not be.

CHAPTER 4

# SIMON MNDAWE

❧

## 'A Pain Without Ending'

W E naively thought that the exposure of inhuman treatment in an
inquest on the death of yet one more detainee would prevent the
death of others. It was a vain hope. Within months of the completion of the
Aggett inquest, Rose Rosenberg, a junior member of the Bar, approached me
on behalf of attorneys Mathews Phosa and Phineas Mojapelo, who were practising in Nelspruit, to do an inquest there. Mindful of the criticism levelled
against the Bar after the Biko inquest by black practitioners that we were only
interested in high-profile cases, I rearranged my programme to take it. The
young attorneys were not known to me then. We later became good friends.
Mathews, now the Premier of Mpumalanga province, had to flee into exile
shortly after the inquest on a tip-off that his name was on the list of a hit
squad. Phineas, who stuck it out, is now the attorneys' professional representative on the Judicial Services Commission and a member of the Law Commission, appointed by President Mandela.

Even though counsel for the police complained that we had turned the
Aggett inquest into a commission of inquiry, which exposed South Africans
and many throughout the world to the evils of detention without trial, it was
not enough to save the life of Simon Tembuyise Mndawe. Was it because,
unlike Aggett, he was not white, but an African? Or was it because he died in
Nelspruit, a semi-rural area, which even the media committed to exposing
apartheid's horrors thought too far and too inconvenient to send a senior
reporter to?

The Mndawe inquest would show that the police and district surgeons outside the metropolitan areas had apparently learned nothing, nor had the
police forgotten how to use crude methods to obtain confessions, be they true
or false. Their lack of sophistication made it easier to cross-examine them
than their more experienced and urbane counterparts in the cities.

The Commissioner of Police, Gen. Mike Geldenhuys, had no hesitation in
proclaiming Mndawe a 'trained terrorist' after the detainee was found hanged

in his cell on 8 March 1983. Mndawe had written a confession the day after his arrest on 22 February, Gen. Geldenhuys explained, and the investigation was thus complete. Now all the police had to do was catch the remaining 'insurgents' – Mndawe's comrades who had infiltrated the country. Due process did not overly concern the General. As Bishop Tutu caustically observed, 'Are the police also judges, determining the guilt of suspects?'

Born in Lydenburg, Mndawe lived in Kanyamazane township outside Nelspruit in the eastern Transvaal lowveld. Bordered by Swaziland and Mozambique, it was often used by guerrillas to enter the country covertly. Mndawe was suspected of being one of these guerrillas. Six months before his death, Mndawe was questioned by the police. 'The police gave me papers and ordered me to write what I know about the ANC,' he said in a statement.

'I told them that I know nothing about the ANC. They put a cloth in my mouth and then another piece of cloth and covered my face, and then put a wet plastic over my head, whereupon they held the plastic against my neck and I felt like I was dying. They hung me on a broom-stick and spinned me around it. They choked me with electricity next to my heart, and even there I nearly died. What is painful is that they used this electricity even on my testes and that is when I wished to die in order to be free from those assaults.'

From the depths of his agony, Mndawe agreed to write the statements the police wanted. He said he was recruiting youths for the ANC, to be trained in Maputo. He told the police that as a reward he was promised a rifle and a car. The police in turn agreed not to charge him, to pay him R3000 for his testimony and for more information in the future, and on condition that he said nothing to anyone of his assault at the hands of the police. Mndawe kept away from the police but they must have heard that, far from suppressing his ordeal, he spoke openly about it.

The bearded 24-year-old was arrested at midnight on 22 February 1983, originally as a suspect on a charge under the Internal Security Act. Three days later he was 'released' and immediately redetained under section 29 for an indefinite period. Following his arrest, he told a visiting magistrate how he had been punched and kicked by the policemen who arrested him. The plain-clothes policemen responsible – Sgt Solomon Bhembe, Cons. Dirk Spies and WO David de Klerk Smith – claimed they had used necessary force to restrain Mndawe. After subduing him, they said they had found a submachine gun, ammunition and ANC propaganda. He was no longer alive to admit or deny their allegations. When Mndawe was brought into the police station, WO Daniel Greyling later testified, his right cheek was swollen, there was sand in his hair and he had a graze on the left side of his forehead. A similar observation was made by a number of other policemen.

Dr Frans Jacobus Viljoen was the part-time district surgeon in Nelspruit. When he examined Mndawe after his arrest he recorded that there were no injuries on 'die swarte'. What sort of examination was it that missed a broken cheekbone and other injuries? But when he again saw the detainee on 3 March, Dr Viljoen noted an 'ingeduikte regte wangbeen' [indented right cheekbone], which Mndawe told him he had received while in detention.

Mndawe had complained of this injury on 1 March to Lt. Gerhardus Oberholzer when the policeman visited him in his cell. Lt. Oberholzer claimed to have seen no sign of injury. The visit followed on an earlier one, that same day, by Senior Magistrate Coenraad Strydom, an inspector of detainees. Mndawe had told him that he had been assaulted by the police when he was arrested. According to Strydom, Mndawe said:

'I have a continual headache since the day of my arrest last week Tuesday. They took me to the doctor on Wednesday afternoon. He gave me headache tablets. I have a broken cheekbone on the right side. I discovered it when I woke up in the police cell. It was swollen. My whole face was swollen when I saw the doctor. I told the Security Police about the broken cheekbone but I did not tell the doctor about it. I was confused but sustained the injury on the day of my arrest. I do not know how it happened. I am sure I was hit by the police. I do not know which one. Yesterday I bled from my nose quite a lot. I also have an injury above my left temple, also from the day of my arrest.'

Although Strydom could not enter the cell, as the key was not available, he noted 'what seemed like a depression on his cheek and also what appeared to be an abrasion on his forehead next to the hairline' on Mndawe's face. When Mndawe was X-rayed on 3 March, the X-rays revealed his right cheekbone was fractured. The inspector also noted that Mndawe complained that he had not been allowed to wash since his arrest. Strydom then forwarded his report to Lt. Slabbert of the South African Police, Nelspruit, and Brig. Jordaan in Middelburg. Lt. Slabbert, who was not a detective, was responsible for investigating Mndawe's complaint. The Lieutenant took a statement from the detainee.

Between his arrest and his death, Simon Mndawe was interrogated by a number of security policemen. They gave him an album of 'terrorists' to page through, and asked him to identify them. On 23 February Mndawe dictated a confession in Swazi, which was translated into Afrikaans. In it he admitted going to Swaziland for political training and distributing pamphlets for the ANC.

The dead man's family and friends could not believe he had killed himself.

Jonas Matsepe Mphachoe was the principal of Sidlamafa school, where he had known Mndawe. He recalled that Mndawe was 'a very quiet and very religious young man. He was not troublesome . . . He was a very balanced young man. I was shocked to learn he had committed suicide.' Mndawe's pastor, the Rev. Matumbu Mdluli, spoke of Mndawe's involvement with the church, and also expressed his shock at the young man's suicide. Mndawe was active in the Student Christian Movement.

After the demise of apartheid, it was revealed that Mndawe was also active in the banned ANC. He operated from Swaziland, recruiting men for military training and disseminating propaganda inside the country. He had evaded capture a number of times before he was finally detained. Whilst he was in detention, and shortly after his death, none of his associates were detained or questioned, an almost sure sign that he did not break down and betray any of his comrades.

Thembi Majola was the mother of Mndawe's children, Fikile and Nkosinathi. She described the caring young man who was her lover: 'Whenever he came to see me he would hug me, kiss me and would show a lot of love and affection to me. Whenever he visited his kids they used to run to him; he would lift them up one by one and kiss them. He spent a long time talking and playing with his children . . . He was soft-spoken and a very warm person. He was very much caring about people's welfare. He used to make me feel like a woman whenever I was in his arms.'

After Mndawe's arrest his family approached the Nelspruit law firm of Phosa, Mojapelo and Makgoba to defend him if he were charged. Before any charges were laid, Phosa received a phone call from a local police officer telling him, 'Your client is dead.'

Mndawe's father was deceased. His mother, Paulina, was a dressmaker for the Shongwe Mission Hospital. The day her son died, two policemen arrived at the hospital. They told her to accompany them, without saying why. When they arrived at their destination, either the police station or the mortuary, Paulina Mndawe heard a senior police officer berating her escorts for not informing her that her son had committed suicide. She did not realise what was happening until the grey blanket was removed from the body of her son. 'Before the police could finish explaining to me, they opened the blanket,' she recalled. 'Since I did not know where we were going, it was a great surprise to see my dead son. I could not hold myself, because they had not told me. I was worried, it was painful because he did not look like the person I knew – swollen forehead, cheek, one eye closed. While I was looking at him, I started crying. A white policeman pushed me because I was making a noise. I fell down, injuring my right leg. I bled and bled until I fainted, and woke up in the clinic.' The police left Mrs Mndawe waiting at the side of the road until they took her home that night, hungry and afraid.

Unable to arrange for a private pathologist to attend the official autopsy, the attorneys attempted to arrange a subsequent examination. The Nelspruit magistrate refused, as did the Department of Justice. The family was preparing to approach the Supreme Court when the state relented and agreed to another autopsy on condition that the state pathologist was present.

In the sweltering heat of February 1984, the men of the Nelspruit police station told the inquest how they had cared for Simon Mndawe. It was not a convincing story. The rules for the safeguarding of detainees were hardly known, much less applied, in Nelspruit and other rural areas. A sorry tale of mistreatment soon emerged, ranging from incompetence to inhumanity. Assuming that Mndawe had killed himself, we would argue that he had done so as a result of the poor treatment he had received while in detention: the injury no one had treated, the social isolation, the interrogation, had all contributed to a depression which gripped the detainee.

The inspector of detainees, as the title implies, was responsible for checking the conditions under which detainees were kept and noting any complaints they might have. Coenraad Strydom had served as inspector for a month when he visited Simon Mndawe in his cell in Nelspruit. Strydom noted the depression on Mndawe's right cheek, but knew little about the conditions in the cell.

During the inquest I asked him, 'Did you ask whether he was taken out twice a day as required by the administrative ruling by the Minister of Prisons?'

'I did not ask because . . . I was not concerned with that and I expected to visit the deceased inside on my next visit. The allegation of assault appeared to be more important to me at that stage.'

'We know that you reported the complaint of the deceased on 1 March.'

'On the same day that I saw him.'

'We know that X-rays were taken on 3 March. I want you to assume that a man with that kind of injury would be in severe pain, would have difficulty in eating solids even though they were particularly soft, and his inability to speak without pain and discomfort would be obvious. Can you say why nothing was done until he took his own life on 8 March?'

'As far as the food is concerned, I asked him specifically as to the food and he said he had no difficulty. If he had complained about difficulty with solid foods I would have taken notice, and I would have spoken about it. I do not remember him mentioning any difficulty to me. I had no indication of that complaint.'

'Nothing happened until 8 March?'

'I am expected when an allegation is made to me to report to the Minister of Law and Order, the Attorney-General and the Commissioner. I realised that if I did not act urgently it would take more than eight days to complete a report, to send it to the Minister, to contact the Minister of Police, and the Department of Security. I went to the Lieutenant on the premises, and also to the Middelburg Deputy Commissioner of Police, Brig. Jordaan. I made a report stating that urgent action was required, in this instance.'

'You did all you could to expedite urgent attention to this person?'

'Yes.'

'Did you ask whether he was given exercise in terms of the code in question?'

'I did not. I was more concerned with the allegation of assault, as there were visual signs that it could be true.'

But even that urgent matter received scant attention.

Maj. Floris Swart was the station commander at Nelspruit, where Mndawe was held. Given his lack of concern for the detainee's well-being it was no surprise that little was done about Mndawe's complaints. Maj. Swart visited Mndawe on 25 February, when he reportedly made no complaints.

The Major was asked, 'On the morning of the 23rd, the deceased said that he was assaulted, and his face was swollen; how do you explain that two days thereafter he had no complaints?'

The Major was resolute: 'I have no knowledge thereof.'

He would have refused to admit the sun had risen on a particular morning.

I persisted: 'But you were the person to whom he said that he had no complaints on the 25th, while on the 23rd and on 1 March, he told Smith that he did have complaints?'

'I don't know how that could have happened.'

'You are the station commander,' Major Swart was asked, 'the person is being detained in your cells, you had a complaint that he was in pain; was there any reason that you know of why the deceased was not hospitalised after 3 March when the fracture became apparent?'

'I see no single reason.'

'Was any reason given to you, after the X-rays, after the fracture, why it was necessary to wait until 10 March?'

'I cannot say.'

'Who was the person responsible for the man's welfare in the station?'

'I was in charge.'

'Who was responsible for the health of the deceased?'

'I was responsible. The man complained to me that he was sick, I must see to it that he receives medical attention, take steps, and I did.'

'Who was the person who was supposed to visit the detainee in the cells?'

'I can't say at that stage.'

'Did the deceased know that he was supposed to go to the hospital?'

'No.'

As far as Simon Mndawe could see, there was no escape from his torment. When his captors were ready to take him to hospital, he was already dead.

The outcry against the Biko doctors almost six years earlier had not made any impression on at least one of their colleagues. He suppressed the truth to help those responsible for inflicting injuries, yet the police officers had no difficulty in admitting and explaining away the injuries the doctor had failed to see.

As acting district surgeon for Nelspruit, Dr Frans Viljoen accepted that he was responsible for Mndawe's physical and mental well-being. Dr Viljoen was asked how it was possible that WO Smith, a police officer, had noted an injury on Mndawe's face, yet he – the doctor – had not.

'Who would you say was in a better position to note an injury, you or Mr Smith?'

'Well, the patient was brought to me with a specific idea that I was to note injuries and to give an assessment of his general state of health, so this was my . . . what I was trying to do.'

'Can you explain how Mr Smith came to see it and you failed to see it?'

'As I have said, all I can think that if it was there at the time, I just did not write it down. I do not know why if it was there, but this is the only possible explanation I can think of.'

It was pointed out that Visser, another police officer, had also noted an abrasion on Mndawe's forehead.

'Are you obliged to note abrasions on a person's face that you examine?'

'I think so, yes.'

'Now can you explain how Mr Visser came to see this and note it in his affidavit and you failed to do it?'

'All I can say once again is that either I did not notice it or alternatively I did not write it down. That is the other possibility.'

'Would you consider that whether it is the one or the other, it was really a breach of your duty?'

'Breach of my duty, ja, probably, that is what it boils down to.'

Even the magistrate had noted an abrasion on Mndawe the same day Dr Viljoen had examined him. No explanation was available for that also.

'Why do you think you were called upon to make a written report?'

'This is . . . that is actually standard procedure. If you examine a patient, as I have said yesterday, this is for your memory, this.'

'In order to refresh your memory and in order that there may be a record?'

'To have a record, yes.'

'As to what happened to this person? Now I want to postulate the following, doctor. If the deceased had lived and had given evidence that he had these injuries, you would have been called as a witness, didn't you foresee that?'

'Yes, this, yes, that is quite possible.'

'And you would have been able to contradict the deceased when he complained of having two injuries on his face because there is nothing in your report?'

'Yes, I would have said no, I did not see it. I did not notice it.'

'You did not see it, and you do agree, doctor, that our courts place much reliance on the evidence of doctors?'

'That is correct.'

'You see, I am going to suggest to you, doctor, with respect, that if injuries are seen by three or four persons and they are missed by a doctor, that it comes to almost recklessness?'

'Ja, well, am I supposed to, sort of . . . '

I cut him short.

'Well, what is your reaction to that question, to that suggestion?'

'That this was reckless.'

'Yes, what do you say? Would a careful doctor, in your position, in retrospect have failed to see or record those . . . ?'

'No, these were obvious injuries apparently to all other people and the accused himself said he was injured at that time and that. Obviously if the other people can see it you should have seen it yourself, there is no argument about that.'

'And no explanation either?'

'No, no.'

When Dr Viljoen finally noted Mndawe's injury, on 3 March, it was as a result of a spontaneous visit. No one had informed him that his patient had a broken cheekbone, or at least an injury. He was never informed that Mndawe had complained to the inspector of detainees. If the inspector's report was made known to him on 1 March, being a matter of urgency, what would Dr Viljoen have done?

'Well, as I said, I would have insisted to see the patient, number one;

confirm what exactly the state of affairs is. Number two, I would have made arrangements or started on a line of treatment. The third thing is the question of possible future injuries . . . '

It was Viljoen's partner, Dr Malan, who had examined Mndawe on 1 March and arranged for an X-ray, as well as an operation.

Although Mndawe had claimed that he was given headache tablets on the 23rd by Dr Viljoen, the doctor was hazy on the matter.

'Now, did you given any medication to your patient on the 23rd?'

'No, not as far as I can remember?'

'Because he . . . not as far as you remember?'

'Remember, no.'

'Is it possible that you gave him medication?'

'No, I do not think so.'

'You do not think so. Because he says that you gave him headache tablets in Exhibit F.'

'It is possible, yes.'

The acting district surgeon, it soon emerged, was also unfamiliar with the duties his job required with regard to detainees. He had never seen the standing orders from the Minister of Law and Order as to the treatment of detainees.

'So therefore you did not know what the minimum requirements were?'

'No. Except being told just by . . .'

'In passing?'

'Well, by the police. By the people that work with these things, that you are supposed to do this, that and the next thing.'

'But isn't the spirit of these standing orders that you, together with the inspector of detainees, really are supposed to be the overseer of treatment by the police? Is it really for the police to tell you what to do or what you should do or not?'

'Yes, I think seen in that light. I do not know what the person who drew up those things, what he had in mind, but as far as I am concerned, as I have said earlier on, the accused or the person being detained is my responsibility and as far as I am concerned I think I may say I do not really consider that I must be told how to do this. I just treat him as another patient, as somebody . . . depending on the circumstances of the case.'

One of the functions of a district surgeon is to treat policemen and their families. One wonders for how long Viljoen would have kept his position if he had treated them in the way he dealt with Simon Mndawe.

Dr Viljoen was unable to comment on the bathing facilities available to

Mndawe, or whether he had sufficient exercise space available. The previous witness, Lt. Louis Slabbert, had testified that the police cells were only holding cells, not suitable for long stays. After admitting that he had not considered whether these conditions met the requirements set out by the Minister, Dr Viljoen conceded that the cell was not suitable for holding a person for a period of over two weeks.

Having agreed that Mndawe's conditions could lead to depression, Dr Viljoen went on to admit that he had made no note of Mndawe's pulse or blood pressure, nor did he ever take his weight. He also made no enquiries as to the detainee's sleeping habits, nor did he warn the police to watch for signs of depression. Neither Dr Viljoen nor the inspector could gain access to Mndawe's cell when they visited him there because one of the keys was not available. This, we argued, would have contributed to feelings of depression on the part of the detained man. Nothing had been learnt by Dr Viljoen, the police officers or, to some extent, the inspector of detainees by the exposure of the dangers and evils made public during the Aggett inquest the previous year.

Not only had the doctor failed to ensure that Mndawe's conditions were adequate, but he had also ignored the standing orders by examining him in the presence of policemen. I asked him if it might have been different had the police not been there.

'Ja,' he replied, 'it is possible that he would have had a different story or had more to say if we were alone, yes, that is possible.'

'Not a different story or more to say, he would have told you that I have got a broken cheekbone and a swollen face? Not so?'

'Ja, maybe, but no, I am going back to the first time that I saw him, he then adopted a sort of attitude of indifference, of just being passive, or just, he just stood there. Well, attitudes is a difficult thing to put in words. You look at a person and he is just, he is negative. You know, one would, under the circumstances, one would expect them to be a bit cocky possibly, or *uitdagend* [challenging], as we say in Afrikaans.'

'Why do you say that?'

'Because you so often find this sort of thing with arrested people. I so often . . . but in any case, that is besides the point. He made that impression on me that he was, just stood there indifferent and not interested, and he just stood, and he was not partaking in any way, he was not doing anything, and . . .'

'He was indifferent?'

' . . . not going to react and he just stood there. That was his attitude.'

'Indifferent to his environment?'

'Ja, and to my sort of, at that stage, questions – what is the matter, what is wrong, what happened, and so on.'

'Didn't it occur to you then, doctor, to send the policemen away and say, "Listen, you know you can speak to me freely, you do not have to be afraid?"'

'No, no, I did not. I did not do that.'

'Any reason why not?'

'As I said yesterday, I just felt for security reasons the police should be there.'

'You are not for one moment suggesting that it was impossible for you to have a private conversation with him?'

'No, no, that could have been arranged somehow, yes.'

We pointed out to Dr Viljoen that Mndawe had no problem in describing how his injuries were sustained when he saw the magistrate on 23 February, yet he told the inspector on 1 March that he had trouble remembering how exactly he had been injured. The doctor admitted that confusion was significant, and that it could arise from concussion.

'And does concussion in its various forms cause headaches?'

'Yes.'

'And does that sort of post-traumatic condition lead to depression? Or might it lead to depression?'

'You mean post-concussion leads to depression?'

'No, concussion leads to headaches, headaches and other surrounding circumstances lead to depression?'

'It is possible, yes.'

Having established at least that, I left the witness for Advocate Dreyer. Counsel for the police tried to establish how difficult Dr Viljoen's job had been because Mndawe had been uncooperative. And when Mndawe had complained, Dreyer pointed out, Dr Viljoen had noted his injuries.

'Did you at that stage ask him if he had any other complaints?' Dreyer asked.

'Yes, oh yes,' the doctor replied enthusiastically.

'Did he then complain of any headache or the fact that he was confused?'

'No, definitely not.'

There was a complete shift in the witness's demeanour. Being questioned by the representative of the police led to confidence.

The pathologist was the Pretoria state pathologist J.D. Loubser, who was also involved in the Biko inquest. He said he was 'surprised' (*verbaas*) to see the X-ray of Mndawe's broken cheek, which was a fresh break. Because of our experience with him in the Biko case, I had a high regard for Prof. Loubser, and wondered how he came to miss the broken cheekbone when he conducted the autopsy. The X-ray was not in the police file. Phineas Mojapelo, Phosa's partner, had obtained it from the hospital as part of the inquest preparation. I feared that there might be some mistake, and treated Prof. Loubser with the respect I thought he deserved by giving him an opportunity to reflect on how he might have missed the injury. He held the X-ray up to the light, and was obviously embarrassed by what he saw. He did not apologise, but said it did not matter because there was such clear evidence to show that this injury did not in any way contribute to the cause of the deceased's death.

He entered the witness box and we questioned him about it. The pathologist said the injury was not serious enough to be life-threatening but would not heal on its own and would cause pain and discomfort. He said it was possible that a blow to the chest with an elbow, such as Mndawe had complained of, could have occurred without a resultant 'kneuswond' [bruise]. During the postmortem no traces were found of the injuries Mndawe had described, although Prof. Loubser said they could easily have healed in the intervening period. With regard to Mndawe's broken cheekbone, he thought it unlikely to have been caused by a kick from someone wearing a shoe, as the skin would have been marked. He thought a punch from a fist a more likely explanation. Ranking the possible causes, Prof. Loubser placed a punch first, followed by a kick and then by a fall.

In order to explain away the injuries, the police argued that they had been inflicted when Mndawe resisted arrest. This at least was what the arresting officers had asserted in their affidavits. But when Sgt Solomon Bhembe came to testify, his story differed from that of his colleagues.

'Did you or your colleague do anything to the deceased during the course of arrest which could have caused one or more of the injuries?'

'We did nothing.'

'Were the injuries found at the time of death inflicted at the time of his arrest?'

'He did not get his injuries during the time of his arrest.'

'Did you use any violence against the deceased at the time of his arrest?'

'No.'

'Even at the time did you use little force as you had to, to put the handcuffs on, did you injure him in any way?'

'Nothing.'

Bhembe denied seeing any blood on Mndawe, or the depressed cheekbone.

'If there were injuries, would they have taken place after he was handcuffed?'

'He did not get those hurts while handcuffed. He did not have injuries before he was handcuffed. I did not see any wounds.'

Bhembe, as an African, probably knew his place. He would never admit that anything untoward was done by his white superiors, nor, possibly for other reasons, by his black colleagues in the police force. Bhembe was then confronted with Mndawe's statement that he had been struck with an elbow in his chest by a black man. Bhembe denied everything in the statement: that he had been struck, that he had fallen down, even that he had cried out. Although he later said that Mndawe had fallen down face first, three times, Bhembe's evidence was extremely unreliable. Under examination by Dreyer on behalf of the police, Bhembe was encouraged to revise his story.

'You told the court the light was poor?' Dreyer asked.

'That's correct.'

'Think carefully, if the man had injuries, and was not bleeding, and did not have the large swelling, would you have not seen it?'

'No.'

'Why do you say so?'

'Because he was full of sand and the lighting was poor.'

'If his *gesig* [face] was injured, would you have seen it?'

'Wouldn't have seen it.'

I noted that Bhembe had mentioned three falls in his evidence, but in his statement he had referred only to throwing the deceased to the ground and pinning him down with force.

'You used the words "threw to the ground and pinned." Was he brought down by you?'

'We fell with him.'

'He landed with you?'

'We fell near to him.'

'You told us he fell on his side?'

'He did not fall, he let himself down.'

Yet another inconsistency in the police version was the entry made in the occurrences book the night Mndawe died. Maj. Swart testified that he was informed of Mndawe's death at 4.50 in the morning by Cons. Smal. But in the occurrences book, it was noted that Smal and Cons. Nkosi were in the cells and that everything was in order at 5 o'clock. When I asked the Major if he did not find this strange, he curtly responded that Smal would give evidence.

Pressed further, he claimed that it was an 'administrative error'.

'How can it be described as an administrative error, an entry in the occurrences book noting that two members visited the police cells and everything was in order, how can such a mistake be described as an administrative error?'

The Major was present when Smal made his later entry. When questioned whether he asked Smal what had happened, Maj. Swart could not remember. He was also unable to explain why someone was noted as coming on duty at 4.30 in the morning, when the next shift only began at 6. When I suggested it was possible that the policemen whom Mndawe had complained of might have come to 'sort him out', Maj. Swart refused to see the possibility.

Although he was only a constable of two years' standing, Renier Smal was in command of the charge office and the cells at Nelspruit police station on the night of 7 March. He was, as he put it, 'the charge office sergeant'.

'And were you responsible that night for the prisoners in the cells?' I asked the soft-spoken young policeman.

'That's right.'

'And you were responsible for their physical and mental welfare there?'

'That's correct.'

'Were you aware of the fact that there was a detainee in the cells?'

'That's correct.'

'What training have you had, to guard detainees?'

'In the police college,' began Constable Smal, so softly that I could hardly hear a word.

'Sorry?' I said.

'I did my training at the police college,' he repeated.

'Yes, and what were you told at the police college in connection with detainees according to the provisions of section 29, if anything? Were you told, what were you told, what is your training on that?'

'No, I don't understand what you mean.'

'Did you receive any special training in connection with supervision and guarding of detainees according to the provisions of section 29?'

'It was included in my training.'

'But can you remember if any special training was given to you in connection with that?'

'I cannot remember.'

It was so difficult to hear the replies, unsatisfactory as they were, that I asked the court to switch off the fan. The traffic department lecture theatre, which was serving as the venue for the inquest, was poorly ventilated. In order to hear Cons. Smal's answers we had to suffer the stifling summer heat of the lowveld.

When I resumed the cross-examination of Cons. Smal, he showed a passing knowledge of section 29. After he agreed that he had to visit the cells hourly, we asked the witness how it had happened that he had made an erroneous entry in the occurrences book. He was unable to explain why he had made an '05h00' entry before 5 o'clock.

'Oh, so you wrote that everything was in order in the cells before you visited the cells?'

'That's right.'

'Now, was this a procedurally correct way to do this work?'

'How do you mean?'

'Was it right that you did it like that?'

'No.'

The supposedly regular visits to the cells did not occur on a clockwork basis, despite what the occurrences book recorded. What was clear was that Cons. Smal had locked away the suspects at 3.15, but only returned to the cells at 4.50.

'If the deceased had needed something during that period from 3.15 to 4.50 – it is about an hour and a half, more or less – what must he have done to attract your attention?'

'If he called me I would have heard him,' came Smal's reply.

This was extremely unlikely, especially as there were forty prisoners in the cells at that time, according to Smal.

'And what is the practice if any of the prisoners shouts, do you immediately go to see what he wants?'

'That's correct.'

'Always?'

'That's correct.'

'Are you serious?'

'Yes.'

And this despite the fact that the cells were in a building outside the charge office, across a cement quadrangle of at least thirty metres, including a flight of stairs and two doors. Even if Mndawe had called, and been answered, Cons. Smal could not enter his cell. The keys were held by two other policemen, WO Graham van Dyk and WO Willem van der Schyff. Since both normally worked the day shift, it was impossible to enter Mndawe's cell after 4 o'clock in the afternoon, until 7.30 the following morning. When the inspector had failed to gain access to Mndawe's cell it was because Van der Schyff was in neighbouring Barberton – both keys were necessary to open the gate.

Cons. Smal had left the police force in November 1983 for reasons he refused to disclose. He would only say that he had bought his release.

It was the same old story. A detainee assaulted, his complaints ignored, medical treatment withheld, inadequate supervision. The result – death – followed by a farcical investigation by a colleague of those who had probably caused his death.

Lt. Denn Alberts, the commander of the Nelspruit detective branch, was charged with investigating the circumstances surrounding the death of Simon Mndawe. In his wisdom he never considered it necessary to investigate Mndawe's allegation that he had been assaulted. When asked why, he explained it had already been investigated.

'The fact that shortly before his death a detainee complained that he had been assaulted, was that relevant in your mind?'

'In my opinion it was not relevant.'

'Not relevant, oh, I see?'

'Correct.'

'And that is why you personally conducted no investigation in connection with the truthfulness or not of the allegations of the deceased?"'

'In connection with the assault.'

'In connection with the assault?'

'No, no interest therein whatsoever.'

During his investigation into the death of Simon Mndawe, Lt. Alberts noted and filed the statements written by his colleagues. He did not question them. He had no reason to distrust them, he explained. With such an attitude to the 'investigation', little was likely to emerge.

After all the evidence had been heard, we obtained a psychological evaluation from the Wits psychology lecturer Alma Hannon, who had conducted extensive research into the effects of detention on detainees. If one assumed that Mndawe had committed suicide, Hannon argued, it was important to note that he had made numerous complaints of assault, but only to the magistrate, the inspector of detainees and a uniformed policeman sent by the inspector. He had not complained to the district surgeon in the presence of the police. He had no access to his family or legal representative; in fact, his only contact was with members of the police force. Despite the fact that he was suffering from a broken cheekbone, nothing was done to alleviate his condition, and he was taken by the Security Police for questioning on 7 March.

Hannon interviewed members of Mndawe's family and associates, but could find no evidence of a tendency to suicide. There was evidence that during his detention, Mndawe had been passive and listless, slept a lot and even lost weight. He had been isolated, in pain, and when he did confide in seemingly neutral people, nothing was apparently done about his situation. 'From the circumstances disclosed in the evidence as a whole,' Hannon concluded her report, 'the cumulative effect of social isolation, injury and the lack of proper care of Simon Thembuyise Mndawe probably led him to take his own life.'

Despite this evidence, the inquest magistrate was unmoved. No one was to blame for Simon Mndawe's death. Neither Mathews Phosa nor Phineas Mojapelo, who either together or in turn attended the proceedings and helped with the preparation, was notified when the verdict was given. Only Simon's older brother Michael made it at the last minute.

At our request, the magistrate referred the matter of Dr Viljoen's conduct to the South African Medical and Dental Council. In October 1985, Dr Viljoen appeared before its disciplinary committee in Nelspruit. Two police-men, a medical expert and Dr Viljoen testified. The doctor's counsel, Advocate Hugo, argued that there was no evidence that the injury to Mndawe's cheek was visible, and if the graze was visible, then it could be attributed to 'menslike feilbaarheid' [human failing], which was not unprofessional conduct. The entire matter, it was submitted, was complicated by the detainee's lack of co-operation with the doctor.

Although the committee accepted that a patient might be uncooperative and this complicated matters such as observation, Dr Viljoen was found to be guilty of negligence for not noticing the graze on Mndawe's head or his swollen cheek. (The other charges, including those relating to Mndawe's conditions of detention, were dismissed.) As punishment, Dr Viljoen received a warning. There was no communication to the deceased's family of the outcome.

Paulina Mndawe still does not know what really happened to her son. 'If he had died because he was ill, or in an accident, I would have forgotten, but this is a question, because I don't understand how such a thing can happen when the government are supposed to look after people.' All that remained of her son were his children, whom she raised as her own.

The Mndawe family remember Simon fondly, and with a sense of pride, as if his death has been vindicated by the realisation of a democratic South Africa. But still they yearn to know what really happened, and, if possible, for justice to be done. 'I've seen we've reached the new South Africa,' Simon's sister Glory explained, 'just as he promised us before he crossed the border to exile. But without the answer to how he died. So to me there is a pain, a pain without ending.'

CHAPTER 5

# GET GLUCKMAN

*'Jonathan Gluckman interpreted justice and compassion the only way that counts: he acted them out. Late in his life he was not content to rest on professional laurels, but saw it as his duty to put his professional reputation at risk in order to test its ultimate integrity as a service to common humanity. He was a man for the people.'*
*– Nadine Gordimer*

I N NOVEMBER 1991, Dr Jonathan Gluckman, then in his late seventies, wrote to State President F.W. de Klerk asking for an interview to discuss 'matters of the utmost gravity which, if they became public, would do the country incalculable harm'. The President's assistant private secretary replied to Gluckman, informing him that De Klerk was too busy to meet with him, but invited him to 'either submit your problem in writing' or to meet with 'a person in National Intelligence who enjoys the fullest confidence of the State President'. Gluckman wrote.

In his letter of January 1992, Gluckman explained that he had performed autopsies on many people who had died in police custody. 'Almost all my colleagues in this branch of the profession have adopted the view that they would prefer not to do any kind of work which might land them in a witness box. This is contrary to my way of thinking and to my general commitment as a doctor and a pathologist.' Moved by 'an increasing sense of frustration and a growing sense of horror by what is being committed by the lower echelons of the Police', the doctor had contacted the Police Commissioner, General Johan van der Merwe, with the details of a murder by a policeman of a prisoner. 'General Van der Merwe could not have been more cordial. In the end result, nothing happened.' Little did any of us then know that the Commissioner was privy to hit squad activities, as he himself would testify before the amnesty committee of the TRC under subpoena at the instance of his men who had murdered many activists. Increasing numbers of suspects, Gluckman went on, usually in criminal matters, were dying in police custody. 'The net result of all this is that after 30 years of doing this work, one is sick at heart as one contemplates the future.'

As a result of this letter, Gluckman met with Ministers Adriaan Vlok and Hernus Kriel. Kriel sent a senior police officer to collect details of five cases Gluckman had selected from around the country. Informing De Klerk of this development, Gluckman wrote, 'As a result of your intervention in this case, for the first time I have some optimism that something will be done.'

Three months later, Gluckman again wrote to the State President:

'It is in a mood of utter despair that I address you concerning the treatment of suspects – not even prisoners – by the SA Police. In my opinion there is no deviation from the patterns which have become all too familiar over the last two decades.

'I realise, of course, that you have enormous worries, involved as you are with the macro-picture of South African affairs. Perhaps I can be said to be involved in the micro-picture made up of small numbers of ordinary human beings, people who are entitled to look to the State for protection against barbarism, particularly at the hands of its servants employed to uphold the law and the sanctity of the individual. That must surely be one of the pillars on which rests the civilised State.'

The letter seemingly had some effect. Vlok contacted Gluckman and arranged for a case to be referred to the Minister of Justice. That was at the beginning of June 1992. Almost two months later, Gluckman broke the story to the press, after yet another death in custody.

The newspapers that appeared on Sunday 26 July 1992 carried the news of Gluckman's disclosures. Of the 22 deaths in custody he had investigated, the pathologist claimed, about 90 per cent were caused by the police. In the ensuing publicity, the media spotlight came to rest on the ageing pathologist. The question they all asked was, Why? What was his agenda? Not political. He was, he told one interviewer, 'a great supporter of the State President', F.W. de Klerk, who had over a year previously made his speech that led South Africa to a democratic form of government. Purely principled, driven by his horror at the violence of the system, he had to do something. This was a man who, speaking at a Wits University graduation ceremony in 1975, bemoaned the tendency of doctors to become more concerned with profit. 'From being a group of professional men inspired by a sense of vocation and idealism, we seem to have become a group of people involved in the universal rat race. We have lost our collective soul,' he said.

When Law and Order Minister Hernus Kriel mused that some of the deaths in custody might have resulted from the trauma of arrest, the political analyst R.W. Johnson gave him short shrift. '[This] takes us back to the worst days of detainees dying through slipping on soap, falling out of windows and the like. Mr Kriel is a disgrace.' Kriel ordered an investigation into all deaths in custody since January 1991. In true Nat tradition, he had his own opinions about what had really happened, regardless of any investigation. In August 1992 Kriel remarked, 'My own opinion is that any death in custody is regrettable. But to come to the conclusion that these deaths are through police brutality, *that* I am not prepared to accept.' Four months later, the police report was leaked to *Rapport* newspaper, which claimed that some of the people who had allegedly died in police custody were still alive.

Gluckman's explanation was simple: when the police had removed his files for the purposes of the investigation, they had taken some which were not relevant. 'I do the odd consultation case on people who are still alive,' he explained. 'My secretary pointed out to the constable which ones were relevant, but she contacted the investigating officer, who said "take the lot." I don't know what was included but what strikes me is that they never called me back to seek clarification on this.' The allegation that he had performed autopsies on people still alive, he added, was 'the most bizarre charge' ever levelled at him. *Business Day* called the incident 'stupefying', demanding that Kriel apologise to Gluckman and make the report public.

When the report was made public, days later, it exonerated the police in 41 per cent of the cases, including the 14 who were still alive. Although denying Gluckman's claims, Kriel announced the appointment of 20 retired Generals and 12 retired magistrates to inspect police stations. Gluckman welcomed this move, even if he doubted how effective they would be. 'I trust that they will do better than the inspectors of detainees appointed after Steve Biko's death. Their appointment did not prevent the death of Dr Neil Aggett and many others.'

Gluckman responded to the report by acknowledging that the figure of '90 per cent' was just a guess. 'Now we are playing the numbers game,' he said, 'and that is not the point. The deaths of people in custody is the important thing.' He took issue with the report, noting that the criteria used by the police to determine who had died in custody were very narrow. They had also separated out those who had died in the homelands. Even the cases in which the police were exonerated were contentious. In short, the report settled nothing.

This did not prevent Hernus Kriel from seizing it as an opportunity to silence the probing pathologist. He told a British television programme, Channel 4's *Dispatches*, 'I think that the report proves that Dr Gluckman's allegations were totally unfounded . . . I think his allegations have been totally discredited.' He added that Gluckman had been guilty of 'making a criminal statement'. The doctor in fact had been told in confidence by a journalist who had interviewed Kriel that he intended destroying Gluckman. Gluckman challenged Kriel to prosecute him.

Dr Gluckman had known his revelations would cause a stir, yet nothing prepared him for the vitriolic response of the Minister of Law and Order. He discovered his office was being bugged. The accuser became the accused. He was a man of integrity who cared much for his and his profession's reputation but was falsely accused of lying, of being driven by false motives. Primarily owing to his efforts, direct lines of communication were established for any district surgeon to report to the Minister of Health if the Security Police interfered with them, as they had claimed in the Biko inquest. Guidelines for the treatment of detainees were published and a comprehensive report by the Strauss Committee warned of the dangers to the lives of detainees after the Aggett case. A man who had been guided by the Hippocratic Oath throughout his professional life, Gluckman was hurt more than he would admit. His wife Lois, who had always taken a keen interest in his work, told me how the controversy now dominated their lives. I promised both of them that should Kriel be foolish enough to bring a prosecution under the Police Act alleging publication of false information, he would regret it as his predecessor had done when a similar charge against Archbishop Hurley had had to be dropped. It must have been of little comfort. Even the possibility of being charged was enough punishment.

Simon Mthimkulu's death was the breaking point for Jonathan Gluckman. The 19-year-old Sebokeng youth was arrested on 14 July 1992, together with his friends Joubert Radebe, Samwell Selebogo and Sikhalo 'Lucky Boy' Maseko. Mthimkulu was the oldest of the four, the others being just 16. They were on an errand in the township when they were bundled into a police vehicle. From their questions, it turned out that the police suspected the three teenagers of burning down policemen's houses. The four were repeatedly assaulted during their journey to the police station. Upon arrival, 'Simon and I were taken into the toilet by five policemen,' Maseko recalled.

'When we got to the entrance, two policemen kicked us. They kept on beating us. They said we must do some exercises. We were told to squat and then to do push-ups. Simon was unable to do the exercises. It looked to me as if he was already tired. He asked for water, but they refused him. They kicked Simon in the ribs. I was still lying face down. I peeped through my hands. I saw a policeman pick up a huge rock, which they used as a doorstop, and throw it on Simon's ribs. I was counting. They repeated this three times. Blood spurted out of Simon's nostrils. Whilst the policeman was doing this to Simon, the other pulled me up and took me to a basin which was filled with water. He dipped my head about three times into the water. I then saw Simon lying down on his back. I then let go of my body and laid down.

'Another black policeman entered, started beating me and ordered me to go home. I tried to pick up Simon, to take him with me. He was lying on his back and blood was dripping from his nose. He was still breathing. They beat me again with a sjambok on my head. I started running and they pelted me with stones. I went straight home and slept.'

Simon Mthimkulu was unable to perform the exercises demanded of him – he suffered from asthma. When he did not return home that evening, his mother, Mapaseka Mthimkulu, began panicking. 'Simon was not a person who was used to running around at night,' she said. She visited one of his friends, who was badly beaten. He told her Simon was sleeping at the police station. The next morning, the police told Mrs Mthimkulu to check the hospital. When she returned from a wasted trip, the police had a different story. 'They said, your child was spanked here and then told to go home.' Mapaseka Mthimkulu found her son three days later, in the mortuary.

Mthimkulu's body had been found by the Internal Stability Unit, lying in the veld surrounding Komasizwa hostel, about three kilometres from the Sebokeng police station and easily accessible by vehicle. WO Paul le Roux was one of those who found the body. He testified there was no evidence of a struggle or blood, leading him to the conclusion that the body had been dumped at its location.

The case was referred to the Legal Resources Centre by the ANC, and Gluckman was engaged to perform the autopsy. Mthimkulu's body was covered with injuries, injuries which, Gluckman said, matched the stories of the witnesses. 'It was the last straw that broke the camel's back. This was a young boy of 19. He could have been my son.'

The inquest began in late 1993 and went on intermittently until October 1994. I appeared for the family, together with Mohamed Navsa and Thandi Orlyn, then Director of the LRC's Johannesburg office. The responsibility of vindicating Jonathan Gluckman's reputation weighed heavily on us. I had to withdraw halfway through the proceedings because of my commitments on the Judicial Services Commission, and Mohamed Navsa completed the task.

The medical evidence was clear that the young man had been brutally assaulted. This was obvious not only from the photographs we had of Mthimkulu's body, but also from Jonathan Gluckman's post-mortem report.

Gluckman died before the inquest was held, but the effect of the evidence he had left behind was devastating.

The initial report, by the Vanderbijlpark district surgeon A.S. Nieman, noted far fewer injuries. The doctor said in reply that he had noted all the injuries he had seen.

'Is it possible', we asked, 'that you saw injuries which you never noted?'

'If it was visible to me, I would have noted it.'

'You say if there were further visible injuries, you would have noted that?'

'That is correct.'

'You are sure of that?'

'Yes.'

We handed in over twenty photographs of Simon Mthimkulu's battered body taken by Jonathan Gluckman in colour. One by one we went through the photographs, asking Dr Nieman to describe the injuries he saw. On photograph number five, he identified an injury on the forehead which appeared to have been made with 'a linear instrument'. Photograph number eight, Dr Nieman said, showed 'signs of linear bruising on the right side of the chest, which often appear when a person has been hit with a sjambok, or sjambok blows'. We proceeded through the grisly evidence, as the images of Mthimkulu's body told of the torture he had suffered. Photograph number 22 showed a haemorrhage of the chest, one which Dr Nieman said would have been caused by much force.

'And a big rock which fell on the chest, could that have caused it?'

'That is correct, yes.'

Following what the district surgeon had described on the photographs, I asked him whether his description of the body when he first examined it was not inaccurate.

'The . . . ,' he stammered. 'At the post-mortem, I broadly described the injuries, and determined the cause of death. I never described every scar in detail, if the photos are correct.'

'You did not do it? Did you not realise that this detail is necessary to determine if an eyewitness's account, if indeed there was an eyewitness, is true or false, so that their evidence can be compared with the findings of the doctor – is that not so?'

'The evidence of eyewitnesses can, in determining the cause of death, agree with that. Every abrasion on the skin is not described.'

I then put Dr Gluckman's report to Dr Nieman, cataloguing once more the damage on the young body. The two linear marks, each about ten centimetres long, running across the chest, were described by Gluckman as 'tram lines'.

'Now the injuries which look like tram lines, could they have been caused by a sjambok?'

'Yes.'

'Are these marks typical scars which we see if a sjambok is used on a person?'

'That is so, yes.'

While admitting that Dr Gluckman's examination showed the correct manner in which an autopsy should be performed, Dr Nieman was at a loss to explain his lack of thoroughness. It was not always practicable, he explained.

'I want to ask you again if you accept that when you saw the body, you came to the conclusion that there was at least a serious assault committed?'

'I am fully aware that it was a serious assault, yes.'

The doctor never communicated with the investigating officer, nor was he aware of allegations that the deceased had died at the hands of the police. If he had known, he said, he would not have done the autopsy, but referred it to the state pathologist.

'I want to put it to you, Doctor, that whether or not you had information, you did not fulfil your duty to the deceased or to the courts.'

'I accept what you say. I can only say to the court that it happens in these recent times, where there is unrest and things, that I am telephoned by the state health department and asked if I am prepared to help if a situation arises. Only brief autopsies will be done . . . '

The medical examination left much to be desired – the police investigation into Mthimkulu's death was even weaker. Mohamed Navsa summed up the incompetent manner in which the investigation was handled, when he put it to Maj. Cilliers of the Vaal Murder and Robbery Unit:

'I want to put the facts to you, as we have now determined them, and then give a conclusion upon which I wish you to comment. Given that it took longer than usual before the investigation began, given that we know that the rock was used in the assault and that it was not sent for forensic testing, given that you ordered the toilets to be sealed and that was not done . . . given that nothing appears in the investigation diary about who was in command of the charge office and what his explanation or observations were, given that we do not know which men were on duty that night, all these givens together tell us that this case was not investigated with the necessary ywer [zeal], that it was not as carefully investigated as it could have been – what do you say about that?'

The rock Sikhalo Maseko had seen slamming down on his friend's body was used as a doorstop in the toilets at the Sebokeng police station. All the policemen agreed that Maseko would not have known of its existence had he not seen it himself.

Under pressure from the Legal Resources Centre, the police agreed to stage an identity parade at Sebokeng. WO Ockert Kruger assisted with the identity parade. He testified that the policemen in the line-up were unhappy about it. There was a general 'moan' before the parade began. WO Kruger explained to them that he was only following orders and they should not be upset with him.

This was not an identity parade like those one sees in American films, with the witness behind darkened glass, and the suspects obeying commands transmitted through a speaker. This parade took place in a large hall, about 20 metres wide, with policemen arrayed from one end to the other in a large semicircle. Sikhalo Maseko and the others were required to approach the man they identified, and point him out while a photograph was taken.

Maseko did not hesitate when he pointed out the man standing at position number 14, as the one who had assaulted Mthimkulu with a sjambok, Cons. Rathai. Samwell Selebogo followed Maseko, but failed to identify anybody. In his testimony Selebogo claimed that when he approached Rathai, the policeman lowered his head and said 'voertsek'. Kruger denied this, although he noted that Selebogo was nervous and hesitant. Kruger conceded it was possible Rathai could have mumbled, but said this was unlikely.

Mohamed Navsa undertook the cross-examination of the policemen accused by Mthimkulu's friends: Rathai, Qabai and Shalale.

Mothlogelwa Morule had been a Detective Sergeant in the police force before he retired in February 1993. He and Cons. Rathai were partners, and on 14 July, he testified, they had returned to the police station at 4 o'clock that afternoon. He was thus unable to confirm Rathai's statement that the Internal Security Unit had been arresting people the entire day. Navsa then asked Morule to consider Rathai's pocketbook relating to that day. At 10 o'clock that morning, according to the pocketbook, Rathai had telephoned the prosecutor to discuss a matter with him. Having only a police radio in the car, Rathai would have phoned from his office. But Morule doubted this could have occurred. After their vehicle inspection at 9 o'clock they had left the police station to investigate their cases. 'Perhaps he made a mistake with the time,' Morule ventured.

The remaining notes in the pocketbook Morule had to accept, being unable to remember what had happened, and not having his own book to consult. His own pocketbook was unavailable – he claimed it had disappeared from the police station, an event he found most unusual. When he was asked about the entry for 1.30 that day, he found himself in trouble.

'Read me the next entry, 13.30,' Navsa asked.

'Wrote in dossiers at office,' Morule read from the little book.

'Now how do you explain that? You said you were out the whole day, from the morning after inspection until 16.00, and here Cons. Rathai tells us that he is back at the office, 13.30, and is now working on his dossiers. How do you explain that?'

'I don't have an explanation. This time is what he wrote there and I don't have an explanation of it.'

'Do you accept the truth of what he says there?'

'According to me, who worked with him, both of us, Rathai did not write the truth here.'

Rathai's remaining entries placed him at the police station before 4 o'clock that afternoon. Morule was evasive, not answering questions. Then he said he was not good with time and he may have made a mistake, although he insisted they had returned to base at 4 o'clock when their colleagues were leaving for home. He had then gone home himself, but was unable to say whether Rathai had remained behind at the police station. Once off-duty it was unusual for any entries to be made in the pocketbook, unless the investigator was still on police business. Yet there was an entry for 16.00 in Rathai's book: 'Out to Vanderbijlpark to fetch my clothes at the drycleaners.' If their superiors saw this entry, Morule said, Rathai could be in trouble. It was incorrect to make such entries concerned with personal business. At 17.05 Rathai noted, 'At Rust-ter-Vaal where I live.' This again was unusual, Morule said. Normally, when leaving the police station one wrote 'from service' only. Why was Rathai so concerned to place his whereabouts that afternoon?

In his affidavit, which he made nine months after the event, Morule stated that Rathai had gone to the drycleaners after work. How had he remembered this mundane event, especially since he had said in evidence that Rathai may have remained behind at the police station? Morule was so evasive on this question that even Magistrate Van Loggerenberg was unable to get clarity from the former policeman. 'It astonishes one that one can receive such answers,' the exasperated magistrate declared. 'It just isn't logical.'

Advocate Barry Roux also chastised the hapless Morule: 'I put it to you that it is irresponsible of you, with respect, to say that Rathai made false entries while it is clear in your testimony that you yourself cannot really remember what happened on 14 July 1992.' Counsel and the magistrate concluded that further examination would serve no purpose and Morule was dismissed.

After a recess that lasted until 22 August 1994, Cons. Sebotho Daniel Rathai, also known as Oupa Cele, was called. He claimed that he had not been in the office on the afternoon of 14 July 1992, had not even seen the young men.

He denied having told Selebogo to 'voertsek' when he was approached during the identity parade. Rathai also had an explanation when asked why Maseko had identified him: 'The people hated me. There was no one who did not know that there were allegations that I went around with white people and killed people. I had been taken to Goldstone. My house had been burnt down. My vehicle was set alight.' Rathai was, his counsel argued, the victim of a vendetta.

When questioned on his relationship with Sikhalo Maseko by Mohamed Navsa, Cons. Rathai said he had never had anything to do with the youth, but had only seen him growing up in the neighbourhood. He was content to answer that there were no bad feelings between the two of them.

'Can we accept that, from the time you first saw him in the neighbourhood until 14 July, there was no basis to come to the conclusion that Mr Sikhalo Maseko had a vendetta against you?'

'No, I don't know. I don't know about that, but personally, between him and I there was no trouble which developed.'

Asked about Sgt Morule, Rathai conceded he had no reason to doubt his honesty. Mohamed Navsa then put Morule's testimony to Rathai: 'He said that the two of you were out investigating the entire day?'

'No, those are lies. He must tell the truth. It appears here in my pocketbook.'

Sgt Morule had also accompanied him on his errand to Evaton, Cons. Rathai claimed. Morule was lying when he denied this. In addition to all this, Rathai denied having told Morule he was going to the drycleaners. The web of lies was beginning to unravel.

Navsa then asked the Constable why he had noted 'back at Rust-ter-Vaal where I live' on the 14th, but not on the following day. That was simple, explained Rathai; he had used his own vehicle, not the police car. Navsa asked the policeman to put down his pocketbook and turn it over. Would he make the same entry if he used the Captain's car, for example?

'And the car which we use, the government vehicle, I would write the same.'

'That day, Wednesday, you did not write that because that was your car?'

'Yes, it was mine.'

Navsa then returned to the pocketbook.

The final entry for that Wednesday read, 'Back at the police station. Gave the SAP 103106 to the Captain and then left with my car.'

'No,' Navsa interjected, 'with his car, his car. It is not "my" car, it is with "his" car . . . ' In Afrikaans, the difference between his and my is only one letter. Rathai acknowledged that the advocate was correct.

'Yes,' Navsa continued. 'Now you did not make an entry here because you told a lie, Cons. Rathai. You don't normally write that you are at home because, according to you, you would not if you took the Captain's car home – you lied twice. Once you said you left with your own car, now it is proved to you that it was with his car.'

'I didn't read this well. It happened long ago, this event.'

Navsa asked Rathai if he accepted what Morule said; that one did not record what happened after hours. Well, Rathai explained, he made such entries in case he was involved in an accident.

'No,' Navsa countered, 'I will tell you why you wrote it in, Cons. Rathai. I put it to you these entries, which are false entries, were made to give you an alibi to put you away from the scene at Sebokeng police station.'

Rathai's denial was unconvincing.

Next up was Cons. Mkwanyane Lazarus Qabai. He was also summoned to appear before the Goldstone Commission, although he alleged it was a case of mistaken identity, there being a number of Qabais in the police force. He also denied being in the office where the assault took place.

Joubert Radebe had stated that he was assaulted by Qabai, and pointed him out at the identity parade. Qabai had an explanation: 'According to me this case has, they point out just any policeman that they know, and he is possibly also cross because my brother left his sister, divorced the sister.'

Qabai was also an evasive witness. At one stage his testimony was contradicted by what was written in the occurrences book. The entry was false, he explained, it was a lie.

The magistrate accepted Mohamed Navsa's argument that there was sufficient evidence that Simon Mthimkulu was killed by the policemen. It was one of the few cases where the customary 'nobody to blame' verdict was not made. The Attorney-General decided to prosecute. The prosecution failed for lack of reliable evidence as to precisely which of the various policemen may have inflicted the fatal blows. The civil case brought against the Minister of Police by the witnesses who survived the assaults was settled. A payment was made to them. It was not necessary to prove which policemen did what in the civil case.

What was clearly established was that Mthimkulu was killed at the police station. The police took advantage of the so-called black-on-black violence then prevailing in the area to dump the body near the hostel reputed to harbour many armed men. The police knew that the best place to hide a corpse was on a battlefield.

What makes Simon Mthimkulu's case more poignant is that his death and the attempted assassination of Jonathan Gluckman's character occurred well after President De Klerk's 2 February 1990 speech, when he and his Minister of Police, Hernus Kriel, maintain that apartheid's evils came to an end.

CHAPTER 6

# THE CRADOCK FOUR

*The Last Days of the Generals*

'HSAW [Gen. Jannie Geldenhuys] sien optredes nie as "moord" nie en definieer dit as volg: " 'n Aanval op 'n individuele (vyand) teiken met nie-standaard uitreiking wapens op 'n onkonvensionele wyse, om nie onskuldiges te raak nie.' [The Chief of the South African Defence Force [Gen. Jannie Geldenhuys] does not see the actions as 'murder' and defines them as follows: 'An attack on an individual (enemy) target with non-standard-issue weapons so as not to affect innocent people.]
– Minutes of Civil Co-operation Bureau (CCB) meeting, 28 April 1987

'The use of terrorism by the government forces must be decided upon at the highest level and it must be so applied as to avoid it boomeranging.'
– Brig. C.A. Fraser, Lessons Learnt from Past Revolutionary Wars

IN THE 1980s Matthew Goniwe was the apartheid regime's enemy number one in the Eastern Cape. In Security Police documents mistakenly left unshredded after 1990, his comrades, friends and colleagues were derisively referred to as his '*trawante*', his hangers-on. When his killers applied for amnesty in the mid-1990s, they became more respectful and called them his lieutenants. Seven years after the killings at least two generals were exposed as having at least conspired to kill him and Fort Calata – two of the so-called Cradock Four. The reputations and careers of the caricature general Johannes Janse van Rensburg and the suave and ambitious general Joffel van der Westhuizen had come to an end. Above all, no longer could any credence be given to the denials of President P.W. Botha and President F.W. de Klerk that they had presided over a state which adopted terrorism in its efforts to survive against the will of the vast majority of its people.

On the morning of 27 June 1985 Matthew Goniwe left the small Eastern Cape town of Cradock together with Fort Calata, Sparrow Mkonto and Sicelo Mhlauli to attend a meeting at the UDF offices in Port Elizabeth. Goniwe told his wife Nyameka that they would return that evening. She remembers that he teased her when she nagged him to sleep over in Port Elizabeth rather than drive home late at night – 'just in case something happened'. Some hours after the winter sun had set, the four left Port Elizabeth to drive back to Cradock. A friend tried to convince them not to travel at night. Goniwe declined, saying that they would not stop for anyone except the police. Little did he know what they had in store for him. The four were never seen alive again.

At about noon the following day a body was found in the bushes in the vicinity of Bluewater Bay; it was later identified as being that of Sparrow Mkonto. He had multiple stab wounds and had been shot through the head. Goniwe's burnt-out car was found the same day. The investigating officer, WO Els, telephoned the Goniwe home to ask what was the registration number of Goniwe's car. Shortly thereafter Molly Blackburn called to find out how Nyameka Goniwe was doing. 'I'm all right beside that thing we heard about Matthew's car was burnt out,' she said. 'A certain Els phoned for us from Port Elizabeth. He said that Matthew's car burned out, but there is no sign of anybody. They want us to believe they were attacked whereas they detained these people . . . The only people who knew Matthew was on the road was the Security Police . . . '

Matthew Goniwe was in the habit of going to Port Elizabeth every Wednesday for a UDF meeting. On Wednesday 24 June 1985, however, he telephoned his colleagues there to postpone the meeting until the 27th. He called again on the morning of the 27th to confirm the arrangement. Apart from his friends and family, the Security Police were indeed the only group of people who knew this: they were tapping his telephone. Transcriptions of the calls were later found in his Security Police file. The security policeman monitoring the calls became a surprise witness called by us at the second inquest.

The body of Sicelo Mhlauli was found near Bluewater Bay the day after the discovery of the burnt-out car. He had been stabbed more than thirty times, his throat had been slit and his right hand was missing. The bodies of Matthew Goniwe and Fort Calata were only found on 2 July after an extensive search. Both had been stabbed numerous times. Dogs had eaten of Calata's flesh. All four bodies had deliberately been burnt, apparently to avoid identification. The car radio was lying on the passenger seat. The car was burnt out but not otherwise damaged. Its numberplates had been removed and a severely burnt Port Elizabeth numberplate was found on the ground in front of the vehicle. This numberplate was a false one, belonging to a vehicle that had been scrapped. It was later traced to one of two vehicles that had received numerous parking tickets in the vicinity of the Security Police headquarters in Strand Street, Port Elizabeth, during 1983 and 1984. The tickets were withdrawn by the senior public prosecutor, as was the practice with tickets received by police officers while on official duty.

Had the murderers not bungled and left one of Goniwe's own numberplates, which had not been burnt or damaged, lying on the ground, the burnt-out vehicle would not in fact have been traced back to him. The scattered bodies would then have been simply more anonymous victims of the political violence then sweeping the country. The Cradock Four, as they came to be known, would have disappeared just as three members of the Port Elizabeth Black Civic Organisation (Pebco) had a few months earlier, and so many others during that period. 'These disappearances are a new phenomenon in the South African conflict. These people are not selected at random – they are key leadership figures in their regions,' commented Raymond Suttner in *The Star* of 5 July 1985. How right he was.

The weekend of 19 and 20 July 1985 saw about forty thousand mourners from across the country flock to the little town of Cradock in hundreds of buses and cars. Accommodation and catering were arranged by committees specially created for the funeral weekend. The atmosphere was, however, more that of a political rally. Before the funeral, Nyameka Goniwe addressed the crowd of people that had gathered in front of the Goniwe family home. The funeral was held at the soccer stadium in Cradock's Lingelihle township. Diplomats from France, Norway, Canada, Australia and Sweden attended and messages of sympathy from the United States, Dutch and British embassies were delivered. The Revs. Allan Boesak and Beyers Naudé were carried shoulder-high to the podium, from where they and several others, including Steve Tshwete, addressed the crowd.

Another guest, Victoria Mxenge, could not control her emotions. Herself an attorney, she had struggled to bring up her family and carry on her legal practice after her husband Griffiths had been brutally stabbed to death, his throat slit and his car burnt. She told the mourners that the dead had gone as messengers to the forefathers. 'Go well, peacemakers. Tell your great-grandfathers we are coming because we are prepared to die for Africa!' Less than two weeks later she was gunned down in front of her home. Since then, Dirk Coetzee and Almond Nofemela have admitted responsibility for her husband's gruesome killing. They have been granted amnesty despite strong opposition from the Mxenge family, who still do not know who killed Victoria. They suspect that those who authorised the killing of Goniwe were closely connected with her death. The killers may even have been spurred on by her declaration that she was prepared to die for Africa.

ANC colours were visible everywhere at the Goniwe funeral as was an enormous Communist Party flag. The coffins of Goniwe and Calata were draped in red velvet, while those of Mkonto and Mhlauli were covered in the ANC's black, green and gold. From the surrounding hills some of the white residents of Cradock watched through binoculars. The police and army were around but kept a low profile. It became known to the mourners, however, that President P.W. Botha was about to announce a state of emergency in the Eastern Cape and Witwatersrand areas, giving the security forces wide-reaching powers. By the end of the following day, at least 133 people had been detained. It was the first state of emergency since the Sharpeville massacre 25 years before and would be the first of several states of emergency by means of which the country was governed for the remainder of the 1980s.

The first inquest into the deaths of the Cradock Four was eventually held in February 1989, more than three years later. It was presided over by Magistrate E. de Beer. Arthur Chaskalson, who is now the President of the Constitutional Court, was then the national director of and senior counsel for the Legal Resources Centre. The families of the deceased had instructed Fikile Bam, the Port Elizabeth director of the LRC, to represent them at the inquest. As Arthur was under tremendous pressure at the time he asked me to do the inquest, but I was not available. He did it himself.

The first inquest remains a testament to Arthur's ability to put pieces of evidence together to support the conclusions he believes to be the truth. There was no direct evidence as to who had committed the murders. Impeccable when it comes to legal ethics, Arthur would never make accusations when the evidence did not support them. But from what he said during his closing argument it was clear who the murderers probably were. 'I propose briefly to review the evidence to show the picture that is disclosed by the affidavits and also, Your Worship, refer briefly to what has happened in court,' he said. He proceeded with what was an almost prophetic assessment of what we now know occurred on that fateful night. There is no better summary of what happened. Indeed those who killed the Cradock Four would say hardly anything different in their amnesty applications from what Arthur Chaskalson had inferred. He told the magistrate:

'Now it seems perfectly clear from all the evidence, and I think I shall be able to demonstrate that from the circumstances of the killings themselves, that the political background of the people from Cradock played an important part in the events and that this was indeed a politically motivated murder.

'The background is really this . . . We know that he [Goniwe] was a well-known political activist. That his phone was tapped, that his car was regularly followed and that he himself had been kept under surveillance and interrogated from time to time. We know that with him in the car was a Mr Calata, who had also been associated with the UDF, and a Mr Mkonto, who had been associated with the UDF . . . We know less about Mr Mhlauli, but three of the four are clearly identified as political activists and well known as such.

'Now everything I suggest to Your Worship points to this being a politically motivated murder. Three of the four had strong political backgrounds and the fourth, Mr Mhlauli, even if his political presence was not as substantial as the others, once one or more of them were to be killed, none could be allowed to go free. All four would have to be killed, otherwise there would have been witnesses. So once one or more of the four was to be a target of murder, all four had to die.

'We know from the circumstances of the killing that it must have been a political murder. Robbery clearly was not the motive. The car was not stolen, nothing was taken from the car. Money was found at the scene . . . and the burning of the car and the bodies and the separation of the bodies clearly point away from some casual robber or highwayman. This was done because the murderers clearly did not want the bodies to be identified or indeed the fact that the Cradock Four had been murdered to be known. There can be no other explanation for what happened. Casual robbers bent upon stealing property for gain could hardly be expected to separate bodies which they had robbed and take them to different parts of the . . . Port Elizabeth area.

'We know a number of factors which point to a carefully planned, well-coordinated and skilful killing. Separation of the bodies, the fact that they were removed from the car and taken to places distant from the car so that the bodies, if found, would not be linked to the car. What other reason could there be for that? We know that the bodies were burnt and if you look at the photographs of those dreadfully mutilated bodies, you will see that each one was lying on his back and that amongst each one the facial features had been burnt. The bodies had been put on their backs, petrol had been poured over their faces and fire had been set to their faces . . .

'A most extraordinary thing happened at the scene. The numberplates of the car, Mr Goniwe's car, were taken off. The front numberplate and the back numberplate were both removed from the car before the car was burnt and a false numberplate was left at the scene. Now why should anybody take numberplates off the car? That is a deliberate action and the only possible reason for taking a numberplate off the car once you are burning the car and seeking to destroy it as far as possible, is that whoever finds the car will not be able to identify the owner of the car, will not know whose car it is; and the false numberplate, to leave a false numberplate at the scene, why would that be? And the only reason would be to lay a false trail.

'Now let us go back to the time. It was night, it was dark. Dreadful murders had been committed. Who sits down at that time to take off numberplates from a burnt-out car or before burning a car, other than a person seeking to lay a false trail? What had happened, clearly what happened is that in the haste, with the dead bodies probably around, with the burning of the car, both numberplates were removed. The false numberplate was put on the scene, but one of the original numberplates was left lying on the grass away from the car where it was subsequently found as well.

'Now nobody travels in a car, a false numberplate at the front and a correct numberplate at the back, and indeed there is no suggestion that Mr Goniwe and these people travelled in anything other than their car with their numberplate in the ordinary way. The killers came prepared. A false numberplate was part of their scheme to set this false trail and indeed, but for their error in leaving one of the numberplates on the grass to the side, their scheme might have succeeded. Because what would have happened? Mr Basson, we know, found the car. He found a burnt-out car which had been hidden, it was pointed out to him by a road worker who had come off the road. It had been hidden in the bushes and he went up there and he found the CAT [Cradock] numberplate which had been left lying on the grass. He radioed through Radio Control and gave them the number of the CAT numberplate which had been removed from the car and had been found lying on the grass. And he was told, "That is Mr Goniwe's car," and immediately it was known the car in which these four people had been travelling had been found, had been burnt out, and immediately the search had to be launched in that vicinity for the bodies, or to see if there were bodies, of those four people.

'But if that numberplate had not been left lying on the grass and if the CB [Port Elizabeth] numberplate had been found, what would have happened? Mr Basson would have radioed through and the information he would have got was, "This is an old wrecked vehicle which had been scrapped in 1983." There was no body near the car because the killers had removed the bodies. They had taken them a substantial distance away from the car. One body was within

1.7 kilometres of the car, two of the bodies were between 4 and 5 kilometres from the car and the fourth body was 14 kilometres from the car. So clearly the plan had been to separate the bodies so when they were found, if they were found – I will show you later that maybe there may have been months or years before those bodies could ever be found – but if they were found, they would not be four bodies together, who might be linked with the Cradock Four. There would be a body, 15 kilometres away another body, 4 kilometres away another two bodies. So the finding of the bodies would mean nothing and the finding of the car would point people in incorrect directions. And indeed if these bodies were left in remote places in the veld, taken away from the car, taken away from the road, they may never have been found before decomposition set in after the faces had been burnt, or if they had been found it might only have been found a long time afterwards, and indeed there were certain fortuitous events which led to their being found at all.

'Now then, what does the evidence then tell us about who might be the killers? . . . We know them, Your Worship, to be a group sufficiently strong and well organised to stop the car, to overpower, to stop the car without doing it any damage, because the examinations show that no damage was done to the car, sufficiently strong and well organised to overpower the four deceased people and sufficiently well organised with petrol, guns and weapons and with transport to move the bodies about and take them to different places. We know from the nature of the killings that they were armed with guns and knives. We know that the gun, Your Worship, had not been used before for unlawful purposes since the forensic laboratories tell us it cannot be linked with any previous or subsequent events. So that was not the gun of a criminal who uses it in the course of his or her trade to effect robberies or otherwise. It was a gun which had apparently never before or never since been used for an unlawful purpose. It was a group of people who knew the Port Elizabeth region well. Well enough to find beach tracks, remote beach tracks at night and leave bodies at isolated places, driving along these tracks. It was a group of people sufficiently skilled to formulate a plan and to leave a false trail. It was a group of people who were equipped with their own vehicle, with their own petrol, with their own numberplates. A group of people who knew who they were looking for, knew the route that they were likely to take and the road that they were likely to be on. It was a group of people who were able to stop the vehicle despite the attitude of the four that they would not stop on the road and a group sufficiently numerous, sufficiently powerful, sufficiently organised, having stopped them to overpower them, burn their bodies, transport the bodies to separate locations, to leave the false numberplate, to disappear and never to be found again.

'Now what clues do we have at the moment? What clues have been laid bare during the inquest? There is the gun. It has been identified as being a Gevarm gun. There are only 700 such guns in South Africa. The killer is likely to be one of those 700 people, or to include within those 700 is likely to be one of the killers.

'As far as the numberplate was concerned, that, fortuitously as a result of traffic tickets, has been identified as having been in use, unlawfully in 1984 by a Datsun motor car. It was in use and so the group that we are talking about, at least one of the people within that group had been, as long ago as 1984, making use of false numberplates and false licence certificates to conceal his activities. He was going about some activity which made it necessary for him not to be identified lest anybody who saw his car whilst he was engaged in such activity, whatever it may or may not have been, would not be able by looking at the numberplate or the licence to lead a trail to the car. So it is not, one would think, a recently constituted group. It includes at least somebody who was engaged in illegal activities a year or so before the murders.'

Putting the blame on feuding black groups was always thought to be a good cover-up. To counter this, Arthur Chaskalson discussed the feud between the UDF and AZAPO and made the point that it was concentrated in the Port Elizabeth area:

'AZAPO had no presence at all in Cradock – there are affidavits to that effect. There were no quarrels, according to the affidavits, between Mr Goniwe and anybody associated with AZAPO, and indeed the affidavits show that he had no part whatever in the conflict which broke out in Port Elizabeth between AZAPO and the UDF . . . indeed the killing is not like the other AZAPO–UDF attacks . . . It is not a case of terror and counter-terror where the victims should be seen to have been harmed so that some fear should be instilled.

'Now there must be a group of persons who were willing to drive around with dead bodies in the dark of night, to conceal and disfigure the bodies, to engage in this macabre and dangerous undertaking, to conceal the identity of their victims, and if it were, as I suggested it must be, a politically motivated murder, why would this be done? Why should people disappear? Who would want people not to be traced? It could be that there would be no inquest. It could be that there would be no funeral. It could be that there would be confusion. It could be that there had been no martyrs, like the Pebco Three who disappeared. But whoever it was, it was a group of persons to whom we have leads through the Gevarm gun and to whom we have leads through the Datsun car.'

At this point the magistrate became uneasy. Was Chaskalson, despite the lack of direct evidence, about to submit that the security forces were responsible? He would surely have pounced to stop him if he dared suggest what the vast majority of the people in South Africa believed to be the truth. Arthur Chaskalson concluded without interruption:

'They constituted themselves into an illegal group which can only be described as having lain in wait for the Cradock Four, constituting themselves as it were into a death squad – stopping, killing them and seeking to make them disappear . . .

'Your Worship, I believe on the evidence, is unable to make a finding as to who is responsible for the killings but Your Worship can, and indeed will, make a finding that they were murdered and that the circumstances of their deaths are as I have described them to Your Worship today.'

At the time of the first inquest even a suggestion of the existence of hit squads within the security forces would have been denied as 'communist and ANC propaganda' and could have exposed whoever suggested it to serious danger. Arthur Chaskalson had to tread a fine line.

Magistrate De Beer did not take long to deliver his finding. After referring briefly to the 'war' between the UDF and AZAPO, he sketched the events on the evening of 27 June 1985, the post-mortem results and the evidence led. His conclusion was:

'Finally, I find that it has been clearly proven who the deceased were, when they had died and what their cause of death was. As I have already said, the only real issue before me is to determine the identity of the actual killer or killers, and from what I have already said, this is not possible.

'The only finding I can make in this regard, which is also a finding to which all parties have agreed, is that their deaths were brought about by a person or persons or group of persons unknown.'

Once again, no one was to blame, but this time, on the evidence led, no other finding had been possible. The magistrate did not find, as Arthur had invited him to, that the circumstances of the murders pointed to the existence of a death squad. He was, however, heard to say privately that he was saddened by what he had heard and that it was obvious to him that there were people who appeared to be doing one thing during the day and other things at night. That is as far as Magistrate De Beer was prepared to go. Any suggestion of the existence of a death squad was akin to an act of treason. It required the courage of Arthur Chaskalson to suggest it.

On 19 October 1989, some eight months after the inquest, Butana Almond

Nofemela, a former security policeman, was awaiting his execution the following morning. Realising he had been abandoned by colleagues who had promised to help him, he made an affidavit to Shanks Mabitsela of Lawyers for Human Rights. In it Nofemela set out the assassinations he had been involved in as a member of what he called the 'Security Branch's assassination squad'. One of these was the killing of Griffiths Mxenge. Capt. Dirk Coetzee, who was named by Nofemela as a member of the squad, had already had discussions with journalist Jacques Pauw and the ANC: he wanted to spill the beans, but was afraid. After Nofemela's revelation, however, Coetzee left the country in a hurry, scared that he might become a scapegoat and be killed by his colleagues to prevent the truth from coming out. Coetzee gave Pauw a full account of what his death squad had done. On Thursday 16 November 1989, Adriaan Vlok, Minister of Law and Order, denied on television that a police death squad had ever existed. The following morning the courageous Max du Preez, editor of *Vrye Weekblad* newspaper, published Coetzee's allegations. They promptly became headline news all over the world.

No great changes occurred even after the death squad revelations were made. Although President F.W. de Klerk unbanned the ANC, SACP and PAC a year after the Goniwe inquest, there was still a lack of transparency in government. From the time of the revelations De Klerk came under tremendous pressure to institute a judicial inquiry into the death squad allegations. But he was reluctant to do so. Instead of a judicial commission Kobie Coetsee, Minister of Justice, appointed the Natal Attorney-General, Tim McNally, and the head of the CID, Gen. Alwyn Conradie, to investigate Nofemela's claims. These two gentlemen did not inspire confidence in the likelihood of their commission getting to the truth. Their report was handed to De Klerk in late November 1989 but was only released a year later. McNally found there was no evidence that Coetzee and Nofemela were telling the truth. In the meantime De Klerk refused to appoint a judicial commission of inquiry, saying that it would take too long. Warrants were, however, issued for the arrest of Dirk Coetzee and his sidekick David Tshikalange. De Klerk's decision caused an uproar. Even the newspapers *Beeld* and *The Citizen*, traditional government supporters, called for a judicial inquiry. John Dugard, a respected legal academic, remarked that the chain of command stretched very high into the upper echelons of government; trying a few policemen would merely serve to create the impression that they had acted on their own.

The government resorted to the old tactic of blaming someone else, and arrested five right-wingers calling themselves 'The Order of Death'. But this did not defuse the pressure on De Klerk. He eventually had no choice but to antagonise the securocrats by reluctantly appointing a judicial commission of inquiry chaired by Judge Louis Harms. From the outset the commission had a major flaw – it could not investigate murders that occurred outside the country, and there were many of these. Moreover, the commission had no teeth. It could not subpoena witnesses and could also not provide protection or indemnity to them. McNally, of all people, was appointed to lead the evidence. The Harms Commission findings were released in November 1990, two months after its report had been handed to De Klerk. Judge Harms headed the report with the Latin phrase for 'Blessed is he who can recognise the truth'. In his report he said: 'The commission has been unable to achieve one of its main objectives, namely to restore public confidence in a part of the State administration.' He found that the Civil Co-operation Bureau had been involved in death squad activities but exonerated the police and defence force. From all the evidence he had heard, Judge Harms recommended further action in only ten incidents. The truth had not after all been recognised – to the relief of De Klerk, who still harboured a number of securocrats in his government.

The Harms Commission has been described as a farce. Both the Minister of Defence, Magnus Malan, and the Minister of Police, Adriaan Vlok, had a vital interest in protecting themselves and their Generals. Documents were not made available to the commission. The identity of senior officers was not disclosed. Some appeared before the commission heavily disguised and under false names took the oath to tell the truth. A large team of counsel representing the security forces and charging exorbitant fees delayed the proceedings by stringing the case out. In retrospect Judge Harms must surely regret that he did not at an early stage impose his authority by seeking greater powers and giving President De Klerk an ultimatum: either extend my powers to do the job properly and order your Ministers to co-operate or I will return the parchment appointing me as commissioner back to you.

At the time of the release of the Harms report a libel action was proceeding in the Johannesburg Supreme Court. It had been brought by Gen. Lothar Neethling against the *Vrye Weekblad*, which accused him of providing poison to death squads. Judge Johan Kriegler gave his judgment in January 1991, finding that death squads did exist and dismissing Neethling's claim with costs. The finding was later set aside on appeal. Although the absence of cogent evidence was again raised by President De Klerk and his men, he nevertheless dropped Malan and Vlok from his cabinet on the ground of ill health.

The inquest into the murders of the Cradock Four would have remained one more in the long line of 'no one to blame' findings, had it not been for the coming to light of a secret signal message in 1992. The *New Nation* weekly issue of 30 April–7 May 1992 reported on its front page that it was 'in possession of proof that the killings of Cradock activists Matthew Goniwe, Fort Calata, Sicelo Mhlauli and Sparrow Mkonto, as well as the disappearance of three other activists in May and June 1985, were probably authorised by the Secretariat of the State Security Council'. The report made mention of a signal 'which was sent by the staff officer of intelligence in the Eastern Province Command to the Secretariat of the State Security Council in Pretoria'. The paper went on to say that the 'four activists were later found dead less than a month after the message was relayed'. At last there was the promise of a smoking gun.

A photographic copy of the handwritten signal was published a week later, under the headline 'Death order from General'. It showed that the signal had been sent by Col. Lourens du Plessis, the secretary of the Eastern Province Joint Management Centre (JMC), on the instructions of Gen. Joffel van der Westhuizen, its chairman. It was addressed to Gen. Johannes Janse van Rensburg, the chairman of the strategy branch of the Secretariat of the State Security Council. The signal had been passed on to *New Nation* by Gen. Bantu Holomisa. It was speculated that he had received it from Col. Du Plessis, but this was not admitted by either.

The signal was classified as top secret; it was marked 'urgent' and was to be dispatched as a 'priority'. It referred to a telephone conversation between Van Rensburg and Van der Westhuizen. It then read as follows:

'2. Name as volg [Names as follows]: Matthew Goniwe

Mbulelo Goniwe . . .

Fort Calata

'3. Dit word voorgestel dat bg. persone permanent uit die samelewing, as saak van dringendheid, verwyder word.' [It is proposed that the abovementioned persons be permanently removed from society as a matter of urgency.]

The signal then noted that wide reaction could be expected locally as well as internationally, because of the importance of these persons to the enemy, especially the first mentioned. Possible reactions anticipated were interdicts, as in the case of the Pebco Three; reaction from leftist politicians like Molly Blackburn; and protest in sympathy. It was dated 7 June 1985, twenty days before the Cradock Four were murdered.

The publication of the signal took the country by storm, as it seemed to contradict what Judge Harms had found a year and a half earlier and showed that everything that President P.W. Botha and the security forces had been accused of was true. The authenticity of the signal was not denied. Although it vindicated Judge Kriegler's judgment in the eyes of those who would see, the government and its Generals were not yet ready to come clean. The very same Van Rensburg, who was implicated in the signal, was given the responsibility of searching the National Intelligence files to find any possible link between the Goniwe issue and the Secretariat of the State Security Council! A pregnant silence from the authorities followed as public pressure mounted. De Klerk knew that the writing was on the wall for the era of securocrats. He eventually instructed Kobie Coetsee to ask the Judge-President of the Eastern Cape Division of the Supreme Court, Neville Zietsman, to reopen the inquest.

The publication of the signal and reopening of the inquest also reopened old wounds for the four widows and other family members of the murdered men. The prospect of reliving the events was painful but was outweighed by the possibility of finally finding the killers. The families approached Clive Plasket, the director of the Grahamstown office of the Legal Resources Centre, for assistance in the inquest and a possible civil claim for damages. Clive had started his legal career with the firm Cheadle, Thompson and Haysom and had thereafter lectured at the University of Natal, before joining the LRC. He is an exceptionally gifted, creative and hardworking attorney. He unearthed vital evidence and answered calls from a number of scared potential witnesses who wanted to give us information but feared for their lives if called to the witness box.

In 1992 I joined the LRC, and was available to take the inquest, whilst Arthur Chaskalson wasn't. He was not only the national director of the LRC but also busy as head of a team drafting the interim constitution. Mahomed Navsa, also counsel at the LRC and at the time director of its Johannesburg office, was briefed to undertake the case with me. He had overcome the disadvantages imposed by the apartheid regime's laws, which not only distinguished between blacks and whites but also between his father and mother, the one of Indian and the other of Malay origin. He could not therefore attend a school intended for either group. He finished up hundreds of kilometres away from his home, in Kimberley, where neither of the two groups was sufficiently large to justify separate schools. He overcame all this to be admitted to the University of the Western Cape where he was elected a student leader and where his sharp mind was moulded. He was awarded the Maurice Zimmerman scholarship by the LRC and, as a pupil advocate to Denis Kuny, helped to research the law relating to suicide in the Aggett inquest. He was an invaluable colleague in sharing the work on the Goniwe inquest in Port

Elizabeth, away from his home and young family.

Another member of the team was Nicolette Moodie, then a candidate attorney at the LRC fresh from Stellenbosch University. Not only did she delve into the documents and records produced, fervently arguing her ideas during preparation, but also acted as my tutor in Afrikaans, often writing out the difficult questions I had to put to the Generals in cross-examination. Mohamed had no such need as his earthy Afrikaans, learned on his mother's knee, earned him respect even from those he took on in cross-examination. He is an exceptionally gifted lawyer and now a High Court judge, having been appointed to the bench at the age of 38.

The more we delved into the documents in the Goniwe case, the clearer it became that the security forces claimed for themselves the right to be the prosecutors, judges and executioners of those they considered to be the enemy of the state. We resolved to try and show that killing and other acts of terror were part of state policy. More and more it became necessary to get on top of the documents in order to discredit the claim we knew would be made by the Generals, that they were officers and gentlemen and would not soil their hands by participating in such unbecoming conduct.

From September 1984 South Africa experienced civil unrest on a scale unprecedented. The apartheid government considered itself to be involved in a war, more specifically a counter-revolutionary war. Already in 1977, in a Defence White Paper, P.W. Botha, then Minister of Defence, stated that 'we are today involved in a war, whether we wish to accept it or not'. He became Prime Minister in 1978 and later President, ushering in an era during which the country was increasingly ruled by militarists, or 'securocrats', as they became known. In a case against the End Conscription Campaign (ECC) in 1988, the South African Defence Force argued before the Cape Supreme Court that the court's jurisdiction over its actions was ousted by the fact that a state of war prevailed in the 'territory of South West Africa and elsewhere in Southern Africa'. The defence force admitted to spreading false and defamatory information about the ECC and to damaging its property but contended that the court could not interfere because South Africa was at war. Sydney Kentridge, QC came back from London to argue the case against this preposterous contention. His arguments were incorporated into an important judgment by Judge Selikowitz, sending out a message that the rule of law was not entirely abrogated.

The 1977 Defence White Paper described a 'total national strategy' to counter the so-called total onslaught. This strategy was based on the theories and philosophy of various authors on counter-revolutionary warfare. What the South African securocrats did was to take these works, written about wars in Burma, Malaysia and Algeria, and apply them to South Africa, targeting those civilians whom they disliked. The work of John J. McCuen, author of *The Art of Counter-Revolutionary War*, was particularly popular.

The essence of McCuen's theories is contained in the following quotation from a summary of his work: 'A governing power can defeat any revolutionary movement if it adapts the revolutionary strategy and principles and applies them in reverse.' McCuen's South African disciple was Brig. C.A. Fraser, a former chief of the army, who wrote *Lessons Learnt from Past Revolutionary Wars*, a work which was much used by the securocrats. According to Fraser, the nature of war had changed and 'the government in power has to conduct a revolutionary war as an interlocking system of actions, political and economic, administrative, psychological, police and military'. In South Africa the National Security Management System became the mechanism which was used to implement this 'total strategy'. It had been dormant since 1979, but was reactivated when civil unrest flared up again in 1984. At its apex was the State Security Council, which had been formed in 1972 in terms of an Act of parliament. It consisted of mandatory members such as the State President and key Ministers as well as others who were co-opted. At the time of the murder of the Cradock Four, the members included the State President, the Defence Minister, the Minister of Foreign Affairs, the Minister of Law and Order, the Minister of Justice, the Chief of the South African Defence Force and the Commissioner of Police.

In theory the State Security Council's function was purely to advise the government on the formulation of national policy and strategy. In reality it was the government for all intents and purposes. It was assisted in the administration of the system by its Secretariat. The Secretariat had a full-time staff and was responsible for the co-ordination of strategic communications and of the formulation of strategy, as well as making recommendations to the State Security Council and passing on decisions to the various departments of government for implementation. At the time of the murders, Gen. Johannes Janse van Rensburg chaired its strategy branch.

On a regional level the system was represented by Joint Management Centres (JMCs). They were dominated, however, by the security forces, and sensitive security matters were only discussed in subcommittees consisting exclusively of security force members. The JMCs were responsible for the implementation of approved strategies. In smaller centres there were sub- and mini-JMCs. Cradock had its own mini-JMC, chaired by Commandant Botha

Marais, commanding officer of the Cradock Commando. The JMCs permeated every level of society and nothing was considered beyond their jurisdiction.

Both Fraser and McCuen describe winning the loyalty of the population as the objective of both sides in a revolutionary war. It is a political, rather than a military, war. Both also emphasise the importance of identifying 'the enemy' and isolating him or her from the population. Another central theme of their philosophy is that the government should sow disunity in 'revolutionary' ranks in order to diminish their power.

In the Eastern Cape a policy was adopted of exacerbating the existing rivalry and disagreements between the UDF and AZAPO. There were cases of bogus pamphlets being distributed and suspicions of informers infiltrating both organisations. Small wonder the perpetrators of the murder of the Cradock Four were not identified during the first inquest – all the evidence had centred on this disunity. This was a deliberate strategy. Col. Eric Winter, head of the Security Police in Cradock at the time of the murders, was heard saying the day after the murders, 'AZAPO het hulle gekry' [AZAPO got them]. More than one witness during the second inquest tried to draw the court's attention back to the conflict between the UDF and AZAPO.

It was not the only case in which this was done. When Dr Fabian Ribeiro and his wife Florence were murdered in front of their Mamelodi home in 1986, the police alleged that they might have been killed by AZAPO, as they had supported the UDF. After Albie Sachs, now a Constitutional Court justice, lost an arm in a car-bomb explosion in Mozambique in 1988, Foreign Minister Pik Botha, a member of the State Security Council which authorised such actions, suggested that the bombing was the result of a power struggle within the ANC in Mozambique. The Security Police have since admitted to giving out such false stories to friendly journalists.

Cradock was especially hard hit by civil unrest in the 1980s. It was one of the 32 municipal areas alleged by the state in the Delmas Trial to be ungovernable. During this case we called as a defence witness Gilly Skweyiya, a member of the Cradock Residents' Association (Cradora). He gave evidence about Cradock, the unrest there and about Goniwe, in rebuttal of the state's case that the unrest in Cradock was inspired by outsiders. His testimony gives one great insight into the period and the people involved. Despite the facilities available to the security forces, they knew little about the lives of those they intended eliminating. They were not even sure whether Mbulelo Goniwe was a brother or cousin of Matthew Goniwe.

In 1973 a black administration board took over the running of Lingelihle township from the white municipality of Cradock. This was in turn replaced by a town council in 1979. The government actively recruited community members who would be loyal to them, to serve as councillors. These so-called community councils were mere rubber-stamps for government policy and did not have the best interests of their communities at heart. The communities could see no improvement in their living standards. It is not surprising therefore that Skweyiya testified that the councillors were seen as useless puppets of the government. They were often the targets of intimidation and attacks. In most townships they were isolated from the rest of the community and lived behind barbed-wire fences and mesh windows. The community of Lingelihle was poor and felt that the amount of rent they were paying was unfair. They had other problems too – there was no electricity, the sewerage system was primitive, the roads were in a very bad state of repair, there were few taps with running water. The services in the coloured township of Cradock, on the other hand, were far superior and the rent was cheaper. The people of Lingelihle did not know what to do about this state of affairs. Matthew Goniwe would change all that.

While teaching in the Transkei in 1976, Goniwe was arrested in terms of the Suppression of Communism Act. His counsel, Ismail Mahomed, now the Chief Justice, argued that the Act did not apply to the Transkei, which was an 'independent country' according to the apartheid state. But the judge, George Anderson Munnik, dismissed this argument, and in September 1977 convicted Goniwe and sentenced him to four years' imprisonment. Mahomed applied for leave to appeal, but Munnik took twenty months to hear the application and had not given judgment on it by the time Goniwe was released. Goniwe thus served his full four-year term.

After his release in 1981, Goniwe settled in Cradock. At first he was not active politically and the authorities thought they would not have trouble from him again. He was subsequently appointed to a teaching post in Graaff-Reinet. He was a teacher of mathematics and physical science and a good one at that, someone who was quite sought after by officials within the Department of Education and Training (DET). After 1983 the DET became responsible for the education of blacks in 'white-designated' areas. Its Minister was Gerrit Viljoen, who was also the Minister of Co-operation and Development. F.W. de Klerk was the Minister of National Education, the overarching department.

Goniwe had been separated from his wife Nyameka and child for years – first through imprisonment and then through economic necessity. She was working in Port Elizabeth and he was in Graaff-Reinet. In 1983 he requested a transfer to Cradock, as his wife had obtained a job there and his family home was there. He was initially appointed as vice-principal of Sam Xhallie Secondary School and shortly thereafter acting principal. This is when he took up politics again.

Before Goniwe took over, the Sam Xhallie school had been in a dreadful state. According to Skweyiya, the school used to be among the top five black schools in the Cape Province. After the 1976–7 unrest, however, the school went into decline and parents would send their children elsewhere if they could afford to do so. There was no discipline. Children would be seen smoking outside school after classes had already begun. They would feign illness and then be seen in town. The school held discos to raise funds but parents felt these were a bad influence on the children. The rate of teenage pregnancy was high. Goniwe's first step was to stop the discos. He and Fort Calata, who was also a teacher at the school, would personally confront and punish children who skipped school or came late. He would visit the parents of wayward students and impress upon them their responsibilities.

In May 1983 Goniwe arranged for the clergymen, social workers and other professionals in Lingelihle to meet. The result was the establishment of committees to organise cultural and sporting activities for the youth. The success of this venture led to the formation of the Cradock Youth Association (Cradoya) on 25 August 1983. The meeting was attended by 600 people. Goniwe was elected chairperson and Fort Calata secretary. In January 1984 Goniwe resigned as chairperson and Calata took over from him. Goniwe's approach to the youth was effective, not so much because he was a strict disciplinarian, although he was that too, but because he put children on their honour. He taught them – and their parents – a sense of self-discipline, and showed them that this was important for themselves, their community and their country. He understood children and gave them a sense of self-esteem. In return they adored him. Not long after the founding of Cradoya, a meeting was called at which Cradora was founded. Goniwe was elected chairperson and Fort Calata treasurer.

Fort Calata was the grandson of Canon James Calata, a venerable member of the ANC. Fort was very proud of his grandfather. He had been an accused in the Treason Trial of the late 1950s arising out of the adoption of the Freedom Charter. After the ANC was declared an unlawful organisation on 8 April 1960, in the wake of the Sharpeville massacre, Canon Calata was convicted on a charge of 'displaying something indicating that he is or was an office bearer or member or in any way associated with an unlawful organisation, in contravention of the Suppression of Communism Act'. The offending items were two photographs of himself and other ANC members: they were hanging, according to the security policemen who gave evidence, 'visible in obvious places'. In one picture he was described as Secretary-General of the ANC and in the other as Secretary-General and Senior Chaplain of the ANC. One of the photographs was found hanging on a wall in the sitting room and another against the wall on a bookshelf in his study. The photographs had been taken more than twenty years before. One may ask what he was supposed to do with previously legal mementoes that were suddenly transformed into incriminating evidence. Judges Jennet and Van der Riet could not find grounds to set aside the conviction of the old Anglican minister and upheld the sentence of 180 days' imprisonment suspended for three years on condition that he did not commit any offence in terms of the Suppression of Communism Act or the Unlawful Organisations Act. Fort received his name because he was born while his grandfather was imprisoned in the Fort in Johannesburg. Gen. Van der Westhuizen, with characteristic lack of sensitivity and insight, later remarked in his affidavit for the Goniwe inquest that he recalled Fort's name because he connected it to the Ford factory in Port Elizabeth! It shows how little the security forces knew about the people whom they branded as the enemy and whose murders they plotted.

Mbulelo Goniwe, Matthew's cousin, and Sparrow Mkonto were also leading members of Cradora. Together with Fort Calata, they were considered by the security forces to be Goniwe's 'militant lieutenants', as one witness put it. Mbulelo and Fort were active in Cradoya as well. In December 1983 Cradora and Cradoya were both affiliated to the newly established United Democratic Front (UDF). Cradora consisted of area committees and street committees, each with its own leadership. This made it very effective in relaying information to its members and taking decisions, without the necessity of large public meetings.

In the 1980s the situation in the Eastern Cape was seen by the security forces as particularly serious and Goniwe was regarded as a major contributory cause. In his affidavit for the Goniwe inquest, Gen. Van der Westhuizen said: 'From about the middle of 1984 the situation in the Eastern Province deteriorated to such an extent that anarchy reigned in certain areas. At that stage the Eastern Province was the burning point of the revolutionary onslaught against the state. Because of this fact, the Eastern Province JMC was in the political spotlight.' He went on to say that Goniwe enjoyed great recognition inasmuch as the plan for the creation of alternative structures in the townships was referred to as the 'G plan' in the Eastern Province, while in other areas it was referred to as the 'M plan', after Mandela. 'Goniwe played a very prominent role in the aforementioned revolutionary onslaught in the EP. He was one of the leaders of the UDF and to the best of my knowledge Cradock was the first place in the Republic where the aforementioned alternative structures were implemented' – a claim later disputed by UDF leaders when those who killed the Cradock Four applied for amnesty. 'Furthermore, Goniwe was a leader of the militant youth movements in the Eastern Cape region and as a result of this he enjoyed prominence with the media as well as with the Security Police and Department of Education and Training.'

It became clear during the second inquest that Goniwe had been such a problem for the security forces that they considered him the 'enemy'. Van Rensburg testified that 'The enemy in the counter-revolutionary war were all the revolutionaries who were focused on overthrowing the state in an unconstitutional manner'. Witness after witness declared that Goniwe was the enemy or that he was a revolutionary. Van der Westhuizen's own opinion was that he contributed to the armed struggle; he was a charismatic leader and drew large crowds whenever he spoke. The security forces thus watched in agitation as the climate of resistance to apartheid grew alongside Goniwe's popularity.

According to Col. Lourens du Plessis, who wrote the signal requesting the death warrant for the Cradock Four, the situation became so critical that Gen. Van der Westhuizen was at risk of losing his job if he did not get it under control. Indeed Gen. Magnus Malan, the Minister of Defence, came down to Port Elizabeth to talk to Van der Westhuizen. The criticism Malan made was so severe, he added, that Van der Westhuizen's secretary burst into tears when the Minister and his entourage were finally on the plane back to Pretoria at midnight. 'They're going to fire our boss,' she cried. Van der Westhuizen himself confirmed that a lot of pressure was put on him by politicians.

A decision was therefore taken to transfer Goniwe back to Graaff-Reinet in an attempt to curb his influence. He was told to report for duty there at the beginning of the 1984 school year. But the Cradock community were outraged. At a meeting attended by about two thousand people, it was decided that Goniwe would not accept the transfer. A delegation of clergymen, parents and members of Cradora and Cradoya went to see Günther Merbold of the DET to discuss the transfer. Merbold was a hardliner who was known to have regular meetings with the Cradock Security Police. He told them that he needed a maths and science teacher in Graaff-Reinet, but the community were not fooled. They told Merbold that they also needed a maths and science teacher and that they knew this was not the real reason for the transfer. The decision was a political one and had been taken in association with the

Security Police. In a telling DET working document later made public for the inquest, it was said about the decision to transfer Goniwe: 'At the request of the security community (for security reasons) he was notified . . . that he was being transferred to Graaff-Reinet . . .' Merbold himself stated in an affidavit that there was overwhelming pressure on him from the Eastern Province JMC to transfer Goniwe. Later Du Plessis would testify that the Security Police had been very upset when Goniwe was appointed acting headmaster in Cradock, as it was then policy that the Security Police had to be approached before a headmaster could be appointed and this had not happened with Goniwe.

Two weeks of negotiations between Goniwe, the school committee and the DET followed. The deadline by which Goniwe had to accept the transfer lapsed while negotiations were still continuing, and Goniwe was advised by telegram that his services were being terminated by the DET. The school committee resigned in protest at the fact that their recommendations carried no weight. They requested a meeting with Merbold, who kept putting them off. Fort Calata took the lead in a campaign by Cradora and Cradoya to start a school boycott should Goniwe not be reinstated. A petition demanding Goniwe's reinstatement was drawn up and presented to Merbold when he eventually met the committee on 3 February 1984. He claimed that Goniwe had dismissed himself by not accepting the transfer but said that he could apply for reinstatement. School boycotts did indeed start, after the students and their parents learnt of Merbold's attitude. By March there was a complete boycott of all the schools in Cradock. A DET document says about this time: 'No discussion was possible with Goniwe at that stage as he was holding a pistol against the DET's head. The SAP agreed on this. The erstwhile Minister of Education and Training was also advised not to talk to him.'

On Sharpeville Day, 21 March 1984, a spirited meeting was held at which Matthew Goniwe, Mbulelo Goniwe and Fort Calata spoke. Thereafter outdoor meetings were banned and on a number of occasions people, mostly school children, were dispersed with teargas and rubber bullets. The community councillors and the headmaster who took over from Goniwe were targeted in petrol-bomb attacks. On 31 March the two Goniwes, Calata and the head prefect of Lingelihle High School were arrested in terms of section 28(1) of the Internal Security Act and detained. A ban was simultaneously placed on indoor meetings. In May the remaining community leaders were detained. Nevertheless the school boycotts continued and eventually involved about seven thousand students throughout the Eastern Cape. In a memorandum from the community council to the Minister of Law and Order, dated 25 May 1984, it was said that 'since March 1984 four ringleaders of Cradora have been arrested and are awaiting trial but in spite of this their subversive activities are still part and parcel of our daily life'. In June and July consumer boycotts were also launched. Detaining Goniwe was clearly not a solution. Nor could evidence of criminal conduct be procured to charge him despite pressure put on other detainees to betray him. ·

After he was released on 9 October 1984 Goniwe immediately resumed his Cradora and Cradoya activities. The campaign against the community councillors and rent increases continued and many rousing meetings were held. The council eventually succumbed under the pressure and resigned on 3 January 1985. It is a testament to Goniwe's leadership that he led the youth of Cradock to the erstwhile councillors' houses to remove the mesh window-guards and barbed-wire fences. It was the only township in the country where councillors were immediately reintegrated into the community.

At the end of 1984 Günther Merbold had invited the community to a meeting in the town hall. He told them that there was a chance of Goniwe's reinstatement and that he should reapply. Both Goniwe and Calata took up the offer but their applications were rejected. During early 1985 community leaders met with Sam de Beer, the Deputy Minister of Education and Training, on two occasions, and with Merbold as well – to no avail. It appeared as if Goniwe's case was closed.

Community members began to realise that there were opposing forces in the government with differing views about Goniwe's position. The security forces wanted Goniwe detained – definitely not reinstated. Merbold, the hardliner in the DET, felt the same way. Van Rensburg testified that Merbold was the 'resistance factor' within his department and felt so strongly against Goniwe's reinstatement that he said that if it were to happen, it had to be done through head office in Pretoria, not his office. On the other hand there were De Beer and his followers in the Department, who felt that reinstatement was not only desirable but also necessary. They were part of a movement within the National Party which, after the September 1984 uprisings, felt that the liberation movements had to be accommodated if there was to be any solution to the conflict. Moves to accommodate Goniwe had to be made cautiously, however, as the securocrats wielded much power. When De Beer spoke to community leaders in Cradock during early 1985, he made promises about Goniwe's reinstatement and socio-economic improvements in Lingelihle. But it seemed that he was in reality powerless to change anything. Unrest flared up again in Cradock and elsewhere. At a meeting of the Eastern Province JMC it was stated that the government was worried about the situation in the country. Firmer action was called for at a meeting of the secretariat.

In the meantime the Security Police were watching Goniwe ever more closely. Extracts from his personal file show the extent to which the Security Police monitored his, and other activists', every move. They did so through observation, informers, listening in on telephone calls and tape-recording public meetings. In Goniwe's case they even went a step further – they placed a listening device, nicknamed a '*tamatie*', in his house. It received and transmitted all conversations within a certain radius. The information obtained in these ways would be transcribed and placed in a Security Police file. The personal files of people who were the greatest causes of concern for the Security Police were classified as 'A' files. Matthew Goniwe, Fort Calata, Mbulelo Goniwe and Sparrow Mkonto all had 'A' files. Goniwe's file was the bulkiest of the four. Unfortunately there seems subsequently to have been large-scale destruction of documents and not much of the contents of these files was still available by the time the second inquest was held. Portions of Goniwe's file were made available to us, however. These showed the intensity with which UDF activities and especially those of Goniwe were monitored.

Reports, classified as top secret, were sent on a regular basis from the Cradock Security Branch to headquarters in Port Elizabeth, summarising recent events. The Cradock Security Police were also responsible for other towns around Cradock, towns where Goniwe was active. It is clear that the Security Police saw Goniwe as the major source of unrest in the Eastern Cape. In the official request for a '*tamatie*' at Goniwe's home, he was described as a 'black power activist who works for black consciousness and who organises underground to overthrow the government. The premises . . . are used to hold meetings where undermining activities, aimed at undermining the state's authority, are held and also where the current unrest at schools are planned and continued by [Goniwe] and his cronies. He also receives visits from restricted persons and other black power activists from elsewhere in the Republic at the premises.'

On 3 February 1985, on behalf of the mini-JMC in Cradock, Commandant Botha Marais sent a memorandum to the Eastern Province JMC regarding Goniwe. It stated they had decided that Matthew Goniwe and Fort Calata should not be reinstated and that nothing had been achieved by the discussions of the last months. There had been too much talk, the document concluded; it was time to do something constructive. 'The enemy is a big strong alleycat. Dogs can't fight alleycats, therefor [sic] you must get yourself a bigger, stronger alleycat.'

In March 1985 Goniwe was appointed regional rural organiser of the UDF and was provided with the ill-fated motor car. He commenced travelling widely, addressing meetings and founding community organisations in small towns throughout the Eastern Cape. Where once he had been, community activism followed. As a result the UDF gained a stronger presence in these areas in the few months of Goniwe's campaign than they had in the preceding two years. Much to the government's chagrin, Goniwe regularly met with foreign dignitaries and overseas journalists. Molly Blackburn, a PFP member of parliament who was later killed in a mysterious car crash, arranged many of these meetings for him. She also helped draft Cradora's constitution.

In April 1985 De Beer met a delegation from Cradock in Cape Town and told them that Goniwe's case had been reopened. The DET wanted to meet with Goniwe in Cradock. When this was reported back to Cradora and Cradoya, Goniwe insisted on the ending of the school boycott. His decision was accepted reluctantly. Because public meetings had once again been banned, permission to hold a meeting was granted to announce Goniwe's decision when De Beer requested it on behalf of the community. On this occasion Goniwe relayed his wishes to the local people. There was much unhappiness, but eventually it was resolved that the children would return to school, while the fight for Goniwe's reinstatement would continue. A week later, on 15 April 1985, students returned to school – fifteen months after the stayaway had begun. It had been the longest school boycott in South African history.

Soon afterwards De Beer came to Cradock but, to the community's disappointment, no meeting was held with Goniwe. Instead De Beer met with the Cradock Chamber of Business. It seemed as if the school boycotts would start again. On 13 May 1985 a meeting was held at the Commando headquarters in Cradock. Present were Jaap Strydom, Chief Director of the DET, members of his department and the Security Police. The topic of discussion was Goniwe. Strydom announced that his department was sympathetically considering the reinstatement of Goniwe. He said that he would arrange with Molly Blackburn to meet with Goniwe to discuss the matter.

The securocrats present at the meeting did not, however, like the idea at all. The information was relayed to the Minister of Law and Order, Louis le Grange, on 23 May. He immediately contacted Gerrit Viljoen, the Minister of Education and Training, asking him to hold over any decision about Goniwe until they could meet on 24 May. It is not known whether they in fact did meet. Another meeting did take place on 24 May: Strydom held a 'collegial discussion' with Goniwe to 'assess his attitude'. The possibility of a meeting with De Beer was also discussed. Such a meeting had been approved by De Beer and the Director-General of the DET.

The security forces were clearly unhappy with the direction things were taking. On 23 May the Eastern Province JMC was informed by Merbold in Port Elizabeth of the impending meeting with Goniwe. At this stage the head of the Eastern Cape division of the Security Police was Col. Harold Snyman, who in 1977 had been in charge of the interrogation team that dealt with Steve Biko. He is recorded in a Security Police telex as voicing his strong opposition to Goniwe's reinstatement at the meeting. Everyone was of like mind. The meeting unanimously decided to send a signal message to the Secretariat of the State Security Council stating that Matthew Goniwe and Fort Calata should under no circumstances be reinstated in any post within the DET ever again. At the second inquest, this became known colloquially as the 'nooit ooit weer' [never ever again] signal. It was signed by Gen. Van der Westhuizen, and delivered to Gen. Van Rensburg by hand, and its contents were relayed to the DET.

Because of the sensitivity of the matter and the conflicting views of the DET and the security establishment, the DET raised the issue of Goniwe's reinstatement at a meeting of the Joint Security Staff on 6 June chaired by the Deputy Minister of Law and Order, Adriaan Vlok. It was referred to a committee under the direction of the Secretariat, chaired by Brig. P.J. Geldenhuys. The committee sat on 7 June 1985, the same day that Du Plessis sent the 'death warrant' signal to Van Rensburg in Pretoria.

According to Jan Vermaak of the DET, who was present, the committee sat for a few hours and, after some debate between the DET and Col. McDonald of the Security Police, decided to recommend Goniwe's unconditional reinstatement. In their report to the Secretariat, mention was also made of the possible detention or restriction of Mbulelo Goniwe and Fort Calata. It is difficult to resist the inference that the securocrats' sudden and apparent change of heart was a bluff, a smokescreen to placate doves like Minister De Beer and to absolve themselves in advance for what was to happen.

In the light of the Security Branch's vehement resistance to the possibility of Goniwe's reinstatement, the lack of vigour with which McDonald put their view to the committee – in fact his very presence – makes one suspect they were merely pretending to give their support to the process, while following their own agenda. On 3 April 1985 the Directorate of Security Legislation, an advisory body, had received a written request from the Security Police for the detention of Goniwe, Mbulelo Goniwe and Fort Calata, the three named in the signal. On 29 April, when the Directorate heard that the DET was considering reinstating Goniwe, it sent a letter to the Security Branch to find out whether they wanted to continue with the request for detention. On 30 May 1985, a week after the 'nooit ooit weer' signal and a week before the issue was referred to Geldenhuys, the Security Police replied that it supported the planned action by the DET. They were clearly lying.

On 25 June 1985 the Commissioner of Police, Gen. Johann Coetzee, sent a memorandum to the Minister of Law and Order. The memorandum is headed 'Recommended action against Matewu Matthew Goniwe, black man, ex-teacher, Cradock'. By this time the Geldenhuys committee had already made its recommendation. The memorandum purports to recommend conditional reinstatement or restriction in Cradock over the alternatives of detention or unconditional reinstatement. But it is clear from a reading of the document that even the recommended options were not seen as viable. The memorandum concludes by saying that, because of the notoriety Goniwe had already received, whatever action was taken against him would elicit serious criticism, nationally as well as internationally. The resemblance to the concluding paragraph of the signal is striking. These documents apparently contradict the clear evidence of Security Police opposition to Goniwe's reinstatement. They seem to be void of substance, as if written for form's sake by people who knew a solution was already at hand, as if they were trying to build an alibi into their own documents. Two days after the memorandum was written, Goniwe was dead.

It is clear from the writings of McCuen and Fraser on counter-revolutionary war, as well as the testimony of security force witnesses at the second Goniwe inquest, and above all the amnesty applicants' evidence, that the security forces were not above killing outside conventional military operations when circumstances demanded such action. Gen. Van der Westhuizen confirmed during his testimony at the inquest that the killing of political activists was always regarded as an option; it was not excluded in principle. Whether it should be done in a given case would be a strategic decision to be taken at the highest level.

During the second inquest, minutes of a CCB meeting of 28 April 1987 were handed in as an exhibit. In it the Chief of the defence force, Gen. Jannie Geldenhuys, gives a chilling redefinition of murder: 'Methods that are applied: The Chief of the South African Defence Force does not see the actions as "murder" and defines them as follows: "An attack on an individual (enemy) target with non-standard-issue weapons so as not to affect innocent people."' In a covering affidavit Gen. Joep Joubert, who was initially in charge of the CCB and who had been present at the April 1987 meeting, said, 'The content of the document is self-explanatory and means exactly what it says. This document is clear proof that there was at all times [army] control over the CCB activities.'

Not only does Gen. Geldenhuys's redefinition show that the security forces were not above murder, it also shows how veiled language was routinely used by them. The wording of the signal may have genuinely offended some of the civilians in the system, but Gen. Van Rensburg was patently lying when he later said in court that it offended him. He admitted that veiled language was used in the military and this was confirmed by both Col. Du Plessis and Gen. Van der Westhuizen. Van der Westhuizen even slipped up once during his testimony and used the word 'uithaal' [take out]. When asked to clarify, he said that it meant to kill.

One can only be amazed by the brazenness (or perhaps stupidity) of the security forces in putting such references to killing on paper, but it seems that this was done regularly in classified documents. One wonders what else would have been discovered had the shredding machines not worked so hard after the dawn of the new era in South African politics.

We arrived in Port Elizabeth on 1 March 1993 to begin the Goniwe inquest. There was great excitement within and outside the courtroom. The large crowd that had come to see justice done sang freedom songs and toyi-toyi-ed outside and packed the public gallery. We had to request our clients not to allow the proceedings to be interfered with by people's excitement at the possibility of at last finding out who the killers of the Cradock Four were. The remainder of the court was filled with counsel in black robes and with attorneys. Judge Zietsman looked a little apprehensive too. He was not given to impose his will strongly and we were to be frustrated at times by his lack of assertiveness against the conduct of Anton Mostert, counsel for the defence force. Mike Hodgen, the Deputy Attorney-General in charge of the inquest, was the first attorney-general in any inquest I had ever been involved in who seemed to have a genuine desire to get to the truth. His enthusiasm was shared by his junior, Nico Henning.

Arthur Chaskalson had told me that at the end of the first inquest Hodgen, then a comparatively junior member of the Bar, was saddened by the lack of proper police investigation and the inevitable finding that no one was responsible for the deaths. He promised that the docket would not be closed and that he would continue looking for the killers. In preparation for the second inquest he and his junior, Nico Henning, had become actively involved in taking statements and confronting would-be witnesses with documents. One of the reasons why we were able to show that the 'death warrant' signal was not sent for an innocent purpose was the result of their efforts. It was a welcome change from previous cases where little effort had been made and sometimes a deliberate cover-up was orchestrated by the 'investigating officer'.

There were four other legal teams aside from ourselves; three of them represented organs of state. Interdepartmental conflicts were coming to the fore. The defence force was represented by Anton Mostert, SC. Our friendship went back to the early 1950s when both of us were attorneys' clerks. He was then highly critical of the apartheid policy and thought his fellow Afrikaners were leading the country to disaster. He became an attorney and I went to the Bar. He often briefed me to argue his appeals. He returned to Wits University to study for an LLB, became the leader of a conservative group of students, joined the Johannesburg Bar, soon became fashionable counsel for the establishment and not very long thereafter was elevated to the bench. He had also been instrumental in exposing the Information Scandal in the 1970s. His junior was Barnard Knoetze.

Doep de Bruyn, SC, assisted by a large red-headed junior, Johan Wessels, appeared for the South African Police. Then there was Nic Treurnicht, who appeared for National Intelligence and had very little to say. All three had been briefed by the State Attorney. It was an indication of the lack of trust that existed between different branches of the security forces that one legal team would not suffice. When thieves fall out . . . This split would be exploited by Mostert at a later stage to protect Gen. Van der Westhuizen, formerly chairman of the Eastern Province JMC. At the time of the publication of the signal and the inquest, Gen. Van der Westhuizen was chief of Military Intelligence and was reputed to be a charismatic character. It was clear that Mostert put Van der Westhuizen's interests above those of any of his other clients. Relying on our friendship during our younger days, Mostert at one stage asked whether we could wrap up the inquest quickly as his client wanted to be considered when an imminent decision was made as to who would succeed the retiring Chief of the South African Army. He was visibly upset when I said that I thought it an unrealistic prospect.

The first witness called was Gen. Van Rensburg, chairman of the strategy branch of the Secretariat of the State Security Council. He was a short, grey-haired little man who did not on the face of it create the impression of someone who could order a murder. Once he started testifying, however, it became clear that he had something to hide. His testimony was filled with contradictions and nonsensical drivel. It was totally incredible.

We commenced our cross-examination of him by asking whether as an officer and a gentleman it was not his duty to report a crime of which he had knowledge. He said yes. He testified that he had been worried about the language in the signal when he read it and that it could be misunderstood. He could not, however, explain why he had not brought the signal to the attention of WO Els, the investigating officer, after he had heard about the murders of the Cradock Four. His reply was that he did not know of the existence of an investigating officer!

Van Rensburg conceded that the signal could be interpreted as a death warrant and made much of feeling 'gebelgd' (which he translated as 'offended') by the language in the signal. At the time, however, he took no steps to correct this and never spoke to its sender, Van der Westhuizen, about it. Col. Du Plessis, former secretary of the Eastern Province JMC, confirmed the obvious, that he would have expected some reaction to the signal from Van Rensburg had he, Du Plessis, misunderstood Van der Westhuizen's instruction and had the signal not been a proposal for a death warrant.

At the end of an incisive cross-examination, Glen Goosen, counsel for Col. Du Plessis, put the latter's version of the signal to Van Rensburg:

'Col. Du Plessis will testify that the signal message is authentic, which does not appear to be in dispute. That he compiled it on the instructions of Brig. Van der Westhuizen and that what is stated therein correctly reflects the order he received and that that order entailed that Matthew Goniwe, Mbulelo Goniwe and Fort Calata had to be killed.'

Van Rensburg answered: 'If that was the case, then this signal was sent to the wrong person and to the wrong addressee. If that was the case, then this signal should have been directed along the line function channels of Brig. Van der Westhuizen and not to the Secretariat of the State Security Council.' The clearly implied admission that there was indeed an address to which requests for death warrants were sent drew gasps from the public gallery.

We then questioned Van Rensburg on the matter: to whom should the signal have been sent, if indeed it was a request for a death warrant? Van Rensburg's answer was dumbfounding: the Chief of the Army! He seemed to be unaware of the enormous implications of his answer. *The Star*'s placard of the day read 'Goniwe – General's shock evidence'. Van Rensburg's own counsel, Mostert, declined to ask him any questions, obviously considering him beyond redemption as a witness. Later, once argument had already commenced, Van Rensburg returned with a new legal representative and a revived memory of the fate of the signal.

After Van Rensburg's initial evidence, Du Plessis had been scheduled to testify the following day. The court was packed; spectators spilled out into the corridors and into the sections reserved for us. People had to be asked to leave. But instead of his appearing, his counsel handed in a new affidavit by Du Plessis. In it Du Plessis recanted the statement in his first affidavit, made before the inquest began, that Gen. Van der Westhuizen had never indicated to him that Goniwe and the others named in the signal should be killed. Now he said that he and Van der Westhuizen both intended the signal to mean that they had to be killed.

He had signed the first affidavit, Du Plessis later testified, under pressure during a consultation with the State Attorney, Johan Wagener, and a General Knipe, the army's legal adviser, on 11 May 1992; at that stage he thought they would represent him throughout the inquest. He recalled that when he told them the signal meant that the people mentioned had to be killed, Knipe almost fell off his chair. He and Wagener would not accept his explanation, saying it was highly unlikely that a senior army official like Van der Westhuizen would put an order to kill in writing. The consultation lasted most of the day during which time he told them again and again that the signal was meant to refer to the killing of those mentioned in it. After all, he said, permanent means permanent – you can't attach another meaning to it. But they would not accept this and eventually convinced him to make the first affidavit. Their attitude was, said Du Plessis, 'we are your friends and we'll look after you.'

Instead, they turned out to be his tormentors. Du Plessis told the court that he had a brief consultation with Wagener and Mostert on 3 February 1993, shortly before the commencement of the inquest. Two days later he received a letter from Wagener, stating that it had not yet been decided whether their services would be available to him personally during the inquest. They would act for him should it appear there was no conflict of interest between him and the defence force. Almost a month later, on 2 March 1993, after the inquest had already commenced, he was informed in another letter that they would not represent him after all. And during the hearing their counsel, Anton Mostert, was merciless in his attack on Du Plessis, who had failed to remain silent.

Did he foresee that the days of the generals were numbered? Did he keep hoping against hope that he would be protected by them? Apparently when he felt this was not going to be the case, he decided to go with the flow of the tide towards transparency, openness and civilian government; he decided to tell the truth. Moreover there was also the possibility of obtaining indemnity, which had not existed at the time of the first inquest.

We expected that Wagener and Knipe would be called to contradict what Du Plessis had said and started preparing cross-examination for them. To our surprise and disappointment, however, they were not called. We were puzzled that experienced counsel like Mostert had not attempted to call them to contradict such damning testimony. The only possible explanation is that Wagener and Knipe could not assist him on this score. Mostert did no more than question Du Plessis about his version of events, trying to discredit him for changing versions. He did not put Wagener's or Knipe's version to him. In argument we made much of Wagener's and Knipe's failure to contradict Du Plessis. Eventually Du Plessis's version of the signal, as set out in his second affidavit, was believed by the court.

Annexed to Du Plessis's second affidavit were extracts from documents relating to a 1986 defence force operation named Operation Katzen, which had been submitted to Gen. Kat Liebenberg, then Chief of the Army. The plan was aimed at overthrowing the government of Lennox Sebe in the Ciskei bantustan by way of a coup, the amalgamation of the Transkei and Ciskei (two supposedly independent countries), and the creation of a united security front in the Eastern Cape against the UDF–ANC–SACP alliance. As the *Sunday Times* put it: 'It was a plan sweeping in its arrogance yet breathtaking in its naiveté – drawn from the textbooks of the "total onslaught" theorists so popular in the 1980s during the imperial reign of PW Botha.' The plan was drafted after President Botha had given an order that the situation in the country be 'normalised' by the end of 1986. The outline of the plan was rewritten by Van der Westhuizen in his own handwriting. In it Lennox Sebe was described as the main stumbling block, who should be removed ['*uit die weg geruim word*']. Possible methods for achieving this were discussed.

Du Plessis testified that the 'removal' of Sebe undoubtedly meant that he had to be killed. In his finding Judge Zietsman later said that more than one of the options set out contemplated the possibility of Lennox Sebe being murdered. His finding about Katzen was that 'the documents and uncontradicted evidence of Col. Du Plessis constitute, in my opinion, *prima facie* proof that Brig. Van der Westhuizen was party to a plan that included, as a possibility, the killing of Lennox Sebe and others'. He went on to declare that Van der Westhuizen had lied in his affidavit when he said neither he nor the Eastern Province JMC had ever planned or executed the murder of anyone. This sweeping exculpatory statement cost the General dearly. In its absence the Operation Katzen documents might have been inadmissible.

As Du Plessis was still awaiting the outcome of his application for indemnity, it was decided that other witnesses would be called in the meantime, of whom one Stemmet, a senior official in the Secretariat of the State Security Council, was the first. Stemmet's testimony would have been the ultimate in vagueness had it not been for the witnesses who followed. Amnesia seemed to beset almost everyone who stepped into the witness box. Stemmet and Van Rensburg had been in telephonic communication with each other on several occasions after the publication of the signal, both before and after they attested to their affidavits. This made their evidence even more suspicious. The Secretariat of the Security Council was in a cleft stick. If the signal was not a request for a death warrant, then why was it not placed before the Geldenhuys committee, which met early in June to decide on Goniwe's reinstatement? In their affidavits the committee members all denied that they had seen it. This was probably true; there were non-security force members on the committee as well. The argument that the signal was intended as a request for detention was, on the other hand, also untenable. This led to incredible answers from those who tried to exonerate Gens. Van Rensburg and Van der Westhuizen.

Stemmet was almost a hundred per cent sure that Van Rensburg discussed the terminology of the signal with him; he was just not sure how he did so.

The judge asked, 'But if the meaning of the signal was that these people had to be killed, would the wording have been too strong?'

'No, it wouldn't have been too strong then,' Stemmet replied. He went on to say it was typically dramatic language used by the security forces and by the military in particular, on a par with words like 'neutralise', 'eliminate' and those sorts of expressions, disingenuously adding that they were words that could mean something different from what the author intended. Stemmet was obviously trying to create the impression that such words had benign meanings but could be misinterpreted because of the dramatic language. Stemmet himself tried to explain the signal as meaning that Goniwe had to be permanently appointed away from Cradock. Later he testified that the words referred to eliminating or removing a person's influence!

During cross-examination Mohamed Navsa asked Stemmet what had happened when the signal was published. The latter said he had been informed by the Director-General of National Intelligence of the content of the *New Nation* report. He told Stemmet that things would happen over the weekend. Stemmet expected that he would be approached, as he had been the most senior member of the Secretariat at the time. He found it strange that no one had approached him by the Sunday evening. He even called Johan Mostert, a senior officer, but was told the matter was in good hands and he need not do anything. He was also called by Van Rensburg at a later stage, but was very vague as to what they had talked about, merely remembering that Van Rensburg had asked about the signal. A few months later Van Rensburg called again, saying he thought he might have given the signal to Stemmet. As Navsa pressed him further on his conversations with Van Rensburg, Stemmet said twice that he had told Van Rensburg he had seen the signal. This was not mentioned in either of the affidavits he had made, because he had told the Attorney-General that he could not remember whether he had in fact seen the signal. But his memory seems to have been revived by Navsa's cross-examination. Thereafter all he would commit himself to was that the signal had looked remarkably familiar to him when he saw it in the newspaper.

When Glen Goosen questioned Stemmet the following morning about the dramatic language in the signal, he extracted a concession that the signal had been unusual. Stemmet added that 'if the compiler had meant anything other than what I understand by "permanently remove from society," then I don't understand why the signal was sent to the Secretariat.'

The following witness was Jan Vermaak of the DET. He had been to interview Goniwe on 24 May 1985 with the late Jaap Strydom and had sat on the Geldenhuys committee. As with other witnesses, he tried to shy away from the obvious meaning of the signal when we asked him what his view of it would have been as an Afrikaans teacher, had it been placed before the committee.

'What would you have thought it meant – the words as they stand there?'

'On the face of it, it can have a very negative meaning.'

'What is it, don't be shy, what is that meaning?'

'No, in that corner you're not going to put me so easily, I'm sorry.'

After some hedging, he said that he did not think the document had been meant for the eyes of the DET – thereby directly contradicting Van Rensburg.

'Whose eyes was it meant for?'

'I don't know. It's directed to Gen. Van Rensburg personally. In other words the DET was not involved in it.'

I kept questioning him as to what he would understand the signal to mean. He tried to get out of it but eventually conceded that the words '*permanent uit die samelewing verwyder*' [permanently remove from society] most probably meant that the persons had to be killed. Mostert spent considerable time in questioning him about semantics, trying to undo the damage and score some points of his own. He put definitions from a number of dictionaries to him and went as far as quoting from an old Dutch dictionary. All the witness was left to do was to say yes now and again.

Vermaak said that Col. McDonald of the Security Police was the only person in the Geldenhuys committee who voiced opposition to Goniwe's reinstatement, but that the eventual decision was a unanimous one. This reinforces one's suspicion that the involvement of the security forces in the committee was a sham. I questioned him about their view on reinstatement:

'In the security community there was a feeling that Mr Goniwe, as leader of Cradora and a member of the UDF, was one of the enemies of the state.'

'Correct.'

'And it was your experience that while you were battling to get him back in his right place, there were people who would maybe have said "over my dead body"?'

'It's possible.'

Next to enter the witness box was the chairman of the committee that supposedly had to decide about Goniwe's reinstatement, Brig. Geldenhuys. He was unimpressive. Geldenhuys's evidence was mostly concerned with technical details.

His committee's report makes mention of a short written input from the Eastern Province JMC. Geldenhuys said he could not remember the *'nooit ooit weer'* signal of 23 May but it was possible that this was the input referred to. I asked him whether the signal of 7 June was ever placed before the committee. He said no.

'And if it had been before your committee, you would certainly have remembered it?'

'I would.'

'Why?'

'Because it deviates quite drastically from what we were busy with. Here it was about reinstatement or not and then a signal arrives that doesn't deal with reinstatement at all. In other words we would have assumed – I am sure that I or another member would have gone back and said that the matter has now changed.'

Later I came back to the signal, but Geldenhuys was not going to admit easily what he understood it to mean. He eventually conceded that he would have considered the wording of the signal as rather unusual and would not have used it himself when referring to someone's transfer.

We returned on 14 June after a three-month postponement, ready to start Du Plessis's evidence. The indemnity board had initially refused him indemnity, but he had on F.W. de Klerk's intervention been granted indemnity for testifying about the signal. The situation was not ideal, but there was nothing we could do.

There was an air of anticipation and excitement in court. Mostert, whom one would have expected to be nervous in the face of testimony incriminating his client, seemed to have regained his composure. I knew why. He had invited me to his home. He could be friendly and charming in private if he thought his or his client's interests would be better served. He informed me that he had hard evidence that the police had killed Goniwe and not the defence force, whom he represented. He swore me to secrecy until he had made the evidence available in open court. In his study he set up a video screen and projected tests carried out by military experts which proved that the 1989 killing of three policemen and an informer at Motherwell in the Eastern Cape had been carried out by the police, not the ANC; they had been killed in order to prevent a leak that the police had planned the execution of Goniwe. He asked for my co-operation and support for his application to pursue what the judge might consider evidence irrelevant to the issue. Never before had there been such a split between army and police. I readily agreed.

On the resumption of the inquest Mostert asked permission to address the court and apologised in advance as he was going to be on his feet for some time. Information had been placed at his disposal and this information had led to the investigation of a number of avenues, he said. 'At this stage the indications . . . are that the police, and particularly the Security Police, should be investigated and examined to determine the existence of any complicity in the murder of Goniwe and the others whose murders are the subject of this inquest.'

Having dropped this bombshell, he went on at some length, drily discussing the nature of inquests and the admissibility of circumstantial evidence. He then placed before the court the record of a previous inquest into the deaths of the three policemen and informer near Motherwell in 1989. He read the affidavits of Capt. Gideon Nieuwoudt relating to the bomb. Nieuwoudt was an investigating officer in the Goniwe case and, as such, had been present in court almost every day. He was also an explosives expert.

Having read the affidavits, Mostert started drawing conclusions about them. Judge Zietsman, rather irritated by now, interrupted him:

'Does this have any relevance to Goniwe?'

'I am coming to that, M'Lord, I am coming to the reason why Your Lordship should investigate this to see whether there is any relevance to Goniwe. And perhaps I should – M'Lord, may I deal with the other matters first and then come to that question?'

Mostert was obviously enjoying himself. Nieuwoudt and Doep de Bruyn, counsel for the Security Police, obviously were not. Mostert came to the point when he said that a possible motive for the Motherwell bomb blast, for which he blamed Nieuwoudt, was that the deceased had been threatening to expose police responsibility for the Goniwe murders and had to be silenced.

Mostert asked that Nieuwoudt, Col. Winter and Col. Snyman be called as witnesses. He asked for Du Plessis's evidence to be postponed – also in order to allow them to get clearance for putting certain classified documents to him.

Judge Zietsman looked concerned: 'There is just one thing I would like to ask you there and that is, what you are in fact saying is that the signal that started the reopening of this inquest obviously involves the army, not the police. The signal as such. And up until now the spotlight has perhaps been on the army because of this particular signal.'

'Undoubtedly, M'Lord.'

'Now, is there any reason why the spotlight must now suddenly be shifted? Should we not carry on dealing with the signal question and can't this question of the police be dealt with later?'

This obviously would not have suited Mostert's purpose at all. He tried to pretend that it didn't really matter in which order the evidence was heard, but then said, "If there is police complicity in both of these murders, the longer you delay – let me say this: if there is police complicity it also means something else, that there has been police cover-up and the longer you delay . . .'

The judge interrupted: 'But I think whoever has been involved, there has been a cover-up.'

This flustered Mostert a little and he simply repeated that one had to avoid a cover-up by getting the police into the witness box as soon as possible.

After the short mid-morning adjournment, Judge Zietsman asked other counsel for their submissions.

I started off: 'Your Lordship correctly indicated that the focus was on the South African Defence Force up to now. Lest what I am about to say is misunderstood by anyone, I would like to make it clear that we on behalf of the family do not intend to allow that focus to be shifted and that focus will remain there. However, M'Lord, it would appear as a result of what my learned friend Mr Mostert has said, that the light can be turned in another direction and for the reasons that I am about to state, we support the application made . . .'

I supported his contention that a postponement would give the Security Police the opportunity to interfere with the investigation and possible witnesses. 'And let me finish off the way I started, M'Lord,' I concluded, 'and that is that we on behalf of the family will submit on the evidence and the information available to us, that it is not either/or, but it may well be that at the end of it, they are both responsible for the death of Mr Goniwe and his associates.' I was, however, very aware of unhappiness at the postponements we already had endured and knew that this change of direction would not be well received by everyone. I ended off by saying that this was a grave concern for us and that whatever the judge decided, we should get on with it.

Glen Goosen, counsel for Du Plessis, said that his client was ready to testify and would be so at any time. He supported Mostert's application.

For his part De Bruyn lashed out at Mostert, saying that 'the way my learned friend tried to implicate Mr Nieuwoudt is not only unfair but is a disgrace' in the light of the political climate. Little did he know that Mostert was on solid ground: not long after, Nieuwoudt was charged with the murder of his black colleagues at Motherwell. De Bruyn could not come up with a substantial reason why the sequence of witnesses should not change, but said that he would need to consult with Nieuwoudt before he could testify. Now suddenly there was no love lost between De Bruyn and Mostert. De Bruyn was very angry, understandably so, but came across as petulant and sulky.

Mike Hodgen supported the application and expressed his hope that this would lead to more witnesses coming forward. De Bruyn again expressed his concern about needing time to consult with both Nieuwoudt and Winter. Discussions followed about De Bruyn's consultation time, during the course of which Mostert cryptically said:

'M'Lord, I don't want to adumbrate or anticipate questions I am going to ask Col. Winter, but my crystal ball tells me that after half a dozen questions or more to Winter, he is going to stand down. I prefer not to say why now, M'Lord, but it will become obvious, Your Lordship will see. I make Your Lordship that promise and I will keep it.'

He did not keep the whole of his promise in the end.

Judge Zietsman directed that Nieuwoudt should take the stand the following morning, with Winter at hand in case De Bruyn was not ready to proceed with Nieuwoudt. Du Plessis was excused. At last the solidarity in the security forces seemed to have come to an end.

The following morning, the atmosphere in the public gallery was electric. The singing of freedom songs commenced again, this time with even more gusto. A Xhosa speaker would understand that the songs were none too complimentary about the witnesses-to-be. But there was immediate silence when proceedings began. De Bruyn looked in an even worse mood than the previous day. He announced that Nieuwoudt and his family had received death threats the previous night.

Because De Bruyn needed to consult with at least sixteen witnesses before he could lead Nieuwoudt's evidence, Col. Eric Winter was accordingly called. He was a stocky grey-haired man with a skin that had obviously seen much sun. He had been in charge of the Security Police in Cradock from March/April 1985 – three months before the murders – having been transferred directly from Namibia where he had been a member of the notorious Koevoet police unit since 1980. Other members of Koevoet were transferred to Cradock during the same period.

At the time of his testimony, Winter was a deputy district police commissioner in Port Elizabeth. He also sat on a local peace structure and tried to create the impression of being a moderate, or even rather progressive, man. Indeed, he went as far as to say he had been in favour of Goniwe's reinstatement, which would have made him a lone voice in the security establishment at the time. It seemed far-fetched to believe that an accommodationist was brought in from Koevoet to deal with the burning point of the security forces' problems. Winter later declared he believed in constructive dialogue with people who could make a difference. This sounded ridiculous coming from someone who had been transferred to the hotbed of unrest in the country on the eve of the first of many states of emergency, after eleven years' continuous service in Namibia.

Mostert asked me to agree that he cross-examine Winter first. I consented, knowing that Mostert would really lay 'r to him and perhaps even had some more information up his sleeve. He wanted to ask Winter about the Security Police memorandum of 25 June 1985 which had purportedly recommended the conditional reinstatement of Goniwe, and the court adjourned for a short while to allow him to read it. The singing and chanting of slogans resumed as soon as the judge left. On his return De Bruyn, already in a foul mood, objected to the noise in the public gallery, saying that it was intimidating the witness. The judge responded that he had not even been aware of any singing but said that if it were to continue, the public would be excluded. This was effective even though it dampened the mood of the spectators.

Winter soon showed himself to be a dishonest and evasive witness who would almost never commit himself to a firm answer – especially not an answer that would show he had had any problem with Goniwe. Because Mostert had a computer expert with him in court who put all their data on computer, including the record of every day's proceedings, he was later able to confront Winter with the extent of his evasiveness:

'You see, 135 times you said "I don't remember," 19 times you said "I don't have knowledge," which is virtually the same thing. Moreover you answered evasively 83 times and then there were answers like "I don't know," "No comment" and so on. Do you want to say anything?'

'M'Lord, I just want to say that I tried throughout to inform the court as well as I can and what I can and if I can't remember then that is that, then I can't remember it.'

'But you see then we get to incidents that also happened in the deep past, but the question holds no threat for you and then suddenly your memory is crystal clear.' To this, Winter had no reply.

When it first became known that Winter was to testify, Clive Plasket, our attorney, was contacted by Fred Koni, a retired security policeman who had been stationed at Cradock from 1978 to 1989. In the apartheid regime black security policemen were usually not made privy to sensitive information. Their white colleagues did not really trust them even though they were at times involved in their crimes. Hardly any one of them had previously taken the witness stand against their white superiors: they needed their jobs; they were afraid for their lives. Kani told Plasket that he had information regarding Winter's behaviour around the time of the murders.

According to Koni, Winter regularly exhorted his staff to try and gather evidence to get Goniwe convicted and sentenced to a long term of imprisonment, as detention had not worked in the past. Dirk Coetzee later told Jacques Pauw that the reason Griffiths Mxenge had been killed was that the police could not obtain enough evidence against him to bring him to trial and have him put away.

Goniwe was under virtually constant surveillance. One of Koni's tasks was to monitor telephone calls and letters to and from activists. The important tape recordings would be transcribed and the transcriptions sent on to Port Elizabeth and Pretoria, after Winter had decided about their importance.

The most important news Koni broke to us was that Winter ordered the monitoring of Goniwe to be stepped up at the beginning of June 1985. Snyman confirmed that this happened around May: further corroboration of the fact that the head office of the Security Branch had on 23 May 1985 urgently requested the Branch in Port Elizabeth to inform it of Goniwe's most recent activities.

Winter was made aware of Goniwe's calls regarding his proposed visit to Port Elizabeth on 27 June. The transcription of the call on the morning of the 27th was actually signed by Winter the same day. Immediately afterwards, according to Koni, he made a phone call and left the office with two colleagues. He did not say where he was going, contrary to his usual practice. Koni did not see them until the following day. On that day, 28 June 1985, Winter was already in the office when Koni arrived. He looked anxious and ordered Koni and his colleague Msoki to keep listening to Goniwe's telephone and not take their breaks together. Koni said that Winter kept coming over to ask what they had heard. He reported to Winter that a friend had called Mrs Goniwe to find out if Goniwe had arrived home. He also reported that WO Els had called the Branch to inform them that a Honda Ballade had been discovered burnt out and that none of the occupants could be found. Winter went into his office and came out later, saying, 'AZAPO het hulle gekry.'

I later put the circumstances of the murders to Winter. He conceded that it was a well-planned murder; that only someone wishing to lay a false trail would remove numberplates from a vehicle; that the dispersal of the bodies was a clever plan; that he didn't know of a group of people outside the security forces who could have carried out the murders in the manner in which they had been executed. When I asked him if his opinion was still that it had been AZAPO, Winter said no, he no longer thought so.

Koni eventually testified and disappointed us by being too eager and full of exaggeration. His testimony was not valued highly in the finding but at least his information gave us quite a bit of ammunition with which to cross-examine Winter. As already mentioned, Winter was vague and dishonest and his favourite answer was that he could not remember. But this tack also meant that he had a hard time refuting Koni's allegations if he supposedly could not remember the events referred to.

I decided to question Winter about Koevoet. Winter was taken aback when I asked him about a memorandum by the Bar Council of South West Africa that had been submitted to a commission of inquiry. It referred to a Supreme Court case and to testimony given by Winter himself on behalf of Koevoet members who had been accused of murder. Winter had testified that he had sent two people to 'warn' someone who had lodged complaints against Koevoet. One could see Winter wondering what else we knew. He said he could not remember the case and that the Bar Council might have been wrong. He could not explain why he would 'warn' people who laid complaints.

Jacques Pauw, in his book on death squads, In the Heart of the Whore, says the following about Koevoet: 'In Namibia, Koevoet was established in 1976 and concentrated on "offensive action in the tracking and eradicating of terrorists." In 1984 [while Winter was a member] Koevoet was described by Lieutenant-General Verster as a "cold, calculated, effective, and ruthless unit and the major thorn in the flesh of the SWAPO terrorists." Countering the claims of brutality levelled against Koevoet, the police claimed the controversy over this unit had arisen "for the simple reason that it was obliged to employ unorthodox methods."'

I asked Winter if he would agree with Verster. He said he would, and agreed that they had used unorthodox methods. Was Winter's transfer to Cradock a few months before the murders a coincidence?

Winter conceded under cross-examination by Glen Goosen that in transferring someone, head office would take into account that person's abilities and the needs of the place to which he was being sent. He agreed that he knew less of the UDF, the Eastern Cape and urban unrest than had his predecessor. The inference was clear – he had learnt other skills from Koevoet that would come in handy in the Eastern Cape.

The next morning I continued my cross-examination. It was clear from Goniwe's Security Police file that Winter must have received information from the investigating officer shortly after the burnt-out car and bodies were found. Winter admitted that this had been the case. This was a surprising lapse on the officer's part, seeing that fingers were already being pointed at the Security Police as possible suspects and such information would have helped them frustrate the investigation. The investigating officer, WO Els, was still on the case and was in court. He looked uncomfortable when I looked at him but gestured that as a warrant officer he would not have been able to deny Winter's request.

Winter continued to try to distance himself from the murders, denying much knowledge of the UDF and saying that, unlike other security policemen, he did not consider people throwing petrol bombs to be terrorists. He did, however, declare that Goniwe was an enemy of the state because his activities were aimed at making the country ungovernable. He also testified that he was never officially asked for his opinion as to what should happen to Goniwe. Winter declared that he never attended the meetings of the mini-JMC in Cradock, as they had no powers. Although he conceded, when questioned by Glen Goosen, that he was in agreement with the policy of fighting the revolutionary onslaught on all levels of society, he denied that it was because of his unwillingness to participate and work with civilians that the mini-JMC in Cradock had been a failure.

When Goosen asked him about counter-revolutionary theory, he had some harsh words for someone who believed in dialogue. He spoke about highly trained insurgents who had been schooled in Moscow, coming into the country and immediately descending on the population, committing the cruellest murders imaginable and destroying existing structures like tribal authorities. He agreed that to counter such an onslaught one had to have unity of effort and that this was the reason for the formation of the National Security Management System. He could not satisfactorily explain his lack of participation in the mini-JMC in the light of this. He conceded that the security forces played the leading role in the system.

Mostert recommended his cross-examination. We sat back with some satisfaction akin to a prosecutor when two accused, separately represented, each try hard to convict the other. Mostert took Winter through the planning of the murders. Winter admitted that the objective and prize of any well-planned murder was that the murderers should not be brought to trial. Mostert continued:

'Let's go back to everything we spoke about. The professional way in which this murder was planned and executed and where it was executed. Will you agree with me that the police had all the abilities to commit such a murder if they wished to?'

'That is correct, M'Lord.'

'Again, if the police . . . committed that murder, it would be one of the reasons, the fact that the police controlled the investigation, why the murderers still have not been traced after eight years, correct?'

'It can be so, M'Lord.'

'Can you tell me on another topic, you remember that you monitored the funeral of Goniwe?'

'That is correct, M'Lord.'

'And several people made rousing speeches.'

'That is correct, M'Lord.'

'Among others, Victoria Mxenge.'

'I can remember that.'

'That was one of the speeches that you monitored, correct?'

'It is possible, M'Lord. I don't know exactly what was monitored.'

'I only ask you this: is it complete coincidence, you monitor Goniwe and Goniwe is murdered, you monitor – may I just say Goniwe and his companions were murdered by being stabbed and shot. One was shot. Was it mere coincidence that you monitor them and it happens to them, and you monitor Victoria Mxenge and fifteen days later she is murdered and she is stabbed and shot? Is it mere coincidence?'

'It is not a coincidence; it is absurd, M'Lord.'

Was Mostert merely inferring that those who killed Goniwe also killed Victoria Mxenge or did he know for certain from the same source that had implicated Nieuwoudt in the Motherwell killings?

Mostert put some information to Winter about two bodies that had been found and had been thought possibly to relate to the Pebco Three's disappearance. More than that he could not offer after having kept us in suspense with hints about investigations and information and documents. He said he might at a later stage ask for the witness to be recalled. Nothing came of it in the end. Mostert must have been told by the highest authority to back off.

The following day saw Col. Snyman enter the witness box. At the time of the murders he was the commanding officer of the Eastern Cape division of the Security Branch. He is a weasly-looking fellow with a grey moustache. It was not the first time I had had dealings with him.

We did not think it possible for a witness to be more evasive than the previous inhabitants of the witness box, but Snyman managed to surprise us. Early on in cross-examination, he showed just how uncooperative he could be.

'Yes, you as a witness who has often given evidence, know that when your answer is "I can't remember" or "It may be so," it is of no value to the court?'

'It is possible, M'Lord.'

This after the question had been put for the third time.

Snyman conceded that sensitive matters would not have been discussed in the presence of civilians and that the police and army knew better about security matters. For instance, confidential information about how dangerous Goniwe was would have been kept in the inner circle of the top structures of the police and army. Snyman was chairperson of the Joint Intelligence Centre, a subcommittee of the Eastern Province JMC, consisting exclusively of security force members. He testified that there was close co-operation between the Security Branch and the army, to the extent that Adriaan Vlok was Deputy Minister both of Defence and of Law and Order.

Goosen questioned Snyman at length but he would not admit, as all the other witnesses so readily had, that he had considered Goniwe an enemy. He obviously feared that if he said Goniwe was an enemy, as he was described in the documents, it meant that Goniwe would have qualified for elimination.

'You have also accepted, if I understand your evidence correctly, that Mr Goniwe was busy fuelling the revolutionary climate in the country through his activities, correct?'

'Correct, M'Lord.'

'So you considered Mr Goniwe to be an enemy, correct?'

'M'Lord, yes, in such a case, possibly.'

'Not possibly. You considered Mr Goniwe to be an enemy.'

'I said in my testimony yesterday that he was considered to be of security interest due to his activities.'

'Yes. I want to put to you that your evidence of yesterday can't be correct in the light of what you just testified.'

'But we were talking about MK members now.'

'But you agreed with me and said that people who fuel the revolutionary climate make it easier for MK members to do their job, not so?'

'Correct, M'Lord.'

'So you accept that you saw Mr Goniwe as an enemy.'

'There was no information that he housed MK members.'

'No, but there was information that he fuelled the revolutionary climate.'

'He was definitely of security interest.'

'He was an enemy, Colonel.'

'He was of security interest, M'Lord.'

'Why are you scared to say you saw him as an enemy?'

No answer.

'You don't have an answer. Why are you scared to say he is an enemy?'

'Well, he acted against the state, that is clear.'

'Why are you scared to say you saw Mr Goniwe as the enemy?'

'I considered him to be of security interest and that is why we monitored him.'

'Colonel, you considered him to be the enemy. Why are you scared, as you sit there in the witness box, to say so?'

No answer.

'Do you have an answer, Colonel?'

'He was a danger to the state, a threat.'

'Colonel, do you have an answer to my question? Why are you scared to say that you considered Matthew Goniwe to be an enemy?'

'He was considered to be dangerous to the state.'

'Why are you scared – listen to the question – why are you scared to say that you saw Mr Goniwe as an enemy?'

'We considered him to be of security interest and dangerous to the state.'

'Colonel, what are you trying to hide? You don't want to use the word enemy.'

'I am not hiding anything, M'Lord.'

'Now why don't you say honestly that you considered Mr Goniwe to be an enemy?'

No answer.

Only when the judge intervened did he concede the obvious.

'Did you see him as an enemy?'

'I saw him as a danger to the state, M'Lord.'

'That is not what I asked. My question is, did you consider him to be an enemy of the state – yes or no?'

'One could describe it like that, M'Lord.'

'What is your answer?'

'Yes.'

Snyman was quite open about the fact that Goniwe was monitored daily by the Security Branch and that he would have been monitored up to the point of his murder. Snyman admitted that the police made use of false number-plates at times, but said that application to do so would have had to be made to him. No such application had been made but it was possible that a blind eye might have been turned to their use in Goniwe's case.

Snyman also conceded that the words in the signal were unusual words, which he would not expect in relation to detention. For the rest his testimony was so vague, its only value for us was to prove he was not a credible witness.

We were then kept busy for some considerable time with the policemen suspected of involvement in the Motherwell killings. There was contradictory evidence as to where the bomb must have been placed and we even had an inspection *in loco* of the underside of a Jetta motor car. Nothing of value to the Goniwe inquest came of it, but it was clear that there was a strong case against the Security Police and that they were lying to cover up. Nieuwoudt and others were subsequently charged and convicted of murder in the Motherwell case and sentenced to long terms of imprisonment.

What has still not emerged clearly is whether Nieuwoudt and others executed the three policemen and the informer near Motherwell in order to cover up the Goniwe murders. At Nieuwoudt's trial Brig. Eugene de Kock, the master assassin convicted of six murders and dozens of other offences, turned state witness and told the court that he had been persuaded to authorise the killings when he heard that the conspiracy of silence was in danger of being broken and the identity of the murderers of Goniwe would be revealed.

Three years earlier Clive Plasket, our attorney, was approached by a senior member of the Ciskei Defence Force and told that the wife of one of the Motherwell victims had informed him of an argument between her husband and Nieuwoudt in her house. They were both involved in stealing cheques posted to the South African Council of Churches and other anti-apartheid organisations which they were monitoring. The fraud squad was on their trail. Nieuwoudt threatened that the blame would be turned on her husband if he did not tow the line. The husband in turn threatened that if this happened he would disclose who had killed Goniwe.

An affidavit by the officer was put in reserve pending the filing of an affidavit by the wife. We were kept on a string for weeks. She eventually refused. The probable reason for her refusal, according to those close to her, was that she was receiving a special grant from the President's Victims of Terrorism Fund and feared she might lose it if it emerged that her husband had not been killed by the ANC. His wife was prepared to live with that. What did she think when it later emerged that he was blown up by the Security Police, whom he had so loyally served?

On 23 August 1993, five months after the inquest had begun, Du Plessis finally entered the witness box. We were a little nervous, because rumour had it that he had a drinking problem and we feared he would fare badly under cross-examination. He looked confident, dressed in what must have been his best suit.

Under cross-examination by Glen Goosen, Du Plessis testified that his chief, Van der Westhuizen, had called him in shortly after speaking to Van Rensburg in Pretoria and instructed him to send the signal. He did so immediately. There was no explicit mention of killing but he did not need to get clarity about what Van der Westhuizen meant. They had worked together closely for a number of years and understood each other well. He was adamant that the signal referred to killing Goniwe and the others. He said he would not otherwise have used the word 'permanent'. He could, however, not remember Van der Westhuizen's exact words, but declared that he would not have sucked them out of his thumb. Spelling out the implications was left to him. He said it would be absurd to think he would have done the whole thing on his own. He had not been surprised when he heard of the murders as he had expected some outcome from the sending of the signal, though he did not know who had been responsible for the actual deed.

Du Plessis confirmed that the prescriptions of McCuen and Fraser were followed in the Eastern Cape in respect of people considered to be the enemy. These authorities were often mentioned in conversations and at conferences. It was policy that people who could not be kept in check, of whom Goniwe was one, should be removed, either through detention or killing. He also confirmed that the security forces would hardly ever say directly that someone should be killed but would use veiled language.

In legal cases of this kind the general rule is that the party most adversely affected cross-examines first. We feared that Anton Mostert would go first and close the gap in advance of anything damaging that we could get out of Du Plessis. We were anxious to bind him firmly on the main issue that the signal was a request for a death warrant, before Mostert had a go at him. Mostert, by nature, would oppose anything we suggested. Thus when Goosen was done, and the judge asked us to cross-examine, I answered that Mostert should really have the first opportunity. Mostert got up and alluded to the warning about the Greeks given to the Trojans: 'We can expect no gifts from Mr Bizos and I would beware of anything even in the nature of a gift from Mr Bizos in relation to this witness and my client.' My trick had worked. It was hardly the first time an opponent had used similar words when I made any concession and I was ready with a retort in defence of the Greeks. 'M'Lord, may I say that we consider that Latin propaganda.' We were asked to start the cross-examination.

Du Plessis confirmed, when I cross-examined him, that the signal could fit within the dictum espoused by Brig. Fraser, who wrote that 'the use of terrorism by government forces must be decided on at the highest level and it must be so applied as to avoid it boomeranging'. He said the murders could be seen as terrorism and confirmed that the signal was sent to the highest authority and the implications were set out in order to avoid the operation boomeranging. He declared it was unlikely that such an act would have been committed without a request for it.

When the Deputy Attorney-General, Mike Hodgen, questioned him, Du Plessis confirmed that any decision about detention lay solely within the jurisdiction of the police. The system was, however, created to facilitate interdepartmental activities. But he could not recall that the decision reflected in the signal had ever been taken at an Eastern Province JMC meeting.

The judge intervened: 'Do you get the impression that Brig. Van der Westhuizen and Gen. Van Rensburg just decided on their own what should happen with Goniwe?'

'If I consider what I know or knew at that stage, then that must be my conclusion.'

'In other words that they virtually ignored all the other people who attended these JMC meetings and decided by themselves what must happen?'

'That is my impression.'

De Bruyn's cross-examination was bent on extracting concessions that the army also had the capacity to commit the murders. The disunity in the ranks of the security forces was working to our advantage.

Mostert started off with his cross-examination very aggressively. When Du Plessis answered that he did not stand by his first affidavit, Mostert said, 'Colonel, let us understand each other very well. It is your choice. You can be there for a day or you can be there for ten days. If you want the assurance that you'll be there for ten days, answer my questions in that manner. Answer my question and I will get you out of there as soon as possible.' He continued his harsh approach towards the witness. We hoped Du Plessis would bear up under the strain.

Almost all of Mostert's cross-examination of Du Plessis was a personal attack against him, with allegations of financial crises, deals with the ANC and a drinking problem. He also tried to get semantic concessions from Du Plessis, but left much of his testimony unchallenged. He did not put Van der Westhuizen's version of events to him. Mostert did, however, score a major victory at the end of his cross-examination when he extracted a confession from the battle-weary witness that he might have misunderstood Van der Westhuizen. This was bad enough for us but worse was to follow. The judge asked Du Plessis whether he could say how strong the possibility of a misunderstanding was and suggested that he could express it as a percentage. Du Plessis's hands began to tremble. He shook his head. He moved his lips twice without saying anything. We were hoping that he was working out a percentage which would convey nothing more than a theoretical possibility. With his head down Du Plessis answered, 'Probably a fifty-fifty chance, M'Lord.' He said he could not understand why he had not made sure whether he had it right. Mostert then triumphantly declared he had no further questions. When the court adjourned he could not resist rubbing it in by saying to his team in a loud voice that he wondered what we thought of our case now.

We were quite depressed. It felt as if all Du Plessis's evidence had been rendered valueless.

The widows of the Cradock Four had earlier asked us whether they could speak to Du Plessis, who on his own evidence had taken part in proposing their husbands' deaths. We advised them to wait until he had given his evidence. They met in the well-marbled hall outside the panelled courtroom. Du Plessis said he was sorry and asked to be forgiven. He tried to explain but the widows moved away. Mrs Goniwe regretted that she had not asked him at least one question, 'Where was your heart when you did this?'

Before Gen. Van der Westhuizen entered the witness box the following morning, Mostert announced that he had advised the witness not to answer questions put to him about Operation Katzen, but to claim privilege against self-incrimination. He would do the same in regard to the phrase in his affidavit 'neither I nor the Eastern Province JMC ever planned or approved the murder of any person'. Indeed, when it came to confirming his affidavit, he refused to confirm that section.

At the outset of our cross-examination Van der Westhuizen confirmed that the main purpose of his affidavit was to prove that he was innocent of the murders of Goniwe and the others. He admitted that he had presided at courts martial and was well aware of the privilege of non-incrimination – he did not need to be warned. We assumed that in order to avoid answering questions to which he had no answers, he would claim that he was not prepared to answer questions which might incriminate him.

We put Gen. Jannie Geldenhuys's redefinition of murder to Van der Westhuizen. He said it looked strange to him. After he had read Gen. Joep Joubert's covering affidavit, I asked:

'Will you agree that the four persons who were murdered at Bluewater Bay were attacked with non-standard-issue weapons?'

'I read that there a .22 rifle was used. That is a non-standard-issue weapon?'

'Knives, petrol, fuel, is not the conventional way the army works.'

'They are not conventional weapons, M'Lord.'

'Yes. And you will agree that the person or persons that murdered Goniwe, the murder was an attack on an individual enemy target with non-standard-issue weapons in an unconventional manner.'

'From the reports I have read, I will agree with you, M'Lord.'

'Do you agree?'

'Yes.'

'So that if members of the army under the control of members of the army, hypothetically speaking . . .'

'Yes.'

'If he wanted to do it, the way in which they were murdered can be placed within the definition?'

'Yes, I think that is correct, Advocate.'

We had managed to extract a very important concession from the most important witness. We were confident that at least the security forces would not get away with murder this time.

Van der Westhuizen said it was unlikely he would have used words such as those in the signal but could not categorically deny the possibility. When cross-examined on the signal he said that the language would not have offended him; his complaint would have been that it was not very clear. If he had seen it at the time he would have told Du Plessis that the latter had mis-understood him. But he conceded, when the judge questioned him, that Du Plessis would not have sent such a signal if he had not ordered it. He con-firmed that there must have been a call between him and Van Rensburg and that the signal was sent to confirm it. At a later stage he admitted that if he had told Du Plessis that Goniwe and the others had to be detained perma-nently, these were the words he would have used, not the ones in the signal.

Van der Westhuizen admitted too that the signal could be seen by an out-sider as a death warrant. But, he suddenly volunteered, it must have been the fatal signal of 7 June that was referred to in the Geldenhuys committee report as the input from the Eastern Province JMC. Mostert objected when I put to the witness that according to previous testimony the reference was probably to the 'nooit ooit weer' signal of 23 May and that the committee never saw the sig-nal of 7 June. Mostert then said that they would argue that the signal of 7 June did come before the committee. When the judge interrupted to declare that the evidence showed exactly the opposite, Mostert responded that the judge was drawing a conclusion without listening to him. Judge Zietsman replied that his questions were legitimate. Before I could continue, Mostert repeated at least three more times that the judge had already found against him.

Van der Westhuizen continued, saying the signal was in fact the input to the committee. But he claimed he would not have told Du Plessis that Goniwe had to be killed. He had to concede, however, that as he could not remember his conversation with Du Plessis, he also could not deny Du Plessis's allegation that the signal referred to murder. He admitted that the signal would have been sent as soon as the order had been given. He said later that if the conversation had taken place in the morning, Du Plessis would not have waited until the afternoon to send the signal. This meant that the discussion between Van Rensburg and him must have taken place around 2 p.m., not in the morning before the Geldenhuys committee started sitting. By that time Van Rensburg would have known which way the committee was leaning. It seemed plain that if there was to be a recommendation to reinstate, the securocrats had their own way of eliminating the enemy.

We scored another substantial victory, with some help from the judge, the following morning. We asked Van der Westhuizen whether the permanent detention of Goniwe, if that were ever possible, would have resolved the problems or not.

'I don't think it would have resolved the complete problems [sic], M'Lord, because I'm not sure how long permanent detention lasted. I think it was six months but I may be wrong.' He added: 'Yes, M'Lord, I think a man goes into detention and if he comes out, then his actions for which he was placed in detention just continue, so I don't think it would have been a solution. It could possibly only have been an alternative during a discussion and it could have been someone's opinion.'

'So it wasn't your opinion on the 7th that your problems here in the Eastern Cape could be solved if Mr Goniwe and his "militant lieutenants" were permanently detained?'

'No, I think it would only have addressed the problem temporarily.'

The judge intervened: 'Were you at that stage on 7 June in favour of the detention of Goniwe and the other men?'

'M'Lord, again, if I have to rely on my recollection, as I say I was in favour of his not being reinstated.'

'Yes, but were you in favour of their being detained?'

'Not that I can remember.'

Again he had to try and cover himself. He attempted to say that what must have happened was that Van Rensburg asked him for alternatives to the Security Police's view of 23 May and he suggested detention as a result. But the signal does not set out alternatives. We put this to him: 'It is completely wrong if Van Rensburg asked you what the alternatives are, the signal is a totally wrong reaction to what you would have said to Du Plessis.'

'It would appear so.'

Judge Zietsman said that he had problems with Van der Westhuizen's testimony and just wanted to understand him properly. He asked him whether he was saying that he had only mentioned detention as one option.

Mostert objected: 'M'Lord, I am trying really hard not to be on my feet this morning, but Your Lordship has put to the witness that "your evidence is this and this and this."'

The judge responded that he was asking the witness whether he understood his evidence correctly and he was fully entitled to do so.

Mostert would not rest: 'But M'Lord, . . . everything with his evidence is that he has no recollection and all these are hypotheses and I would be grateful to Your Lordship, my learned friend has done that, and I would be grateful if Your Lordship also puts it on that basis. He is dealing with a series of hypotheses and no more.'

Van der Westhuizen tried to undo the damage he had created earlier when he recalled his opinion that detention would not resolve the problem, by saying that he could not remember at all what his view about detention had been.

Judge Zietsman was frustrated. 'See, I find it very strange. This was a very serious problem that everyone sat with. They had to decide what must happen to Goniwe and I find it very strange that you tell us every now and then that you can't remember at all. You can't remember anything about the telephone conversation, you can't remember what you would have said to Du Plessis, you can't remember what order you would have given Du Plessis.'

Van der Westhuizen's explanation was that he had been very busy at the time. Shortly after the signal was sent he had time to go on leave, however. He was on his hunting farm in 'South West Africa', as he still called it, and only returned on 15 July 1985.

What had happened at the time the signal was published? Van der Westhuizen said he was telephoned at home on 2 or 3 May 1994 by Gen. Kat Liebenberg, then Chief of the Army, who asked him if he knew of any involvement with the report about Goniwe. Van der Westhuizen said he then went to Sun City for a week and only saw the New Nation report on 9 May. He seemed to have convenient times for his holidays. Although he was implicated in the first New Nation report, no one, he testified, contacted him until the following Saturday, after the signal was published. At that stage he was Chief of Military Intelligence. He did not use any of the sources available to him to try and find the signal. He did not call Du Plessis to find out what was going on. He was taken straight to attorney Wagener's office when he returned. He made a statement without any preliminary investigation.

We asked Van der Westhuizen whether he had ever asked Van Rensburg where the signal was. He said the matter was discussed but he could not remember if he had asked him. He may have done so in a Port Elizabeth hotel in the presence of the legal team when they were all together at the beginning of the inquest. He had not asked Van Rensburg at the time of publication.

It was Goosen's turn to cross-examine Van der Westhuizen. Goosen moved on to covert operations and read to him from an American dictionary of military terms, in which covert actions are defined as being 'so planned and executed as to conceal the identity of or permit plausible denial by the sponsor'. Van der Westhuizen agreed that these two aspects would be considered in the planning of a covert operation. He said that one of the ways the planners of covert operations could conceal their identities was by using non-standard-issue equipment or weapons. He also declared that one of the ways in which plausible denial could be established was by the use of a cover story.

'Given these core aspects of a covert operation, you will agree with me that the murder of Mr Goniwe and the other three can be seen as a covert operation?'

'Yes.'

'For example, we don't know today who was responsible.'

'Correct.'

'You will then also probably agree that it appears to have been a very well-executed covert operation?'

'Yes, there at least must have been thorough reconnaissance.'

'There must have been reconnaissance, there had to be thorough planning of the equipment that was used. You probably know that a Gevarm .22 rifle was used.'

'Yes.'

Then Van der Westhuizen made a major concession.

'General, can you think of anybody that possesses all those abilities and characteristics needed to have committed the murders?'

'M'Lord, the South African Police and the defence force.'

'So you accept that the army also had all of those abilities and characteristics?'

'Yes, M'Lord.'

'Yes. Can I deduce from your answer that the bodies you mentioned are bodies that form part of the security forces?'

'Yes, M'Lord.'

'Correct. There is no other body that you can mention?'

'That had all the abilities?'

'Yes.'

'For the planning and reconnaissance, no, M'Lord.'

'So you agree that it could have been the police or the army that was responsible for the murder of Goniwe and the others?'

'Yes, M'Lord.'

He agreed that the elimination of key members of the insurgency was always a possible option and that it would be a tactical or strategic decision whether this was done. Such a decision would be taken at a high level – at least at the level of the State Security Council. He conceded that if the army wanted to recommend that someone be killed, this suggestion would be addressed to the highest authority. He accepted too that a decision in principle about the killing of activists would be taken at a strategically coordinated level, though the actual operation would lie with a line function department and not with a central organ such as the State Security Council. Such an operation would necessarily be covert. He agreed that the cover-up story that AZAPO had been responsible for the killings was very effective: it had lasted through the first inquest and was still being espoused.

Van der Westhuizen admitted that before stepping into the witness box he had never mentioned the fact that Du Plessis might have made a mistake. Nor could he remember any other case where Du Plessis had completely misunderstood him. The fifty-fifty concession made by Du Plessis was looking much less problematic for us in the light of Van der Westhuizen's testimony. He also doubted whether AZAPO would have had the ability to execute such an operation, even though they may have had the intention. Goosen asked him whether he would agree that if a body not involved in the conflict between the UDF and AZAPO wanted to take covert action against members of either, the conflict and mutual bloodletting would offer ideal cover for such action. Van der Westhuizen agreed. He also agreed that the security forces, having the ability to take covert action against Goniwe, would also have been able to act in such a way that the murders would appear to have been committed by one of the conflicting groups.

When Mostert re-examined Van der Westhuizen he failed to undo the damage. Even if he was not indicted, Van der Westhuizen knew that his career had come to an end, a serious blow for the handsome and debonair young general who aspired to become the Chief of the South African Army. On 31

March 1994, two months before the judge's finding was handed down, Van der Westhuizen retired as Chief of Military Intelligence for 'medical reasons' – a reason given by a number of high office-bearers in order to secure a full pension. Never had so many Generals been afflicted by poor health within such a short period of time.

Testimony of a few peripheral witnesses was completed in September 1993. The final record ran to three and a half thousand pages. We faced the daunting task of preparing our argument. In February 1994 we reconvened. It had been almost a year since the inquest had begun.

Arguing first, we said that Gens. Van der Westhuizen and Van Rensburg together with Cols. Du Plessis, Snyman and Winter planned and carried out the murders. We spoke about the circumstances of the deaths and who had the means and motive to commit the murders; about the signal and the lack of follow-up to it; the patent lie that the signal was meant for the Geldenhuys committee; the destruction of documents. We discussed counter-revolutionary theory and Van der Westhuizen's testimony relating to a strategic decision being taken at the top. We discussed the pressure on Van der Westhuizen placed by Goniwe's increased activities and profile and the resulting intensification by the police of their monitoring of Goniwe. Seeing that the Security Police would have monitored him on the day of his death, his disappearance could only have taken place with their knowledge and connivance if they themselves had not done the actual killing.

We argued that the judge should believe Du Plessis's version of events. We put the fifty-fifty concession in the context of three and a half days of cross-examination and threats. Then we dealt with Van der Westhuizen's evidence. Mostert had obviously realised that he was facing a serious problem and had argued that his client had been 'good on fact but bad on hypothesis'; he was a 'poor conceptual thinker', who had had a hard time picking his way through a minefield of hypotheses. This was the Chief of Military Intelligence whom Mostert was talking about. We pointed out how Van der Westhuizen's lapses of memory concerned important facts, not trivialities. We argued that his affidavit was cleverly drawn up in order to leave his options open.

The following morning Mostert dropped a bombshell. He said he had the previous night received a fax from Gen. Van Rensburg enclosing a statement by him. He declared he could not tell the judge what was in the statement as it was privileged. That morning, he went on, he had faxed a letter to Van Rensburg, withdrawing as his counsel. All he would say was that it was a Bar rule that when a client departs substantially from a previous version, counsel is obliged to withdraw. Van Rensburg would have to decide whether he wanted to engage new counsel before any further steps could be taken.

We decided to carry on until we had word from Van Rensburg. Navsa and I continued with our argument. It was rather strange carrying on as if nothing was amiss, when we all wondered what Van Rensburg was up to. We managed nevertheless to do some damage to Van der Westhuizen's and Van Rensburg's credibility in our argument. The following morning Hodgen announced that he had been informed that Van Rensburg had engaged a new attorney and counsel.

The news was that Van Rensburg was terminally ill and that he had not long to live. We thought of the possibility that his conscience had led him to come clean and he would tell us whom he had handed the signal to, who had killed the Cradock Four, and confirm that the Geldenhuys report was a charade. How naive we were. Instead he stuck to his story that the signal was not a request for a death warrant, and gave a long, hardly comprehensible and contradictory account of what he had done with the signal. Nobody took his new explanations seriously. We wondered how such a foolish man could have risen to the rank of General and secretary of the Secretariat of the Security Council. I was reminded of the aphorism that tyrants towards their end are served primarily by fools, thugs or eunuchs. Mostert was heard to mutter at the end of his evidence: 'With Generals like him, no wonder we lost.' He was concerned about the political fall-out. In informal discussions about dates he asked the judge to consider delaying his judgment beyond the general election that was to be held in April 1994. Judge Zietsman said he would deal with the matter without regard to such extraneous factors.

Towards the end of the proceedings Mostert applied to the judge to recuse himself. The grounds advanced were hardly worth serious consideration. The application was an attempt to take the sting out of the adverse findings which were likely to be made. Judge Zietsman's patience was being put to the test, but the dignified manner in which he suffered the attacks on him was exemplary.

Mostert's argument was lengthy and thorough. Every possible contradiction or improbability in any evidence favourable to us was drawn to the judge's attention. Excuses for the shortcomings of their witnesses' amnesia, contradictions and highly improbable conduct were advanced. In reply we stressed the inherent improbabilities in their versions and persisted in our submission that Gens. Van Rensburg and Van der Westhuizen as well as Cols. Snyman and Winter should be found guilty of having conspired to kill the Cradock Four.

We returned to Port Elizabeth on Saturday, 28 May 1994 for the reading of the finding. The public gallery was packed with friends, family and community members of the victims, members of the public and journalists. It had been a long haul and we were hoping for the best. A hush fell over the courtroom as the judge entered, sat down and started reading.

He commenced by saying that the only matter he had to decide upon was whether in terms of the Inquest Act 'the death was brought about by any act or omission *prima facie* involving or amounting to an offence on the part of any person'. We had anticipated that the technical nature of this test was to prove quite important to him, and had argued at length about it. After setting out the facts, the judge borrowed from Arthur Chaskalson's argument in the first inquest, saying that 'whoever planned and carried out the murders had to have the ability to formulate such a plan and the resources to carry it out'. He then went further than Arthur had dared to go and declared that 'the South African security forces, which included the police, the Security Police and the army, had the necessary ability and resources'. We felt more confident of getting the finding we had argued for. The judge went on to say there was no evidence that AZAPO had the ability to carry out the murders and that witnesses including Van der Westhuizen had opined that it could only have been the security forces. In any event AZAPO would not have considered it necessary to go to such lengths to try and avoid the identification of their victims.

Judge Zietsman discussed the evidence regarding police involvement extensively and concluded that it 'raises a suspicion that Col. Snyman and Col. Winter knew that Matthew Goniwe and the others were to be murdered and that they could have taken part in the planning of the murders', but that the evidence did not establish a *prima facie* case as required by the Act. We were disappointed but had not realistically expected a positive finding against the police. We were hoping for, and had strenuously argued for, a finding of conspiracy or incitement to murder by Gens. Van der Westhuizen and Van Rensburg as well as Col. Du Plessis even though he was indemnified.

After dealing with Operation Katzen, Judge Zietsman discussed at length Van Rensburg's evidence about the fate of the signal. He concluded that 'the evidence surrounding the signal is in practically every important respect unsatisfactory'. No other conclusion had in any event been possible. He then set out a number of facts about the signal and said that these 'support the submission made by certain of the counsel appearing at this inquest that this was not the innocent signal suggested by Mr Mostert, and by Maj.-Gen. Van Rensburg in his evidence'. We were heartened by this. He further found that Col. Du Plessis had intended the words in the signal to mean that Goniwe and the others should be killed and that this was also the meaning Gen. Van der Westhuizen intended should be conveyed in the signal.

We knew that the only hurdle we were still facing was the link between the signal and the murders that had bothered Judge Zietsman so much during argument. Our fears were realised when he said: 'the problem is that we do not know what happened to the signal after it had been received by Maj.-Gen. Van Rensburg. The evidence of Maj.-Gen. Van Rensburg is contradictory and unsatisfactory, but a rejection of his evidence does not justify a finding that the signal was sent on to higher authority and was then acted upon. There is no evidence to prove that the recommendation of the signal was adopted and carried out. There is no evidence to prove that the person or persons who murdered Matthew Goniwe and the others knew of the signal or its content. Evidence to link the signal with the murders is lacking and the set-up of the National Security Management System does not in itself justify the assumptions and inferences I have been urged to make.'

It was ironic that Van Rensburg had succeeded in his purpose, despite his evidence being rejected. We knew we had lost any chance of a recommendation that Van der Westhuizen and Van Rensburg be charged with conspiracy to murder. Judge Zietsman went on to say that it was not his task to speculate on possible offences which had not been proved to have brought about the deaths as required by the Act. 'I accordingly decline to comment upon whether there is *prima facie* proof that an offence such as conspiracy to murder or incitement to murder has been committed, in the absence of evidence to show a link between such possible offence and the death or deaths of one or more of the four deceased persons.'

He concluded by saying that the murderers were members of the security forces and that a case of suspicion had been made out against certain members of the police force including Snyman and Winter, and against Van der Westhuizen, Du Plessis and Van Rensburg, 'but suspicion does not constitute *prima facie* proof'. This would require some link between the deaths and acts committed by the persons under suspicion, which the evidence led did not establish. In the formal finding he concluded with no mention made of the security forces. He merely said: 'I am not able, on the evidence placed before me, to identify the murderer or murderers.' There was a groan of disbelief and disappointment from the public gallery.

Our clients were, in Nyameka Goniwe's words, 'terribly disappointed'. She told reporters she was 'delighted' that the judge had placed the blame on the security forces and said she was trying to think positively about the finding, but she had hoped for more. She spoke for all four widows when she said: 'I can't forgive and forget, or go on with my life until I know the actual killers. We cannot close this chapter yet. Our lives have been involved in this case for years. I don't know how it feels to be without it. The crucial thing is to know who did what. We know the reasons, but we want to know who actually did it.'

Mbulelo Goniwe's wife commented that 'in the spirit of the reconciliation mood we are not suggesting revenge against the people who were involved, but we want to know exactly what happened on the night of June 27, 1985'. Nyameka Goniwe added that she hoped there would be some kind of mechanism to deal with their pain.

The split between South Africa's Afrikaans and English language press was clear from the following day's headlines. 'Security forces did kill Goniwe,' said the *Sunday Times*'s front page; 'Signal for death' was the large headline of the *Weekend Post*; 'Permanent removal indeed meant death,' read the *Sunday Nation*. 'Signal was plot to kill,' the *Sowetan* announced on Monday. 'Nie genoeg getuienis in Goniwe saak,' [Not enough evidence in Goniwe case] read the headline of *Rapport*, the National Party mouthpiece.

Les Roberts, Attorney-General of the Eastern Cape and Mike Hodgen's senior, was to decide on the possible prosecution of those involved in the signal. A few weeks later he announced that he would not prosecute anyone for the Goniwe murders or for conspiracy or incitement. 'The available evidence is not strong enough for a reasonable chance of a successful prosecution against any individual or individuals,' he said. 'If any further evidence comes to light which could strengthen the chances of a prosecution on any of these charges, then this decision will be reconsidered.' He added that he was still investigating the Motherwell case.

Ours was a partial victory in that for the first time in South African legal history it had been found that the security forces were not above murder and that they were in fact responsible for the murder of Matthew Goniwe, Fort Calata, Sparrow Mkonto and Sicelo Mhlauli. But we were disappointed, if not surprised, that the judge had not gone beyond the strict letter of the law. No prosecutions would follow. No one would be held accountable. In the eyes of the law, no one was to blame.

In asking Judge Zietsman to hold Harold Snyman and Eric Winter responsible for the deaths of the Cradock Four we were not far wrong. In the mid-1990s six Port Elizabeth security policemen applied for amnesty for the murder of the Cradock Four: E.A. Taylor, G.J. Lotz, N.J. Janse van Rensburg, H. Snyman, J.M. van Zyl and H.B. du Plessis, while Eugene de Kock applied for amnesty as an accessory after the fact. De Kock insists that Col. Eric Winter was involved even though Van Zyl and the other killers have kept Winter out of it, probably because they thought him incapable of sustaining the half-truthful version they would offer to the amnesty committee.

In their applications Snyman and the others declared that the order to kill came from Snyman. Because he was too ill to appear at the amnesty hearings, the killers, taking advantage of this, said that they were sure that a soft-hearted man like Snyman could not have initiated the plan but that the order must have come from high up. None of them visited him on his sick bed to ask him who had authorised it nor did the attorney and counsel acting for them. We suggested at the amnesty hearings that the very least they could do was to take a short affidavit from the bedridden Snyman saying who had authorised the killings. But the invitation was not accepted.

Gen. Joffel van der Westhuizen did not apply for amnesty for the Cradock Four killings although he did so for other crimes which he committed. He was apparently confident that he would not be charged with incitement to murder or conspiracy.

Whilst preparing to oppose the applications for amnesty we received a copy of a statement by Jacob Jan Hendrik van Jaarsveld, known as 'Jaap' to his friends. He disclosed that in the middle of 1984 he received an order from Major Craig Williamson, the head of Intelligence of the Security Police in Pretoria, to investigate if it was possible to 'take out' Matthew Goniwe. (He added that it meant to kill him.) Van Jaarsveld had worked in the Secretariat of the State Security Council before being transferred to the Intelligence section headed by Williamson. Van Jaarsveld travelled to Port Elizabeth with Col. Gerrit Erasmus, who also assigned ex-Koevoet member Sakkie van Zyl. They first went to Henry Fouché, the head of the Security Police in Cradock, who proudly showed them the room in which the bugging of Goniwe's home was monitored. They also went to the Goniwe house where they found Mrs Goniwe. No special reason was given to her: she was accustomed to raids of her home. Here Fouché showed Van Jaarsveld where the microphones were hidden. On his return to Pretoria the next day he reported to Williamson that Goniwe could not be killed at home. There were too many people in the vicinity who might compromise the operation but suggested that he should be followed and killed along the way elsewhere.

Van Jaarsveld's recommendation must have been borne in mind. When more than a year later Goniwe was finally killed he was stopped on the road from Port Elizabeth.

Van Jaarsveld thought that Williamson's orders came from Brig. Piet 'Biko' Goosen or Brig. Herman Stadler of the Security Police. In his opinion, based on his knowledge of the workings of the Security Council Secretariat, it was possible that they authorised the killings. Retired army general Van Rensburg was in fact a serving policeman and Stemmet was his second-in-command. Had Van Jaarsveld's evidence been given before Judge Zietsman the nexus between the army and the police might have been established in court.

Van Jaarsveld's evidence, however, was denied by Craig Williamson, who said the former was more suited for academic assignments rather than surveillance of this sort. But he would not name anyone in his section who was well suited for the job. Williamson's testimony was made in cross-examination in his own application for amnesty for the bombing of the London office of the ANC and the murders of Ruth First and Jenny and Katryn Schoon. The main applicant for amnesty for the London bombings was the head of the Security Police, Gen. Johann Coetzee, who was Police Commissioner at the time of Goniwe's death. He, like Williamson, maintained that the police had done nothing unlawful within the country. This opened the door for us to ask how the system worked and what they knew of the many hundreds of deaths of their 'enemies' within and outside the country. We heard of meetings of the 'sanhedrin' and target identification committees. Whoever chose the name 'sanhedrin' apparently knew the real purpose of the meetings of the heads of the Security Police sections, which were attended from time to time by guests from the army and National Intelligence. Was this where authority was given to kill the Cradock Four? Gen. Coetzee, who presided over the sanhedrin from 1980 to 1983 and who, as Commissioner of Police from 1983 to 1987, would have known about its functions, was not keen to give us information about how decisions to kill were made.

In his evidence before the TRC, Coetzee avoided all questions relating to killings by saying that he was not prepared to give answers to general questions, but would only respond to specific instances. We were ready to deny him this easy way out. We put to him one case after the other drawn from Jacques Pauw's book *Into the Heart of Darkness*. Gen. Coetzee was adamant: he denied any knowledge of them. 'I never gave an instruction that someone should be assassinated, or killed, inside or outside the country,' he declared.

To rebut his assertion we asked him to read an account from De Kock's autobiography of a 1986 police raid into Swaziland in which they killed three people and seized ANC documents. Having completed their task the group arrived at Coetzee's home at 5.30 a.m. and found him in his dressing gown. He shook everybody's hand. De Kock says, 'When he got to me he said he did not know whether he should touch my hands since they were covered in blood.' Like so many others, Coetzee was not prepared to contradict De Kock directly in cross-examination. He fudged an account of the event in order to deny the obvious, that as commander of the Vlakplaas unit, the execution squad of the apartheid regime, De Kock had killed many people.

We asked, 'Did you ever suspect the deaths of so many ANC people inside and outside the country may have been the work of members of your police force?'

'I did not suspect the police force was involved.'

'If you drew up a list of suspects, who would be number one suspect, organisationally?'

'I don't know, sir.'

'You are one of the most experienced policemen the country has ever produced, General; please tell us!'

'It could be anyone. It could be an outside agency, that was involved in the East–West situation. There were many allegations made, for instance, against the CIA.'

'Did it come to your knowledge that the ANC Swaziland representative was blown up in 1982?'

'Yes, it must have come to my notice.'

'Who did you think was the fairy godmother who got rid of yet another ANC chief representative in another country?'

In the *Sunday Times* that appeared after this testimony, the once debonair and overconfident Gen. Coetzee was pictured as holding his head under his ruffled toupee and described as a 'wimpy warrior'. Under the heading 'Mampara of the week' the paper commented, 'Isn't it sad how the ruthless leather-booted blue-shirts of the old police force have been reduced to pathetic whimpering mamparas before the Truth Commission.'

Craig Williamson must have decided that he was not going to be called a mampara the next week. He admitted that he realised that ANC activists in and outside the country were being killed by the security forces. He was adamant that he did not take part in any of these killings. He was obviously disappointed with the evidence of Coetzee, who said that he would not have authorised the killings of First and the Schoons. Coetzee also declared that Williamson was guilty of breaching the trust he had in him and that if he had found out what Williamson had done he would have disciplined or even charged him. Williamson was non-committal in his responses. Although his mentor had let him down he remained loyal and true to Coetzee to the end.

The six security policemen who applied for amnesty for taking part in the murder of the Cradock Four were joined by a seventh applicant, Eugene de

Kock. Although he did not take part in the murder of Goniwe and his friends, he applied for amnesty as an accessory after the fact of their murder because Sakkie van Zyl had asked him to use his good offices with the police forensic laboratory in Pretoria to remove any evidence to connect the rare gun that killed Sparrow Mkonto with other crimes. He agreed to do so. It was Van Zyl's revelation to De Kock that helped flush out the six murderers.

The story told by all of them was that the order to kill Goniwe and his colleagues was given approximately two to three weeks before the murders. If true, this corresponds with the dispatch of the signal on 7 June to the Secretariat of the Security Council that they should be removed permanently from society as a matter of urgency. This evidence created a high degree of probability that there was full co-operation between army intelligence, a probability not sufficiently established in the second inquest to enable Judge Zietsman to come to a definite conclusion. That there was army and police collaboration in murders became apparent from the evidence of Williamson and his application for amnesty for the murders of Ruth First and the Schoons.

But as we have seen, the plan to kill Goniwe was not originally hatched in 1985 but more than a year earlier in March 1984 when Van Jaarsveld received instructions from Williamson to go to the Eastern Cape to investigate the possibility of killing him. If head office had sent Van Jaarsveld in 1984 to arrange for the killing of Goniwe, why should the superiors of Van Zyl, Snyman and Van Rensburg not have been told about it? How did it come about that the killings were actually carried out in the manner suggested by Van Jaarsveld? We asked the amnesty committee to find that Snyman, Van Rensburg and Van Zyl knew this.

The applicants could not make up their minds as to who gave the order to kill Goniwe and 'his hangers-on'. In one version the plan appeared to have originated between Van Zyl and Du Plessis and was taken to Van Rensburg, who suggested that they approach Snyman as their officer commanding. They went to Snyman, who according to one of the versions said, 'Do what is the best for South Africa.' The applicants could not, however, make up their minds about who was meant to be killed. One said it was the Cradock Four, another Goniwe and five or six others in the discretion of those that were to put the plan into operation. When it became clear that Snyman would not be giving evidence, they all testified that Snyman would not have taken the decision on his own. Instead they suggested that it must have been Minister Louis le Grange, who had since died. No one suggested that it might have been Minister Adriaan Vlok, who had presided over a meeting of police and army commanders the day before the signal was sent asking for a death warrant.

Their difficulties were compounded by their knowledge that the Geldenhuys committee had sat at the same time and was considering a recommendation to the Minister as to whether Goniwe should be reinstated. They had no answer to the question, How can you assume that the authority to kill came from the top if you knew that a recommendation had been made that he should be reappointed? In reply they seriously suggested the ludicrous answer that this subcommittee of the Secretariat of the Security Council was dealing with a political matter raised by Deputy Minister De Beer, whereas they had a grave responsibility to maintain the security of the state. The conclusion is inescapable that the order came from the top, that the Geldenhuys committee was a sham intended to appease Sam de Beer with a decision to reappoint Goniwe. The hawkish generals, brigadiers and colonels were planning to kill Goniwe and anyone else that was with him at the time, and blame it on AZAPO. How could anyone therefore blame the government for the killings? Even Gen. Coetzee, the Commissioner of Police, had recommended in a confidential memorandum that he should be reappointed. Who could have thought of a more neat and ingenious way of getting rid of an enemy and at the same time reconciling the opposing tendencies within the National Party?

From evidence before the TRC and a number of amnesty applications it became clear that such decisions were made at the highest authority. Gen. Coetzee and Craig Williamson said so in so many words. Unhappily for the administration of justice, both suffered from amnesia when asked who was present at meetings where such matters were discussed. Neither Coetzee nor Williamson remembered any discussions about any killings within the country. Although Williamson admitted that there was a target identification committee that would identify who was to be killed, he was only concerned with actions outside the country and could not name a single person who sat on such a committee. Was Van Jaarsveld sent by Williamson to Cradock after the target identification committee brought Goniwe within its sights?

Another unanswered question was whether Sicelo Mhlauli was killed because he was a high-profile activist or just because he was there, as suggested by Arthur Chaskalson at the first inquest. Whatever reasons the Security Police may have had to kill the others, we established almost beyond any reasonable doubt during the course of the amnesty hearing that Mhlauli, who came from Oudtshoorn, was killed because he happened to be in the company of Goniwe. In their amnesty applications, Snyman, Van Rensburg and Du Plessis were unequivocal in their assertions that all four of the victims were identified and prioritised by the sharpened information-gathering functions of the JMC. The decision to include Mhlauli was based on the fact that he was a leadership figure and activist in the south-western Cape and in regular contact with Goniwe.

Despite the contents of their written amnesty applications, the oral evidence of the applicants before the committee shifted significantly so as to become consistent with the amnesty application of Van Zyl. The latter claimed that Van Rensburg originally ordered that Goniwe and 'his closest cohorts' were to be eliminated and that he and Du Plessis had referred specifically to Goniwe, Calata and Mkonto. Although Van Zyl claimed that they already had information that Mhlauli, under the leadership of Goniwe, was in the process of furthering the aims of the UDF, he was only identified for elimination in the two or three weeks' monitoring period prior to the actual murders. The applicants laid it on thick. Mhlauli was said to have been a pivotal figure in the organisation in Oudtshoorn, furthering the aims of the UDF and introducing the Goniwe plan into the south-western Cape; he was recruiting youths for training abroad (although they had the grace to say that they could not verify this information); he was in regular contact with Goniwe; and he visited Cradock often and attended Cradora meetings. On the evidence we were able to submit that the applicants were not only lying about the nature and extent of Mhlauli's political involvement, but were also lying about the crucial fact that, far from his being a priority target for elimination, they did not even know or care who he was prior to and at the time of his death.

In order to defeat their applications for amnesty we concentrated on Mhlauli's case. We tried to establish that without a Security Police file in existence relating to Mhlauli they were hard put to explain how they could have identified him as a priority target. The applicants believed that the documents relating to the murders had been destroyed. But they were wrong. In the Attorney-General's possession a copy of a telegram was found dated 2 July 1995 in which the local Security Police wrote to Security Police headquarters to report the deaths of the Cradock Four. There was information about the three. About Mhlauli the word 'onbekend' [unknown] stood out starkly. How could they maintain that they had killed him because he was a high-profile activist?

Consistent with the applicants' duty to tell the truth, it would have been better for them to say that they did not know who Mhlauli was; that he was present, and if they killed one, they had to kill all, and this was their only opportunity to eliminate Goniwe. If they had argued this version they could even have claimed Mhlauli as an innocent casualty of war. But they did not. In fact they went further and stated categorically that in terms of their own order and authority they would have been obliged to abort the mission if there had been an unknown person in Goniwe's car. The murders were inextricably linked. If they lied about one, how can they be believed about the others? It was not the first time that untruths were told in order to improve a case but had the effect of making it much worse.

The widows of the Cradock Four had been put through another ordeal but felt that the full truth did not come out. They want to know who gave the order to kill their husbands. There are people in high places who know. They have remained silent for too long. Will they ever come forward?

The Cradock Four, who according to Victoria Mxenge were the messengers to their great-grandfathers, will not be forgotten. One can only hope that those at the top who ordered their deaths will eventually be exposed.

CHAPTER 7

# EPILOGUE

*'It is a strange thing what authority the opinion of mankind generally grants to the intervention of courts. It clings even to the mere appearance of justice long after the substance has evaporated; it lends bodily form to the shadow of the law.'*
 *– Alexis de Tocqueville*

*'How easy it is to judge rightly after one sees what evil comes from judging wrongly.'*
 *– Elizabeth Gaskell*

IN 1988 I was invited with Professor Stephen Ellmann by Jack Greenberg, then dean of the faculty of law at Columbia University, to teach a course on legal responses to apartheid. Jack had a special interest in South Africa: he inspired Arthur Chaskalson, Sydney and Felicia Kentridge, and Geoff Budlender to form the Legal Resources Centre.

A conference was then arranged for September 1988 with a theme that must have appeared both premature and optimistic to many. Academics from North America, the United Kingdom and South Africa met with representatives of the liberation movements to discuss the constitution of post-apartheid South Africa. It was there that the question was raised of what was to happen to those who had violated human rights.

A member of the ANC executive in exile lost no time in responding to this issue. He related some of his personal experiences and alluded to what was common knowledge. He insisted that the only course open would be to appoint special tribunals similar to the one that dealt with the high-ranking Nazis in Nuremberg. There could not be forgiveness for murderers, torturers, bombers and saboteurs acting on behalf of the racist apartheid government. They should be charged with and convicted of crimes against humanity. He referred to them derogatorily as 'Boere'. His assumption was that they would be defeated: a compromise or settlement was out of the question.

A number of hands swiftly went up, accompanied by murmurs of both approval and dissent. As chairman of the session I chose to recognise the cut-off arm of Albie Sachs. Everyone knew that whilst in Mozambique teaching law his car was booby-trapped. He did not only lose his arm above the elbow but suffered serious injuries to the upper part of his body. Albie said that calls for acts of revenge would delay the dawn of freedom. Addressing the previous speaker directly and instinctively raising his damaged arm across his chest, he said, 'Comrade, if I can forgive them I am sure many more will do so.'

Laurie Ackermann was also present. He had been a judge but resigned shortly after he had presided over a 'terrorist trial' to become a human rights law professor at Stellenbosch University. His rulings on the admissibility of evidence and the comparatively light sentences he imposed were welcomed by those of us who regularly did political trials and raised eyebrows among his colleagues who were habitually chosen to do them. Struggling to control his emotions he said he was an Afrikaner; he knew what oppression was. His grandmother had died in a concentration camp during the Anglo-Boer War in 1902. He said nothing more. He rightly assumed that we all knew that the tar brush should not be directed at all Afrikaners.

Shortly after President F.W. de Klerk announced the unbanning of political organisations, including the ANC, PAC and SACP in 1990, negotiations between the apartheid state and the liberation forces began in earnest. One of the questions that had to be decided as a matter of urgency was what was to happen to those on Robben Island and in other prisons.

During the negotiations for the independence of Namibia, SWAPO had insisted that its imprisoned combatants were political prisoners. Although this term upset the South African government, it had to agree to the appointment of Prof. C.A. Norgaard, a Danish jurist, to interpret and give advice on the application of paragraph 7(b) of the United Nations settlement proposal, which provided for the release 'of all Namibian political prisoners or political detainees held by the South African authorities'. In the absence of a definition of 'political prisoner' it was agreed that the meaning given to the words 'political offence' in the law and practice relating to extradition should guide the parties to the agreement and Professor Norgaard. On behalf of the prisoners, however, it was contended that regard should be had to the context in which the term 'political prisoner' was used as part of the settlement plan, which had reconciliation as one of its fundamental aims.

Once Nelson Mandela was released in February 1990 and the liberation movements unbanned in South Africa, a process began that secured the release of political prisoners and allowed political exiles to return, indemnifying them against prosecution for political offences committed during the course of the freedom struggle. The terms for this were laid down in the Groote Schuur Minute, which adopted the approach of Prof. Norgaard in the Namibian situation.

De Klerk began releasing political prisoners on an *ad hoc* basis. Temporary indemnity was given to those returning from exile – but not fast enough for political prisoners, who threatened to go on a hunger strike until they were released. Consequently the Pretoria Minute was drawn up in August 1990, which instructed a working group to devise a plan 'for the release of ANC related prisoners and the granting of indemnity to people in a phased manner.' The Norgaard Principles were published. Two indemnity Acts were passed, which spoke of the promotion of peaceful constitutional solutions and reconciliation.

The Pretoria Minute saw the suspension of the armed struggle but not the end of state-sanctioned violence. In an attempt to bolster its chances in a democratic election, the National Party government employed a variety of delaying tactics, insisting on minority rights and impossible concessions. All the while people were dying in a systematic campaign to undermine the support of the liberation movements, themselves struggling to operate as political parties.

While South African security forces who had committed serious crimes against the people of Namibia were never particularly concerned about their future, being sure of government protection, those in South Africa feared that they might be held accountable for the wrongs they had done in apartheid's name. Their wrath was not directed against Mandela but against F.W. de Klerk and his equally spineless politicians for having capitulated. The least De Klerk could do was to provide in the interim constitution for unconditional indemnity or amnesty for every policeman and every soldier irrespective of rank for anything they might have done. 'Let us start with a clean slate,' said De Klerk. He was met with a chorus from the ANC: 'The very least that we must do is to write on the slate what happened and then decide who is entitled to amnesty and who is not.'

There had been debates within the ANC about the fate of those members of the security forces who had committed gross violations of human rights. In general three options emerged: Nuremberg-type trials, Chilean-style blanket amnesty, and collective amnesia along Argentinian lines. During the negotiations the ANC abandoned the Nuremberg option, and made it abundantly clear that the South American route was out of the question. The liberation movement was not going to have anything of the Argentinian solution, which instructed those who felt they had to confess to go to their priest and not to the newspapers, nor with the Chilean formula that the price to be paid for the partial withdrawal of a tyrant should be the perpetuation of a conspiracy of silence. Kader Asmal, the well-read law professor, found support for his and the ANC's view in Alexander Solzhenitsyn: 'By not dealing with past human rights violations, we are not simply protecting the perpetrator's trivial old age; we are thereby ripping the foundations of justice from beneath new generations.'

It was only as the turbulent negotiations for an interim constitution were drawing to a close towards the end of 1993 that a breakthrough was made on the vexed question of amnesty. Two paragraphs were handed over to the drafting committee, who were told not to change them but to incorporate them in the constitution. Both sides feared that any attempt to alter even the grammar might give those who had reservations about the ambiguous provisions relating to amnesty an opportunity to change their minds. There was no time to polish them up or even to number them in the appropriate place in the interim constitution. They were tacked on as a postscript at the end of the constitution under the heading 'National Unity and Reconciliation'.

'This Constitution provides a historic bridge between the past of a deeply divided society characterised by strife, conflict, untold suffering and injustice, and a future founded on the recognition of human rights, democracy and peaceful co-existence and development opportunities for all South Africans, irrespective of colour, race, class, belief or sex.

'The pursuit of national unity, the well-being of all South African citizens and peace require reconciliation between the people of South Africa and the reconstruction of society.

'The adoption of this Constitution lays the secure foundation for the people of South Africa to transcend the divisions and strife of the past, which generated gross violations of human rights, the transgression of humanitarian principles in violent conflicts and a legacy of hatred, fear, guilt and revenge.

'These can now be addressed on the basis that there is a need for understanding but not for vengeance, a need for reparation but not for retaliation, a need for ubuntu but not for victimisation.

'In order to advance such reconciliation and reconstruction, amnesty shall be granted in respect of acts, omissions and offences associated with political objectives and committed in the course of the conflicts of the past. To this end, Parliament under this Constitution shall adopt a law determining a firm cut-off date, which shall be a date after 8 October 1990 and before 6 December 1993, and providing for the mechanisms, criteria and procedures, including tribunals, if any, through which such amnesty shall be dealt with at any time after the law has been passed.

'With this Constitution and these commitments we, the people of South Africa, open a new chapter in the history of our country.'

The newly appointed Minister of Justice in the first democratic government, Dullah Omar, lost no time in calling for a law dealing with amnesty to be passed by parliament. Omar was particularly concerned that the law should pay particular attention to the treatment, feelings and rights of the victims. After all, he had been one himself. Not only was he put in jail without a hearing but the third force conspired to kill him as he left or approached his home and, when that proved impracticable, by substituting dangerous drugs for the prescribed medication when he was in hospital. As Geoff Budlender, national director of the Legal Resources Centre, had made it known that the LRC would assist when called upon in drafting human-rights-friendly legislation, Omar asked whether Mahomed Navsa (then counsel at the LRC) and I would try to define 'an act, omission or offence associated with a political objective'. We did that. We also suggested the removal of what we thought were objectionable provisions in the draft not in consonance with the Bill of Rights in the interim constitution. We were called to a meeting of the Justice Portfolio Committee to explain the published draft bill.

It was my first visit to parliament. The lobby, the passages and the room in which the whites-only parliament had sat from 1910 to 1984 were covered with portraits celebrating white supremacy. But now the majority of the members of parliament present at the committee meeting were black. Some were fellow legal practitioners before they went into exile, others were clients who had been imprisoned on Robben Island.

Many members of the Justice Committee are lawyers. Judging by their questions, those from the National, Democratic and Freedom Front parties were concerned about the impartiality of the persons to be appointed to the amnesty committee. They wanted to know who would appoint them, what qualifications would be required, what their powers would be, and, above all, whether they would treat wrongdoers from both sides on an equal footing. We drew attention to the provisions of the draft bill, which spoke of persons broadly representative of the South African community possessing knowledge of the content and application of human rights in order to record their gross violation. The chairperson of the amnesty committee had to be a judge. What was meant by full disclosure of all the relevant facts? Would amnesty be refused if the applicant had lied or covered up in the past? No, provided he told the truth now and did not remain silent or lied about his own role or the role of others, more particularly those who had given orders to commit the crime or delict. Why was it necessary for the applicant to show that he was doing the bidding of a known political organisation or liberation movement? In order to exclude those who might say they had formed their own little underground cell so as to enable them to claim a political motive for crimes committed for gain or motivated by racial hatred or to settle old scores. How would employees of the state show that they had acted in good faith or had reasonable grounds to believe that they could commit murder, torture people, cover up their deeds and defeat the ends of justice? If they had orders to do so, there was no other way to achieve their objective and they did not use excessive means. After much debate, inter-party negotiations and drafting and redrafting, the Promotion of National Unity and Reconciliation Act was passed. As the TRC chairman, Archbishop Tutu, later reflected, 'The commission remains a risky and delicate business, but it is still the only alternative to Nuremberg on the one hand and amnesia on the other.'

When the Biko family and others applied to the Constitutional Court for the amnesty hearings of the TRC to be declared unconstitutional, Ismail Mahomed, then sitting as Deputy President of the court, turned down the application, stressing the importance of reconciliation in South Africa, and quoting the epilogue to the constitution. He said it was a difficult, sensitive, perhaps even agonising balancing act between the need for justice to victims of past abuse and the need for reconciliation and rapid transition to a new future; between encouragement to wrongdoers to help in the discovery of the truth and the need for reparations for the victims of that truth; between a correction to the old and the creation of the new. It was an exercise of immense difficulty involving a vast network of political, emotional, ethical and logistical considerations. It was an Act calling for a judgment falling substantially within the domain of those entrusted with law-making in the era preceding and during the transition period. The results might well often be imperfect, supporting the belief of Kant that out of the crooked timber of humanity no straight thing was ever made. Mahomed concluded that parliament intended to offer 'amnesty' in the fullest sense, 'so as to enhance and optimise the prospects of facilitating the constitutional journey from the shame of the past to the promise of the future'. The Act establishing the TRC, with its power to grant amnesty, was not unconstitutional.

One can understand the feelings of members of a family when amnesty is given to those who murdered their loved ones. When the conspiracy of silence was broken by Nofemela, Coetzee and, later, others in the De Kock case, one could understand their sense of revulsion and their demand for justice. But, on the other hand, if amnesty had not been promised there would have been no political settlement. If there had been no settlement, there might have been civil war, from which untold injustices would have resulted. It may not be perfect justice, but justice is not something that can be found in its perfect state, and compromises have to be made to avoid even greater wrongs.

One must also admit that amnesty has been crucial in exposing the truth. The granting of amnesty and indemnity has persuaded people to talk who might otherwise not have done so, and has exposed the wrongdoers who otherwise might never have become known. Moreover, there is provision for reparations, though obviously these are not as good as being compensated or having the satisfaction of seeing the wrongdoer punished.

Indeed, there can never be adequate compensation for the murder of a loved one. The wrongs of the past can never be put right. They are written in blood, on the floors of our jails, in our hearts. Those killed by apartheid are there to remind us, to accuse us when we falter in our quest for a just society. Such a quest is less likely to be achieved by the call for blood than the just call for full disclosure of the truth.

Amnesty can only come with truth: pardon cannot be given for nameless crimes, nor forgiveness for concealed sins. There is no better evidence than that coming from the perpetrators, freely and voluntarily, given publicly. Had it not been for the litany of violence which has flowed from the mouths of perpetrators, the false denials would have gone on, the history of the country might have been distorted for ever. Full disclosure has to be made. Nonetheless, many applicants have said no more than what they knew was known to the victims, their relatives and the amnesty committee, thereby protecting their comrades who have not applied within the prescribed period. Many applicants have not been prepared to say that they received direct instructions from above, preferring to rely on the implied authority of political speeches exhorting them to battle. At times it is clear that their loyalty lies not with the truth but with their partners in crime.

Indeed, right at the top, both P.W. Botha and F.W. de Klerk maintained that they did not know. If that is so, they must have worked diligently at distancing themselves from the truth. Botha refused to appear before the TRC, variously offering as excuses his ill health and the so-called bias of the commission (which he described as a circus). His public statements when charged for failing to answer a subpoena and his behaviour in and out of court have led many to believe that the clown's headgear would suit him best. De Klerk, on the other hand, agreed in his suave manner to testify. But when counsel for the commission, Glen Goosen, started his cross-examination, there was a theatrical withdrawal. The reason given was that the documents emanating from the Security Council and the archives had not been shown to him earlier. He made it clear he would not come again.

All the same much has emerged about our tragic past from the proceedings of the TRC. Amnesty applicants in respect of the killing of Biko and Goniwe confirmed the correctness of what we said all along, though we and our clients had been accused of being liars, propagandists for and willing tools of the enemies of South Africa. Archbishop Tutu is right – for all its flaws, the TRC remains the best chance we have of discovering the truth, believing it, and living with it. In truth lies catharsis. The perpetrators are not expected to suffer like Oedipus, who gouged his eyes out to rid himself of guilt.

And yet we quail at allowing murderers to walk away from their heinous crimes with not even an admonishment. It cannot be otherwise. The rush for amnesty was not born of remorse or even regret, but as a result of Attorney-General Jan D'Oliveira's successful prosecution of Eugene de Kock. It was the thought of sharing the dock with him that drove the flood of applications. Once De Kock was convicted and received two life sentences plus 212 years' imprisonment, his declaration that he would tell all forced many to apply for amnesty who would otherwise not have done so. De Kock gave notice that he would submit his application for amnesty at the very last minute. He did not want to be in this alone; he wanted all to come forward and, in particular, he wanted to implicate the politicians and the generals who had abandoned him. His submission ran to over a thousand pages. Those who suspected they may have been implicated could not afford to take the chance, and applications flooded in.

At the same time it must be admitted that with the exception of Biko and the Cradock Four, no new material information has come to the fore concerning human rights abuses prior to the 1980s. It seems that the security policemen of the 1960s and 1970s were more disciplined, and no fissures have appeared in their defences. For decades the conspiracy of silence has held – Ngudle, Haron, Timol and Lenkoe are among the dozens of victims from this period whose deaths remain a mystery. There are many out there who know what really happened, who lied while persuading magistrates that they spoke the truth and the public that they acted only in their best interests. Their reward was exoneration. Old men now, most of them have receded into obscurity, but they carry the knowledge of their crimes, with only a magistrate's words to salve their conscience. The same is true of the wrongdoers in the defence force who have maintained a stony silence, as evinced by the failed prosecution of Gen. Magnus Malan and others. Had they been convicted, how much more might we have learnt?

Of equal concern is that attempts are being made to discredit the work of the TRC and the amnesty committee. Despite the evidence that has emerged, the bodies unearthed, some people still try to bury the truth. The most common charge is that the TRC is not evenhanded, that it favours the ANC, while it humiliates the Afrikaner. Yet much of what we know about the killings and atrocities of the apartheid regime is the product of the courageous work of Afrikaners such as Jacques Pauw and Max du Preez and even, for his own reasons, Dirk Coetzee. One diatribe masquerading as journalism moved Du Preez to express his anger with people 'trading on an Afrikaans surname to inform the world of how "Afrikaners" feel and think'. Antjie Krog dedicated her book *The Country of My Skull* to 'every victim who had an Afrikaner surname on her lips'.

Apartheid politicians have taken refuge beneath this ethnic blanket, claiming, oblivious of the irony, that they are being subjected to racial persecution. There have been exceptions. Leon Wessels was the first member of the former government to apologise. At a conference in Denmark at which Nelson Mandela was a member of the audience, not long after his release from prison, Wessels offered a personal apology for what he had done. He left the podium to shake Mandela's hand. Mandela was moved and in his usual way he embraced and thanked him. In giving evidence before the TRC, Wessels said, unlike P.W. Botha, De Klerk or even Pik Botha, 'We did not want to know.'

'No President can know everything which takes place under his management' is De Klerk's answer. Expressions of regret have been mouthed by senior police officers, who nevertheless continue to speak about 'terrorists' (but cannot bring themselves to utter the words 'liberation movement'), 'confessing' that mistakes were made on both sides. President Mandela was infuriated when that phrase was incorporated in De Klerk's Nobel Prize acceptance speech in Oslo. One has only to contrast this attitude with that of Brian Mitchell, who has offered to go and work in the Trust Feed community which he wronged; hardly any have followed his example. Eugene de Kock has accused P.W. Botha, his Ministers and Generals of refusing to accept responsibility for the deeds they authorised. 'They want to eat lamb, but they did not want to see the blood and guts,' said De Kock.

Those responsible for such dark deeds have found it difficult to respond to the revelations of unspeakable acts of barbarism at the TRC hearings. The perpetrators have in turn accused their victims of equally serious acts of terrorism, which could not be proved. They said that they relied for their information on informers whose identities they were not prepared to disclose. Some documents which they did not manage to destroy contradict their versions. Moreover, those who knew the victims have given circumstantial accounts that also contradict the official stories. They were killed because they were active against the apartheid regime. In a democracy their activism would have been considered lawful democratic activity.

Have the amnesty hearings led to reconciliation? On a personal level and in the short term, probably not, especially when the one side accuses the other of not telling the truth. But reconciliation cannot be an instant affair – for one thing, the constitution does not expect it. The perpetrators have themselves appealed for understanding and for at least an acknowledgement that they alone were not entirely to blame. After all, to be understood is a form of forgiveness. Their suffering has been visible too: few of their families have accompanied them to the amnesty hearings; many have struggled to form meaningful relationships with their children; and a number of families have fallen apart.

On 28 October 1998 the TRC handed its report of over three and a half thousand pages to President Mandela. The President, on receiving it, praised the Commission for its work and made the report public. The handing-over ceremony took place amid allegations of bias, applications to court and threats of further legal action. In finding that all the major protagonists, both in defence of and in opposition to apartheid, were guilty of gross human rights violations, the report did not please any of them. Among its main findings, the report held the National Party government, its security forces and their collaborators primarily responsible for a host of violations, including the torture, abduction and assassination of opponents, and the training and funding of hit squads. Although the report also found that the ANC had fought a just war, leading members of the ANC objected strongly to the findings which might be interpreted as the 'criminalisation of the liberation struggle'.

The debate will go on. The amnesty committee still has over a thousand cases to hear, including those involving high-ranking security force officers. Of those already heard, the findings in some cases, including Biko and the Cradock Four, have still to be made. We do not know what will emerge.

Once again the divisions in South African society have come to the fore. There are calls for blanket amnesty – an option likely to have the same effect as the Chilean and Argentinian solutions. There are calls too that we should put an end to the whole sorry past. What would be the response of those who have already applied for amnesty or those whose loved ones have been killed? Yet others call for the prosecution of the perpetrators, attracting the criticism that they are wanting Nuremberg-style trials. These are questions that will have to be answered, decisions that will have to be taken. The process will have to go on, and the pain caused by the conflicts of the past will have to be dealt with.

The search for the truth will continue. Why, how and by whose hand so many died in detention is not yet fully known. We owe it to their memory to keep the dockets on their deaths open in the hope that those who know will not take their secrets to their graves.

# ABBREVIATIONS

| | |
|---|---|
| ANC | African National Congress |
| AZAPO | Azanian People's Organisation |
| BCM | Black Consciousness Movement |
| BCP | Black Community Programmes |
| BOSS | Bureau for State Security |
| BPC | Black People's Convention |
| CCB | Civil Co-operation Bureau |
| CODESA | Convention for a Democratic South Africa |
| Cradora | Cradock Residents' Association |
| Cradoya | Cradock Youth Organisation |
| DET | Department of Education and Training |
| ECC | End Conscription Campaign |
| JMC | Joint Management Centre |
| LRC | Legal Resources Centre |
| MASA | Medical Association of South Africa |
| MK | Umkhonto weSizwe |
| NUSAS | National Union of South African Students |
| PAC | Pan Africanist Congress |
| Pebco | Port Elizabeth Black Civic Organisation |
| PFP | Progressive Federal Party |
| SABC | South African Broadcasting Corporation |
| SACP | South African Communist Party |
| SADF | South African Defence Force |
| SAMDC | South African Medical and Dental Council |
| SAP | South African Police |
| SASO | South African Students' Organisation |
| SWAPO | South West African People's Organisation |
| TRC | Truth and Reconciliation Commission |
| UDF | United Democratic Front |

# NOTE ON SOURCES

Records of proceedings in the magistrates' courts, including inquest proceedings, are destroyed within five years of their date of occurrence. I have thus had to rely on copies of the proceedings in private collections or, when these did not exist, newspaper reports. The latter have proved an invaluable aid in reconstructing the past and supplementing my own recollections.

The following sources, arranged by chapter, were used in writing this book, and may prove interesting for those wishing to read further.

### From Ngudle to Timol

Newspaper reports of the inquest were used, as no record was available. The evidence of members of the Timol family forms part of the TRC record.

*Timol v The Magistrate of Johannesburg* 1972 (2) SA 281 (T)

Joel Carlson, *No Neutral Ground*. New York, Crowell, 1973

### The Passion of Steve Biko

Microfilm records of the inquest are available at the Department of Historical Papers, University of the Witwatersrand.

Documents relating to the amnesty applications in the Biko case are held by the LRC.

*S v Mushimba* 1977 (2) SA 829 (A)

*Azapo & Others v TRC* 1996 (4) SA 562 (C)

*Azapo & Others v The President of the RSA* 1996 (4) SA 671 (CC)

Steve Biko, *Black Consciousness in South Africa*, ed. A. Millard. New York, Random, 1978

Steve Biko, *No Fears Expressed*, ed. A. Millard. Johannesburg, Skotaville, 1987

Steve Biko, *Black Viewpoint: Study Project on Christianity*. Durban, SPRO-CAS, 1972

Steve Biko, *I Write What I Like*, ed. A. Stubbs. London, Bowerdean, 1978

Hilda Bernstein, *No. 46: Steve Biko*. London, IDAF, 1978

Donald Woods, *Biko*. New York, Paddington Press, 1978

Mamphela Ramphele, *Mamphela Ramphele: A Life*. Cape Town, David Philip, 1995

'Bantu Steve Biko: Beacon of Hope' (documentary film), produced by Nkosinathi Biko and Nhlanhla Dakile

'Dear Tata' by Nkosinathi Biko, *Tribune* magazine

### Neil Hudson Aggett

The record of the inquest, and various related papers, are held by the Department of Historical Papers, University of the Witwatersrand.

The evidence of Dr Elizabeth Floyd to the TRC.

Helen Joseph, *Side by Side: The Autobiography of Helen Joseph*. London, Zed Books, 1986

Nikos Kazantzakis, *Zorba the Greek*. London, Faber & Faber, 1961

### Simon Mndawe

Portions of the record of the inquest proceedings are in the library of the LRC.

Interviews with Mathews Phosa and members of the Mndawe family.

### Get Gluckman

Dr Gluckman's files are held by the Department of Historical Papers, University of the Witwatersrand. Related papers are to be found in the LRC library.

Interviews with Mrs Lois Gluckman and members of the Gluckman family.

### The Cradock Four

The record of the inquest and amnesty applications are in the LRC library.

Interviews with the widows of the Cradock Four and members of the Cradock community.

### Epilogue

Presentations to the TRC by the judiciary and legal practitioners in *South African Law Journal*, 115, 1–3, 1998

Stephen Ellmann, 'To resign or not to resign', *Cardozo Law Review*, 19, 3, 1997

### General

Catherine Owen, 'A survey of twenty years of deaths under security legislation in South Africa, 1963–1983,' BA(Hons) dissertation, University of Cape Town, 1983

Jacques Pauw, *Into the Heart of Darkness: Confessions of Apartheid's Assassins*. Johannesburg, Jonathan Ball, 1997

Jacques Pauw, *In the Heart of the Whore*. Johannesburg, Southern Book Publishers, 1991

Antjie Krog, *Country of My Skull*. Johannesburg, Random House, 1998

Thomas G. Karis and Gail M. Gerhart, From *Protest to Challenge: Nadir and Resurgence*, vol. 5. Bloomington, Indiana University Press, 1997

The activities of the Truth and Reconciliation Commission were widely reported in the press, and supplemented by documents produced by the Commission itself. Recordings of the proceedings of the Commission are available, and several documentaries on the process were screened by the SABC, most notably those by Max du Preez.

# INDEX